Moon City Review 2011

An Annual
of Poetry, Story, Art, & Criticism

Other Books from Moon City Press

robert e smith: Paintings, Drawings, Poems, and Stories, selected and edited by Eric Pervukhin and Carla Stine

Confederate Girlhoods: A Women's History of Early Springfield, Missouri, edited by Craig A. Meyer

Moon City Review 2010: An Annual of Poetry, Story, Art, & Criticism, edited by Lanette Cadle and Marcus Cafagña

**Moon City Press titles are distributed through
The University of Arkansas Press:**

<http://www.uapress.com/titles/mcp/mcp.html>

Moon City Review 2011

An Annual
of Poetry, Story, Art, & Criticism

Edited by Marcus Cafagña and Joel Chaston
Missouri State University

moon city press
springfield missouri
2011

www.mooncitypress.com

Cover Design: Lanette Cadle
Cover Photograph: Bruce West
Text Layout: Angelia Northrip-Rivera

ISBN: 978-0-913785-32-4

Contents

I. Featured Work

II. Direct From Moon City

III. Archival Treasures

For Michael: teacher, scholar, editor, colleague,
and one helluva poet

Marcus Cafagña

Introduction

This volume in the MCR book series focuses on alumni in the broadest sense of the word. Some of the best writers in and from the Ozarks are included, but luckily for us, the best writers include a generous mix of student, faculty, and others, the primary measure being excellence. Readers from the Ozarks may recognize some old friends and other readers will get a better idea about "where we're from." My co-editor Joel Chaston and I invited work from not only alums but from the entire region of the Ozarks and beyond: Missouri, Arkansas, Oklahoma, and Kansas, including writers who share no direct connection to Missouri State University, but who understand this region, its people, and the distinctive voices that originate from the Ozarks.

In order to better understand what I mean by *distinctive voices*, let me quote a famous Ozark poet, Miller Williams: ". . . many poets have developed distinctive voices without gimmicks, without distorting the language as it is spoken."[1] Poetry is "good talk," as Williams or Michael Burns, his former student and founder of our creative writing program, would have it: poetry that when "read aloud . . . without affectation," offers the "compelling illusion of conversation." Clearly, Michael Burns' leadership is evident in these pages. Many of the writers in this Alumni volume were his students and his colleagues, and many of his past students have gone on to successful careers in other parts of this country. Others included here are currently students at Missouri State

[1] I quote Miller Williams here from *Making a Poem: Some Thoughts About Poetry and the People Who Write It* (Louisiana State University Press, 2006).

and at other institutions in the Midwest. Ultimately, the poetry, fiction, and creative nonfiction within these pages talk to their readers and, at the same time, extend a longer conversation begun by writers and readers who know this area and its concerns well. As editors, we hope that the work here speaks to you also, and if you now live somewhere far away from the hills and hollers, it brings you back.

In the spirit of this celebration of "where we're from," the Featured Works section opens with a suite of poems by former Missouri Poet Laureate Walter Bargen. We are proud to include these poems and hope that those of you unfamiliar with his work enjoy them as much as we do. Next, there is more poetry from Missouri Staters Alexandra Teague, C. D. Albin, Jessica Glover, and Sara Burge, who recently returned to Missouri State soon after the publication of her first book of poems to join us as poetry faculty. Also in the featured section are Travis Mossotti and Sarah Wangler, whose work was included in the *Best New Poets 2010* anthology. For a volume that went out of its way to include a significant amount of fiction, *MCR 2011* has notable work from the poetry world, including an interview with former U.S. Poet Laureate and Pulitzer Prize-winning poet Ted Kooser, by Missouri State alums Mantooth Miller and Lee Busby. Kooser was gracious enough to send us a poem, which we placed next to the interview.

Our Featured Works this time has two extraordinary offerings in creative nonfiction. The first piece of writing we accepted for this volume was Clark Closser's incomparable "The Summer I Carried a Gun," an essay from his autobiography in progress. Recent Missouri Staters may remember hearing Closser read an earlier version of this piece at Plaster Student Union Theater last spring to a packed and very appreciative house. Additionally, we have the compelling first-hand account of Meg Worden's incarceration inside a women's prison, an essay from her yet to be published memoir. Other creative nonfiction in the volume includes Tita French Baumlin's essay "Evening of a Fawn," which is not to be missed; nor is the creative nonfiction of graduate student Heather Cook, who offers an unabashedly personal take on an eating disorder and the Pill.

Many of those presented in *MCR 2011* are no longer "yet to be published": Brian Shawver published his first novel, *The Cuban Prospect*, with Overlook/Penguin and a second, *Aftermath*, with Doubleday; Alexandra Teague's first book, *Mortal Geometry*, won the 2009 Lexi Rudnitsky Prize in Poetry and was published by Persea Books; Sara Burge's first book, *Apocalypse Ranch*, was selected for the 2009 De Novo Prize. Of course, former faculty members Michael Burns, Roland Sodowsky, and Laura Lee Washburn are no strangers to publication, and each make a strong contribution.

The Featured Works section is not the only site for work by notable (and promising) writers. In the Direct from Moon City section we offer a poem by Dustin Macormic, who recently had his Missouri State nominated poem selected for the 2011 Associated Writing Programs Intro Journals Project Award. Liz Breazeale's short story, "Chapel Bluff," was chosen as the winner of the inaugural *Moon City Review* Short Story Competition by Kevin Brockmeier, an MSU alum who has become one of our leading American novelists. From the other nine finalist stories in the MCR competition, editors chose the short story by Anthony Bradley for inclusion in this volume. We chose work from standout alums like Kerry James Evans, Chad Woody, D. Gilson, Susan Dunn, and Ben Pfeiffer, who have begun to publish their poetry or fiction more widely in literary journals. We also welcomed many newcomers, like Lora Knight, Daniel Iacob, Allys Page, and Andy Myers to our regional community of writers. Current faculty is also included, in poems by Lanette Cadle and fiction by Jen Murvin Edwards and by Shannon Wooden.

We are honored to present two fine translations, one

of a short story by Mexican novelist Ana García Bergua, translated from the Spanish by Toshiya Kamei, and the other a poem by François Villon, translated from the French by our translations editor John DuVal. We appreciate the opportunity to include English renditions of the work of these distinguished writers.

Our Archival Treasures feature both a poem by one of the best loved professors of our department, the late Robert Henigan, and an illuminating lecture entitled "On Not Teaching Poetry" delivered by a distinguished Springfieldian, the late Robert Wallace, a poet and editor gone but not forgotten by thousands of college students across the country that learned in part how to craft their poems from studying *Writing Poems*, his textbook, now in its eighth edition from Pearson Longman.

Finally, in the production of this third volume, I want to thank my co-editor, Joel Chaston. His generous spirit lent an openness to the proceedings. I want to thank Lanette Cadle, our MCR Book Series Editor, who designed the cover using Bruce West's photo of a dictionary from Meyer Library. She guided us through the editing process. As editors, we owe much to many. *MCR 2011* is partially funded by the Missouri State University College of Arts and Letters and Department of English; many thanks to Dean Cary Adams and the English Department Head, W. D. Blackmon, for their continued support. Editor for Moon City Press James S. Baumlin, as always, has been an endless source of ideas and Rock of Gibraltar.

We thank our production assistant Anna Robb, who helped us manage submissions for *MCR 2011*, served as a student reader, and worked on promotions and mailings for other Moon City Press books, all while completing her second year in the M.A. program at Missouri State. Angelia Northrip-Rivera did the text layout, while Bruce West contributed the cover photography and interior black and white photographs from his *Landscapes* series. We also give thanks to the staff of Meyer Library's Special Collections and Archives—David Richards, Anne Baker, and Tracie Grieselman-Holthaus.

We owe additional thanks to the creative writing faculty for getting the word out about this volume and helping drum up the addresses of former students who, in some cases, we had not heard from in years. We thank faculty who served as readers, especially Jane Hoogestraat. We thank undergraduate and graduate student readers Kristen Cypret (poetry), Ben Bogart (fiction), and Heather Cook (creative nonfiction). Of course, we always appreciate the fact that so many of our alumni and other interested writers accepted our invitation to contribute. Without such a large group of submissions to draw from we would not have had such a strong book. With such a strong community of writers, great things can happen. As editors, we believe this current volume is our best. We hope you agree.

I. Featured Work

(And Some New Arrivals)

WALTER BARGEN

Day's Receipt

What a block of life has past.
—Robert Lowell

The book marked by a yellowed cashier's receipt date December 21, 1991,
the shortest day of that year
and nineteen years later it's still the shortest day, and memory grows shorter yet,
though the day remains
24 hours long and not at all. But I'm worried about last week, having not fully stopped
at a traffic light, rolling through
and turning right, as a mounted camera clicked away. This doesn't deny the last
megafauna extinction of giant ground sloths
and mastodons, except that Arctic ice cores are revealing dust from yet another
meteor collision, dating back
12,000 years before traffic cameras. There's no turning back from a moving violation
and living through a failure
to stop anything—hurtling planet, meteor, ticket and fine. Maybe it was never clear,
decades ago a new job,
now decades of alarm clocks ring in my head, the miles between here and there tallied
under a diminishing sun.
What was I doing?
A day passed that had no beginning and no end?
A night where surely the stars
and vast vestments of space collapsed inward and if I stared upward at all, I was lost,
the sky wasn't having never been found.

At least the receipt has a time and place printed but fading.
At 10:24 a.m. money exchanged, the transaction
completed. I would like to think I was satisfied as I turned to leave,

2

having found what I wanted

or a satisfactory substitute. But there must have been more. A name

for the young clerk, say Hannah,

in her haste to beat back the clock, she dropped two pennies that spun off

across the floor

and were lost under the next counter. She apologized to the person behind me

for her clumsiness

and taking too long, which wasn't long at all, if she recalled saber tooth tigers

and mammoths,

and it was even shorter than a meteor burning through the stratosphere.

The receipt for one day

out of 21,000 comes back to me as fiction like all the rest.

WALTER BARGEN

Exposure

For Robin Albee

The flea- market photo
bought 50 miles south of here, printed on stiff gray card stock,

with the town's name, Ashland,
in silver across the bottom. Maybe there's a relative who still lives there.

The man pictured
stern, severe, dour, nearly a morgue shot. But even in black & white,

nothing stops his gray steel stare,
penetrating the camera and the other end of a century. Behind the foot-long beard

tapering to a blunt point,
the face of old-time religion, ready to suffer, ready to make others suffer.

Seated in an office,
I explain this morning's tardiness: feeding the cats, taking out the garbage,

taking the man in the photograph
to the local newspaper. My ex-Peace Corp coworker exclaims, *Oh no, it's the camera.*

In Niger,
the people were so animated, always laughing, singing, ready to play, but when he aimed

his camera,
all activity stopped. Everyone buttoned their shirts, buttoned down their collars,

straightened their dresses,
grimly lined up to be executed for posterity. He stands up behind his desk,

both arms nailed to the sides
of his body, pine-board straight, shoulders squared, chin thrust slightly up,

his face cold clay,
as if he'd already been in the office eight hours.

WALTER BARGEN

Thumbing Through the Book of Days

What if you knew you only had a few days left to stare at your thumbs?
Take my thumbs for example: not overly long or out of proportion
with the rest of my hand, though longer fingers might have helped,
if I'd ever followed through on racing up and down
the neck of a guitar, stretching for impossible chords, or the reaching
down into a warm moist cleft for that other music. They are pinkish,
though more a light blowing sand unless flushed with blood, but more likely
on a cold day carved a statuesque alabaster from poor circulation. Held
next to each other, not quite mirror images, fraternal not identical twins,
their two quarter moons nailed to prehensile tandem orbits, working together
even when unscrewing a tight jar lid and the twisting torque is in opposite directions.
If thumbs up is a little phallic, it can't be helped, they are only commiserating
from different sides of the same dismal dilemma. The scattered scuff of clouds
that drift slowly across their sickle moons toward the nail clippers, bruises
or seasonal vitamin deficiency, I don't know. The soft wrinkled details
of hairless cross-hatched skin along their length and the deeper furrowed joint
where motion is planted and replanted—so many details, but not the fumbling
"all thumbs," not the vulgar "sitting on his thumbs," not the soccer stadium
in Santiago, early 70's, where thumbless meant the guitarist's hands
butchered by soldiers. Even Ozymandias could not save his thumbs
from a vast sand sea, and you have only a few days left.

WALTER BARGEN

Forced Bussing

This is what the old do after giving up the future—recalibration: 50 the new 40,
60 the new 50.
Falling backward as they stumble forward. Denial finally the viable strategy.
Held close,
holstered to the chest, a concealed weapon that fires blanks at every party,
every birthday
as it creeps closer through the underbrush of days. No candles, no cards,
not even a half-day off
from work, certainly not a vacation to hide within or without. So this is what the old do,
grow more
and more stateless as borders blur, and it's not just because of retinal detachment,
visions clouded
by storms of floaters, the cascade of cataracts turning traffic lights into shimmering pools,
macular degeneration
abandoning the tunneled light for a dark room in eternity. The old buy busses
to convert
into compassed destinations but are quickly lost in installing the light-weight cabinets
with fixed shelves
to slow the breakage to a rattle, or lost in the bolting of mattress frame to floor
and wall
to lessen the careening, too soon confused, believing there is time to sleep off
another chance,
to awaken from all the comas of love's past collisions. The old bleach the water
reservoir,
secure the propane tank,
reread the instructions for the composting toilet, grow tired of the inventions,
the ingenuity,
the space savers, the estate planning, the automatic bill payments, and resort to
realphabetizing
the map drawer,
choosing another destination, this one is too much like the last one, segregating
distance from the distant.

WALTER BARGEN

All It Takes

For Roger Egling (1945–2009)

It was only a moment and not even that long.
    That's all it takes and even that is too much and not enough.
Not even time for a thought much less a second thought.
    Afterthoughts are for the rest of us
trying to disentangle the quotidian and ourselves,
    our breathing so sympathetic to our cause.

There were halcyon moments:
    my son, nine or ten, long before you imagined
the faces of your two sons, and during that night
    while we slept, an unexpected snow, maybe ten inches.
What else for the three of us to do but fall with the snow,
    the improbable heroics of diving catches into a frigid softness.
The football soon too slippery to catch, we were off
    tramping a sled path through sloped woods
that ended at the creek bank and our brief impossible flights
    of sled and rider before the contusive landing on ice, on rock.

Then standing on the steps to the altar,
    dressed in the regalia of a groomsman,
the vaulted ceiling enough to induce vertigo.
    A little uncomfortable and ill-fitted in rented apparel,
light-headed having just received,
    in the back of the church, my first haircut in twenty years,
fulfilling a promise that I'd made that you hadn't asked for.
    Friends in the pews searched for me, not seeing me
as I stood on the third step. Now we are looking
    for you, wondering which step you are on,
and not seeing you, you who are too quick for the living.

WALTER BARGEN

Art Market

For Betty Thompson

1

           One of many paintings that hung
     in the living room of her apartment:
a broad nineteenth century London street,
      nearly abandoned or just empty
           except for the soul of moonlight muted
by backlit broken clouds, and a cloaked
        rider leaning forward, the horse
     so defiantly galloping against the stillness
a viewer can hear hoofs echoing off
      the coal-stained Romanesque buildings.
          It's easy to imagine hiding behind one
of the shadowy fluted marble columns,
        hoping not to be found out, handed
     the urgent message, that always
arrives too late for fate, for destiny,
      for the tired rider.

I set the gilded frame outside one overcast
          spring day, rain a threat, so a need to hurry.
     The painting upright, backed by books,
at a slight angle to the vertical, facing away
      from the darkly muted sun that could
        almost have been moonlight. An odd
centerpiece for a wrought-iron picnic table.
        With a flash I took eight or ten photographs.
     The developing done, the appraisal requested,

the photographs mailed to Christi's.
   Odd, no matter how I tried
      to avoid the flash's glare, each frame held
its bright blind eye, as if the oil resisted
      this perspective. Her husband, recently dead,
   this was her inheritance, a European painting
hanging on a forgotten Midwestern wall.
   Informed it was not an original, not worth
      the hundred thousand dreamed dollars—
a copy by a student studying the master's
      strokes, the tradition of the time. Worth
   something, but not enough for a lifetime.

2

What about the Sumerian pottery handles
      used for bookends, the cuneiform clay tablets
   that sat on a shelf with their message of bushels
received and promised, the noseless bust
   of a pharaoh mounted on a small steel post,
      the brass wheel of fire encircling the many-
armed Kali, dancing by herself on the howling
      upturned gutted body of creation, her necklace
   of skulls wreathing the lamplight?
In what century are they again lost?

In the penny jar shoved to the back
      of the kitchen counter near the sink,
   the heads of Lincoln deeply stacked
on the tarnished heads of Lincoln,
   and there a small glint, a drop of silver
      toward the bottom of a copper sea.
Pennies heaped on the table, I held
      a small thick coin, an imperfect circle,
   edges broadly rounded. The portrait

ancient, a heroic Greek profile
　　　　with unkempt swirl of hair, the lion's head
　　　　　　hood swallowing the back
of his head as if he were being devoured
　　　　　　　by the power of history. The reverse,
　　　　a god or king, seated, staff in hand, eagle
at his feet. Later, we would know it's
　　　　a hemidrahm, one Alexander the Great
might have spent in his empire. Later still,
　　　　it was a present, the small change of our past
　　　　　　that fills jars and gets casually spent.

3

Who can say what happened? What's left,
　　　　　　ashes. Friends wondering. Eight years
　　　　ago, she turned away. Refused to answer
phone calls, knocks on the door, shouts
　　　　through open windows, letters, except
　　　　　　for the occasional collison in grocery stores,
and to say fine, return quickly to her list.
　　　　　　She must have found aisles
　　　　that no one wandered looking for cheese
and cereal. What's left is a 911 phone call,
　　　　an unidentified voice, dirty pots and pans
　　　　　　scattered across the living room floor,
dozens of jeans worn once, panties bedded
　　　　　　in each one, the pockets stuffed with dirty
　　　　tissue, nothing her size, her car
in storage but no record of its location,
　　　　in fact no records of bank transactions
　　　　　　or utility bills, her monthly rent always paid
with money orders. Eight years ago,
　　　　she became her art.

ALEXANDRA TEAGUE

Holy Water

My father brings me Ganges water
in a plastic bottle stamped *Hampton Inn*
Shampoo. He wears kurtas now, moccasins
when I was young. He voted for Reagan,
keeps a framed photo of being kissed
by Minnie Mouse, the blessing of her hard,
immobile mouth against his forehead.
He says the Hindus say everyone is Hindu;
unseen and seen, the divine lives everywhere.
He shows me photos of women wading
in bright saris, men shaving waist-deep, stiff hair
of dead dogs, floating candles. The water
he's given me looks clear as Florida pools,
as the lit tank where the Little Mermaid sang
with such pure longing. Even in my twenties,
I cried. For legs, she'd trade a lifetime of sequins,
walk on knives. I keep the bottle on my desk.
Travel-sized, slim as those new Norwegian waters.
Sacred Ganges, he's written in fine, permanent marker.

ALEXANDRA TEAGUE

Rehearsed by Sorrows

Already, she woke with sand
in her eyes every morning. Blank white
desert of the sheets. A thousand paces
from the dresser to the bed, a chasm.
The Persian rug's plateau stretched on
for days. Unsweepable light
the maid kept breaking on the floor.
On the stairs: spillways of stained glass,
slow green rapids. In her ribs, a globe's rusted axis,
a continent turned to the same intractable sun.
Dust reticulating everything. Gray evergreens
against glass. All that space
for silence inside the piano's sounding board.

ALEXANDRA TEAGUE

B Side

When Angel unleashed a storm of records,
we shielded our faces, jumped shrieking
to the bed. Sharp, starlit planets swerved

out of their orbits, our futures spinning at us
not as the circus lady had promised—
pinwheeling, sequined, smiling inside the rain

of knives—but flailing against sheetrock walls,
birds caught in the pressed air of Fort Worth
summer. Music was an arsenal left unattended

by the grown-up world—parents working,
older brothers sleeping as Greased Lighting
drag-raced through our dolls. *Chicks cream*

meant something feathered; *automatic,
hydromatic, systematic* like the rhymes in fairytales
that unlocked castle doors. Inside,

we grew from 7 to 20 with a graceful click.
No one sang about cars motionless on
concrete blocks, broken sidewalks, the mirrored

blades that Angel—fat, mean, and almost thirteen—
hurled across the bedroom they shared;
high jail window curtained with tiny pink flowers.

TOSHIYA KAMEI, TRANSLATOR

"Japan"
by Ana García Bergua

At fifty he doesn't remember preparatoria well. He's stayed away from it ever since he graduated and went to Japan to study engineering. He got married there, got divorced, and when he came back to Mexico, he hardly knew anyone except his family: his parents, his brothers. His brothers say he's changed—withdrawn, solitary, he hardly mixes with anyone outside his company, where he works more than eight hours a day. As he himself admits—his difficult divorce from Fumiko, endless arguments with his Japanese in-laws, and some old habits hard to break—all this makes him a bit aloof, rather defensive. These days he's thinking perhaps he should start socializing more often, apart from Sunday family dinners. Maybe he should take up his brother Sandro's repeated invitation and go out with his friends on Friday, but he's not sure. Sandro, his youngest brother, is much younger than himself, and interested in other things: overcrowded discos, cult movies—in Tokyo he saw too many of them, which ultimately bored him—unfamiliar online games. He didn't have children who'd bring him up to date on these things. He feels he marches alone at his own pace, on his own path. One morning he receives a phone call:

"Felipe? Felipe Pardo?"

Yes, it's his name.

"Hello, I'm Sonia. Remember me? Sonia Cabrera, from the Preparatoria 26, the Hernán Cortés."

Sonia Cabrera. The name means nothing to him, but out of politeness he says hello back as if he knew her.

"Oh, of course, Sonia. How are you? Long time no see."

Sonia Cabrera says she's trying to locate their former classmates so that they can get together soon, talk about their lives, and relive the memories of that important period of their lives. She speaks with sentimentalism tinged with enthusiasm. Her voice sounds almost like a teenager's, and he wonders what she's like, whether there's a terrible contrast between the voice of a twentysomething girl and the image of a fifty-year-old matron, the same age as he. She asks him what he does for a living, what he has been up to. He gives a brief account, tells her he used to live in Japan. He doesn't ask her anything, feeling shy. She asks for his e-mail, and assures him she will soon write him and the classmates she has found—I already spoke to Manolo, Joaquín, Adela, and Curly. Remember them? And we're close to locating Frida Galván—so that they can decide about the reunion.

After hanging up, he wonders how she got his number. Maybe she called his parents, that would make sense. He goes to work with his head full of those names that don't sound familiar. He tries to remember preparatoria, a dark classroom with sixty teenagers crowded together who, supposedly, would change the world, but realizes that period has grown rather hazy over time. He remembers some friends, but none of the ones Sonia mentioned. For instance, Sonia doesn't ring a bell. Susana, yes—he liked her, a girl with jet-black hair, green eyes, and they kissed briefly in the dark during a school trip. Will she, perhaps, go to the reunion? Will Sonia find her? He also remembers Adolfo Sáenz, a friend in those days, but surely they have no longer anything in common. None of his classmates has been outstanding in the public sphere, as far as he can tell from newspapers or TV news. He thinks they're probably as gray as he is. He remembers his teachers best, a couple of them, the math teacher and the PE teacher. He remembers their faces, their figures, but isn't sure about their names: Baeza, Boeza? He feels a little ashamed

15

that his mind goes completely blank, and thinks maybe he suffers from some serious problems.

In the following days, he feels a bit anxious. Every day he checks his e-mail, waiting for Sonia's message. He's worried he might have given a wrong address, or she wrote it down incorrectly. At times he prefers not to receive anything, to forget the whole matter: what will he talk about with a bunch of strangers? Maybe he'd rather go to the movies with his brother's friends. A new secretary with prominent Japanese features has just joined his company. He likes Japanese women. The memory of Fumiko has somewhat faded away, but now that he sees the new girl every day, he remembers his life in Tokyo, where he spent so many years, virtually all his life. It's a good excuse, perhaps, in order to ask her out for tea, to tell her he wants to practice his Japanese, which is already a bit rusty.

But he has always taken time to make this kind of decision. He lives methodically, each day almost identical to the one before, which suits him: exercise, shower, breakfast, work, lunch, more work, dinner, reading or TV, and sleep. And Sundays with his family. While doing one of those activities, he tries to figure out what he wants or whether he really wants to change his life. At last, on Monday, he receives Sonia's e-mail. His address is part of a very long list. He finds it admirable that she has found so many people just for the reunion by herself, like someone who makes a cocktail he doesn't taste. She talks about "those days," the follies of youth, the spirit of the Prepa 26, nostalgia for the sixties, and asks everyone to suggest a date and a place of the reunion. He cautiously waits to see if the others reply. Over the course of the weekend, messages arrive now and then. Many add memories of their experiences; others send even pictures, in which he eagerly looks for himself. None of those faces that appear hugging, making the V for victory sign or diving into Chapultepec Lake seems to be him. He doesn't remember anyone in the photos either. When he moved to Japan, he left all his school papers with his mother. He wonders if there is any photo among them, he'll ask her later. After a small disagreement in which he doesn't take part, they fix the date and time of the meeting. It'll be at the empty apartment someone called Lucas Roldán has just rented. In an act of daring, he confirms his attendance in a brief message. He even agrees to pitch in and bring some drinks and snacks. He's looked for Susana's name in the list. Maybe she's the one with suspiros@hotmail.com, but he's not sure. In this excited mood for the reunion of the whole class, it may not be appropriate to ask for someone specific.

Over the next few days he feels nervous, worried. Even the new Japanese secretary ceases to exist for him. He wonders what to wear and looks himself in the mirror, measuring the ravages of time on his appearance. He asks his mother for his photos. She doesn't have many: you didn't like having your picture taken, she says, especially at that age. You spent many hours studying, you were quiet. In the few photos from that period, a skinny boy appears, a bit dull, with a big nose, long black bangs over his tiny eyes. Except for his hair, which now he keeps very short to hide his incipient baldness, and a few crow's feet, he hasn't changed much. He still has a slim, firm body. Surely they'll remember him. In the official photograph of the preparatoria, he appears with his classmates. They're numerous, and the picture was taken from far away, so he can't quite make out the faces. He looks for Adolfo and Susana, but he doesn't see anyone he knows, not even himself. Perhaps the voices, the anecdotes, the atmosphere. Something will turn up.

The night before the reunion he can't sleep. In the morning he skips his exercises and arrives at work, exhausted, with dark circles under his eyes. Precisely on this day the new secretary with Asian features approaches him.

"I see you here every day," she says. "But we haven't been introduced. My name is Guadalupe."

He feels a bit disappointed; he expected an authentic Japanese woman, but she must have been born in Mexico.

"How are you?" he answers. "Nice to meet you, I'm Felipe."

"I wanted to tell you if you need anything, just let me know. Mr. Ojeda told me to help others, and I see you're overloaded with work, you don't even get up from the desk to drink coffee."

This is his chance to ask her out. She's offering it to him, as if she were taking off her blouse in front of him. But he just stares at her, as if looking for her real Japanese name behind her almond eyes and her shiny black hair.

"Thank you very much. Of course."

He doesn't know what else to say. She lingers for a while, confused, then murmurs a polite goodbye and walks away toward her area. She's very thin, and hardly sways her hips while walking. She's his type. He wonders why he didn't take advantage of the chance. He could have asked her to accompany him to the reunion, but he doesn't feel like it. Somehow he feels excited about meeting Susana. Perhaps she keeps herself young, recognizable, perhaps she still feels nostalgic for the kiss in the dark.

He leaves work in a hurry to buy drinks and snacks to bring with him. Then he goes back to his apartment and does his best to dress up: he takes a shower, shaves carefully, puts on lotion, brillantine, his black suit, the only one he has, his polished shoes, blue shirt, red tie. Then he takes off the tie, thinking it's too formal for a reunion dinner. But it occurs to him everyone must have achieved success at that age, they may be subconsciously competing to show off their social standing, and he puts it back on. Then he hesitates, and stuffs it into his jacket pocket. Perhaps he manages to see how others dress through the window and get ready. His stomach is upset because his nerves are frayed, and doesn't know if he can eat something, let alone drink.

The place is far away, and the drive is a long one. While he drives across the city, the party seems as far away as those years. He's given up trying to recall and is somehow ready to give himself up to whatever this night may bring. He doesn't want to get his hopes up too high either, wait for things that never will happen, and this desire to lower his expectations makes him more tense than usual, causing the journey to seem too long. The freeway ends, and he takes a narrow road, which supposedly leads to the residential area where Lucas Roldán lives or is going to live, Residencial Los Robles, a dime-a-dozen name. He drives past several condos named after trees, passes through several crossroads, and at last arrives at the residential area where he looks for H 201. For a moment he feels fear of being so far away, but calms down as he goes up the stairs and hears music drifting from the apartment.

"Who are you?" asks the woman who opens the door, a dyed blonde in a floral shirt that hides her rather robust body. She must be Sonia, he thinks. When he tells her his name, she looks at him, a bit puzzled, but then hugs him as if she missed him terribly and invites him in.

"You've really changed, wow. Come, I want you to meet Paco Marín. Do you remember him? Look, Paco. Here's Felipe Pardo."

Paco, a bald man in a jacket and tie telling jokes in a folding chair, gets up and hugs him. He forces himself to give him the most enthusiastic hug he can manage, trying to remember the faces around him.

"I was telling them about when Fito, you, and I stole copies of the math exam from the principal's office. Remember?"

And Paco continues his anecdote, making his audience laugh. Felipe doesn't remember, but smiles as if he did. Someone else says:

"Of course, Felipe! Felipe Pardo, I'm Miguel, Curly. We locked all the restrooms in our school and hid the keys, remember? Everybody was desperate."

Remember? Remember? These people have a lot of memories that include him, but he doesn't remember anything except a series of gray days and science courses. He feels a bit embarrassed to ask for his friend Adolfo or Susana; by now everyone seems to know everyone else perfectly. They even begin to act like teenagers: they shout, joke, and take off their jackets and ties. He doesn't know what he did with his jacket, maybe he handed it to the woman who answered the door. The interest stirred by his arrival fades quickly when other former classmates arrive, some equally disconcerted. The man next to him says he heard he was in Indonesia; he doesn't bother to tell him it was Japan, and just nods.

"It's been a long time," he says, trying to find excuses for whatever mistakes he may make in the next few hours, so sure that whatever he says will reveal his lack of memory, which makes him feel like an imposter.

Another woman with somewhat showy hair and fake jewelry gives him a drink in a plastic cup, and he gulps it down. Amid laughter, music, and shouts, he loses himself and manages to relax. Not only he still doesn't recognize anyone, but also he feels himself younger than the others, people of a certain age, who make him think of family reunions of elderly aunts, uncles, and grandparents in which young people feel a bit out of place. He wonders if he's really like them, if there's some mistake; some look quite worn out, as if life had been excessively cruel to them. Curiously, they're the most enthusiastic ones. Some women sing protest songs, and he searches their faces for the features of his old crush, Susana, whom his mind has reconstructed as a woman with

20

black hair, light eyes, fine features, but none of them matches her as he remembers; the ones with green eyes are too tall, too fat, or too sour-looking. If she's any of them, he'd prefer not to know it. What's more, the woman he's thought was Sonia turns out to be someone else, an Ángela. He tries to pay attention to names that come up, here and there, as new arrivals are announced as if in old-fashioned balls in movies —the Marquis of Such-and-Such, the Duke of Something-or-Other—and those who get up from their folding chairs to greet them, asking "Do you remember me?" launch into some anecdote everyone seems to remember with exclamations, nods, and clarifications. He's possessed by a desire to imitate, like the protagonist of a movie he saw, the one who became a Jew or a Chinese depending on the company he kept, and also by a desire to be accepted, to belong, and not to be a stranger. He drinks up every cup he is offered, and even gets up to dance. A woman draws him toward her, inviting him to dance—a gaudy redhead with sweet eyes. "I always liked you," she says. For a change he doesn't know her name and is not going to ask. He searches for Susana's features in her face, certain she's not her, but he doesn't care. The lights dim, the music surges up, and the drunken partygoers form pairs and groups to dance. He's swept away by the mood, and even gets excited. He's dead drunk. It's been a long time since he's been with a woman, since Fumiko. A relationship that ended, paradoxically, in bed, has kept him from seeking companionship, apart from his own shyness. He leads the woman across the dark empty rooms and gives her a kiss, which she accepts as if she had been waiting. They stumble into an empty closet, shut its sliding doors, and make love on the floor, awkwardly, between laughter and whispers. He accidentally bangs his head, but endures the pain in silence. He wants to keep it going, and he doesn't want to faint.

He wakes up in the empty closet, frightened, feeling ill. For a moment he doesn't remember where he is. Then he slides the door open and goes out into the dusty, empty room. Outside lies a forest, and he hears the chirping of birds and a distance noise like the buzzing of a chainsaw. His head hurts terribly. Feeling ashamed, he wonders what the woman thought when he passed out like this. He doesn't know, anyway, why she didn't help him. He imagines he will find other drunken men lying here and there, and prepares to appear in a pitiful state before his classmates. But there's no one outside or inside. He feels a strong urge to urinate, but the bathrooms are locked. Plastic cups are strewn across the floor, and a large black garbage bag in the kitchen is overflowing with cigarette butts and leftovers. The air reeks of liquor and smoke. His jacket is gone. So are his keys, his wallet, his cell phone. At least the exit door is unlocked, but he sees no one outside. His car is missing from the parking lot. I must be imagining this, he thinks while emptying his bladder behind a tree.

He begins to walk, resigning himself to the idea that he has to cover a long stretch of road in this condition, before he can take a cab to his parents' house. Far away on the road, he sees two other men walking like him. One has no shoes, and the other seems to be hurt. It crosses his mind that there may be more people ahead of him, going back to the city. Perhaps many of those who came to the party were pretending and didn't really know anyone. While he wonders whether he should approach them, he decides not to ask them their names.

Sara Burge

Jobless Pantoum

Unoffered jobs eye us at our dinner table
tonight. Another day without
and I've begun deciding which bills will go unpaid.
Fear sets in and silences us

and for another day we'll go without. Tonight
our gutterless roof pours torrents of run-off.
Fear sets in and silences us.
Words only make things real.

Our gutterless roof pours torrents of run-off
and the cat yowls for an open door.
Words will only make this real
and pity is in short supply.

The cat yowls for an open door
because we have nothing for him.
Pity is in short supply
and desperation stretches itself out on the couch.

We have nothing,
so plans include ramen and peanut butter.
Desperation stretches out on the couch.
We know we will last only so long

when plans include ramen and peanut butter,
survival requires perfect health.
But how long
can we go with no fever? No broken bones?

Survival requires perfect health.
My husband's hands are aching.
We hope for no fever, no broken bones
while our son falls into fitful sleep.

My husband's hands are aching.
They know something is amiss.
While our son falls into fitful sleep
he makes nervous clicking sounds.

He knows something is amiss.
He doesn't understand
and makes nervous clicking sounds
in the back of his throat—

he doesn't understand
and doesn't know how to help.
In the back of his throat
a trapped cricket calls out

and he doesn't know how to help.
The refrigerator has stopped working.
A trapped cricket calls out.
The AC has stopped working.

The refrigerator has stopped working.
We are losing it.
The AC has stopped working.
We are choking.

We are losing it,
deciding which bills will go unpaid
while we choke
on mouthfuls of jobs unoffered.

SARA BURGE

Display

I blame my bout of melancholy on split ends
and search for Beauty Salons, find them facing

Bereavement upon a sprawl of phonebook
in ordered incantation, alphabetized display.

In my kitchen arrangements fade, sunflowers
pucker up plump seeds. If I do not throw them away

they'll start to stink, water already filming
with pestilence and green. The seeds say

Let yourself go.
The moment before they fall holds

nothing together. The illusion of gravity
may loosen. The leaves, the petals may be pressed

into forms that remind us something mattered.
But they are dead, nonetheless.

Bereavement is a good excuse
until beauty raises its unsightly head,

smoothes imperfections, promises all will become
tolerable as long as we make ourselves pretty

before marches toward husbands, sons,
pyres fueled by bodies we once loved.

Sara Burge

Clay and Wax

For Ken

Peter married Eva in Manila during mission work.
It ended with cancer. He is no longer Mormon.

I do not know she is six months dead when I first enter the house
where he and his sons have huddled.
I do not know to feel sorry.

Peter says, *Call me Pops*
He insists. Becomes all our fathers.
He drinks too much and falls into walls and soon
his sons will fall apart. Only more slowly.

I didn't survive the last funeral I went to.
It was my brother's. A black hole
opened in the ceiling and devoured me.
I flew apart into atoms of grief.

Eventually, I marry.
Pops visits my home with a gift—
he's been taking pottery classes and trying to drink less.
I've been practicing my domesticity,
waxing the hardwood floors. He leans close,

tells me that in the Philippines they use coconut halves,
strap them to their feet and skate. Eva used to do that.
His words are whiskey.

We waver there between nobody's business
and a dangerous urge to be honest.
Children holding secret boxes, lifting one corner
to let each other peer into our dark.

Pops hands me a blue-flecked bowl
amidst smells of liquor and waxed wood.
Embers of ourselves, dying for these quiet comforts.

The Summer I Carried a Gun

"What kind of gun you carry?" These were the first words I ever heard from A.T. Boone's mouth.

"I don't carry a gun," I said.

"I mean, what kind of gun you got in your car?"

"I don't carry a gun in my car."

"You mean to tell me you brought mah little girl all the way down to Georgia from Arkansas without a gun in your car?"

Aubre Tillman Boone was incredulous. He was speaking slowly and without anger, but his expression was that of a man suspicious he was being kidded but more afraid that he was hearing something true but unnatural and contrary to good order and morality. We were sitting at the kitchen table, and A.T. startled me when he suddenly raised his voice: "Bubba!" My thirteen-year-old brother-in-law appeared in the door. The boy's real name was Aubre Tillman Boone, Junior, but everyone called him Bubba. A.T. told him, "Bring me some handguns in heah."

It took Bubba a couple of trips to place six or seven firearms on the table, politely positioning the barrels so that they pointed away from us. A.T. told me to pick out one for myself. There was a black .32 automatic of Italian make that I recognized as identical to a pistol my father owned. Seeing an opportunity to impress A.T. with my acquaintance with guns, I pointed to it and was about to speak when he broke in. "Naw, you don't want that damn thing," he said. "I shot a man five times with that gun and he didn' fall down till he was *outside* the pool hall."

It was March of 1966, and I was wishing I had not worn a Madras sport coat on my first visit to Georgia not only because of the cold drizzle that began as I unloaded the car, but also because I could sense A.T. couldn't believe a white man would wear such a colorful garment. I soon got the idea that A.T. couldn't believe a lot of things about me, one of them being that in spite of his never having heard of me, I had recently married his only daughter and was now sitting in his kitchen and drinking his beer. To top it off, he had discovered that contrary to reason and custom, I was unarmed.

I managed to tell A.T. that I didn't intend to ask for the .32, just wanted to point out that my father had one like it and didn't think much of it either. There was a handsome silver Smith & Wesson .38 police special that I liked, but A.T. said he was thinking of "putting it in the green Foad." He pronounced *Ford* to rhyme with *toad*. I was twenty years old and had grown up in Little Rock thinking I lived in the South. No one I knew talked this way. (Later, I would hear a Georgia man ask A.T. if he had a "ridiatah for a foe-ty foe Foad.") We talked over the weapons for a while, A.T. deciding that he had a special plan for each of the pistols I selected. Finally, I was left with an antique—a .38 caliber revolver called a "lemon-squeezer" because it did not possess a traditional hammer. The firing mechanism was powered by a spring concealed within the handle. The safety was also unique. The gun could not be fired unless the back of the handle was being "squeezed" by the grip of the shooter.

I hadn't even shed my absurd jacket and already I had been given all the beer I could drink as well as an unusual handgun. The next day, I blew apart numerous cans with my strange pistol. I found to my delight that I was a pretty good shot, especially if the target was moving. Young Bubba

29

would toss the cans in the air or send them rolling along the ground, and I would blast away. I learned to point the gun rather than try to aim it. The pistol made a satisfyingly loud BLAM and shuddered in my hand when I squeezed the trigger. Since I had to buy the ammunition, we didn't play this game for very long. And that was how I came to have a loaded gun in my glove compartment.

One morning soon after our arrival, as I was shaving I happened to look out the open bathroom window. A large yellow dog of no discernible breed was standing in the backyard and looking back at me. As we regarded each other, the dog's skull suddenly exploded in a pink cloud and the animal dropped out of my sight. I watched as the old black hired man took one of the dog's legs and dragged him off into the woods behind the house. When I went in the kitchen, A.T. was sitting at the table. He asked me whether I had seen what happened earlier, and I said that I had. The unfortunate stray had "taken up" around there sometime back, and it seemed to A.T. that the dog had been trying to have an unnatural sexual relationship with Samson, my mother-in-law's testy male Chihuahua. Apparently, A.T. had had enough of the stray that morning and had used the .22 that leaned against the wall behind the kitchen door to put an end to this foolishness. He asked me not to mention it to my wife, Gloria, or her mother. No need to upset the women.

A.T. didn't seem too concerned about them the next evening. We had finished supper and night had fallen. My wife and I were sitting with A.T. at the kitchen table when Bubba came in and said that he thought he'd heard a noise coming from the back yard. Gloria was at the end of the table facing me with her back to the porch door. I watched over her shoulder as A.T. strolled out and pushed open the screen door that opened on the back steps. I didn't realize what was about to happen, or I would have warned Gloria. A.T. had somehow produced a .45 automatic, and crossing the arm that held the gun across the arm that propped open the screen door, he fired four shots into the darkness. He was only a few feet behind my wife who was unprepared for the terrific explosions that rang out over the concrete floor of the porch. We watched as her father turned the side of his head to the open door. Though his ears must have still been ringing, I realized that he was listening for any sound from the yard—a moan perhaps? Something trying to crawl away? A.T. said he'd go look around in the morning, I suppose to check for a puddle of blood. Mary, my mother-in-law, who had gone to bed, now came rushing in, fearing the worst, I suppose. We had a good laugh at my wife's shocked reaction, but I was a little shaken myself. I'd had enough gunfire to last me for a while and was ready to get back to Arkansas. Mary, by the way, could never accompany us to our gates when she took us to the Atlanta or Augusta airports because she, too, packed heat. What she called "my little gun" was a four-barrel Derringer loaded with .22 caliber long-rifle hollow point bullets. There were four firing pins, and when she squeezed the trigger, the rounds would go off simultaneously. I never fired her gun nor saw it fired. I didn't even like to look at it much. Mary kept it in her purse with her car keys and wallet.

We returned to Georgia in June when we learned that my mother-in-law, who was only forty years old and had never smoked in her life, had been diagnosed with throat cancer and was to undergo a radical resection to remove the lymph, healthy and malignant, from both sides of her neck. And so began the summer of my Southern education. We drove back and forth from the hospital in Macon until Mary was able to come home to recuperate. I found myself spending a lot of time with my new father-in-law.

A.T. was in his late forties when I first met him, but a hard life and heavy drinking made him look considerably older. He was tall and still strong, but his shoulders were rounding

31

and his long arms were losing their bulk. His gray hair was cut short and usually kept beneath a fedora indoors and out. He wore his pants low on his hips, his pockets bulging with his pistol, keys, lighter and—held by a thick rubber band—a huge roll of cash, hundreds and fifties on the outside. I know he could read because I watched him carefully inspect contracts and warranties and the occasional life insurance policy he took out on his teenage son as a sort of investment given the boy's proclivity for finding trouble and violence, but I never saw A.T. read a book or even a newspaper. The library in his office at the junk yard consisted of Tijuana comics starring Dagwood and Blondie and a couple of tattered nudist magazines. All in all, he was a solitary, silent man, spending his days and nights drinking and brooding. Under the circumstances, he and I got along pretty well. A.T. provided room and board, but I needed to make some money. We clashed when he pulled some strings to get me hired at the Washington County garage and couldn't believe that I was so ignorant of basic auto mechanics that I turned down the job. When I told him, he suddenly stood up and shouted that nobody was going to make a goddamn fool out of him. He gave me a look so fierce that adrenaline shot through me. I truly believed that we were going to tangle, but after I managed to stutter out an apology, A.T. settled down, and we went back to our beers. I got pretty good at brooding myself.

Since Sandersville didn't provide any employment opportunities for a twenty-year-old college student with no mechanical ability, A.T. hired me at something like minimum wage to help him at his metal salvage business. I spent my days doing odd jobs like cleaning brick or painting model numbers on transmissions or sorting metal from iron. (The iron is the stuff with rust on it; the metal is the stuff without rust on it.) Of course, I was incompetent labor. Once, when A.T. told me to cut the spindles (whatever they were) off an old Cadillac, I managed to set the car's tires as well as the surrounding grass on fire with the acetylene torch. It didn't help that the bucket I brought down from the shelter contained kerosene and not water. Much of my time was spent sitting with A.T. in his office, whose plate glass windows overlooked piles of various metals and acres of wrecked cars. We spent our evenings after supper smoking and drinking beer in the kitchen. I came to understand that long silences were more in order than conversation, but little by little I came to know something of the man and his history.

A.T.'s mother, Mamie, lived in one of his better rental houses. She paid a reduced rent, true, but she still paid. The one time I was in her place I nearly passed out because although it was a fine spring day, the wood-burning stove in the living room was going full blast. It must have been ninety degrees. Mamie, a shrunken old crone barely four feet tall, could walk beneath the cloud of heat. Her late husband, A.T.'s father, was a brutal alcoholic who beat his only son frequently and well until A.T. was big enough to fight back, which he had to do only once. In the ninth grade, rather than suffer a whipping with a belt at the hands of the school principal, A.T. left the building, but he didn't go home. Instead, he waited for the school day to end, waylaid the principal, and thrashed the man in a fight fair enough that A.T. escaped prosecution. That ended his formal education. When World War II came along, A.T. was drafted.

As he boarded the bus that would take him to boot camp, Mamie called out, "I'll pray for you, Aubre." A.T. replied, "Pray, hell, it's too late. I'm done gone!" A.T. came out of basic training an infantryman, but his mechanical know-how got him assigned to the motor pool. He spent a lot of time in the stockade, but his C.O. would spring him because he needed men like A.T. to keep the tanks, Jeeps, and trucks running. The young soldier wound up in Italy, and one day got to visit Rome, where he was very impressed by the

Coliseum, a place he was told people "who had done some meanness" were thrown to the lions. His outfit was in on the assault of Monte Casino, and A.T. was supposed to play a combat role, but he declined to participate. "I saw them going up the road," he said. "I sat there drinking that dago red and watched them go. Hell, them Eye-talians never done anything to me." I didn't feel like pointing out that Monte Casino had been defended by German troops.

A.T. came home to Georgia with a small fortune he had made playing poker in the Army. Having survived the Depression and a world war, not to mention a brutal father, A.T. was determined—in spite of his lack of education or connections—to make something of himself by going into business. He bought a small grocery store that failed. He ran a pool hall and beer joint for a time until they, too, went under. After a costly adventure with chickens, he went in for pig farming, believing there was much money to be made. He put everything he had into his swine operation. He built a farrowing shed for his sows, but right after they delivered, a rare and record-breaking Georgia snow storm collapsed the roof, killing the sows and their issue and wiping A.T. out. Through it all, though, he managed to buy land and hold on to it. The three-mile stretch of highway connecting Sandersville and Tennille came to be known as "Boonetown," since A.T. owned nearly all the land on either side of the road. He made some money from the shotgun shacks he built and rented, even for a time running a drive-in theatre.

But his fortunes really changed when he discovered metal. It began with his buying wrecked cars for next to nothing. Some cars and trucks he repaired and sold—repossessing many of them to be sold again and again. But real money was to be made in salvage. A.T. liked to impress me now and then by loading up a flatbed truck with aluminum or copper or whatever when the price was right and hauling it to Macon to sell. I went with him on one trip which brought

34

in over four thousand dollars. He gave me some hard-earned business advice when he told me, "Son, never deal in anything that eats or that people eat." After all, iron may rust, but it will be there when the crops fail or the pigs die or the grocery store goes out of business or the honky-tonk closes. Those eyesores of scrap metal and wrecked cars piled on one another that dot Southern highways are really gold mines. A.T. put the money he made from metal into more and more land, another commodity that doesn't have to eat to keep its value.

By the time I knew him, A.T. was well known as a tough and shrewd businessman who knew his way around deals, deeds, and lawsuits. He was basically honest—no one was expected to tell the government the truth—and his personal word could be trusted. When it was necessary, he was not above getting his hands dirty or bloody to protect his interests. It was said that the KKK once tried to recruit him, but he told them he didn't need them. Both black and white citizens of Washington County gave A.T. Boone plenty of respect. Now and then, an episode like the pool hall shooting would reinforce his reputation as a man to be taken seriously.

During my Georgia summer, a nearby rendering plant—what amounted to a glue factory for the disposal of animal carcasses—began to put out more odor than previously. A.T. called to complain, but the stench only got worse. I listened as he telephoned the plant's owner one last time and told him, "You're stinking up the place because your insinuator ain't working right, and that's a dangerous situation. No, sah, a faulty insinuator can cause a fire that will burn your whole operation to the ground." The odors soon ceased.

One lot on Highway 15 that A.T. had been unable to acquire belonged to the congregation of a Pentecostal church, and they refused to sell. It was particularly galling to A.T. because the church's land was not far from his own house, and when the church's windows were open in the

35

summer, the noise of their singing and holy roller hullabaloo was audible and annoying. I asked A.T. once whether he ever went to church, and his comeback was quick and calm: "Son, the Bible says to avoid all *appearance* of evil."

Once, a delegation from the church came calling to demand that A.T evict one of his renters. An old black woman who called herself Princess Little Dove was operating a fortune-telling business out of her home. The princess was long gone by the time I got to Georgia, but I asked about her after cleaning out a storage shed and coming across a large signboard with her name painted on it along with the outline of a hand divided into sections like a butcher's schematic of a cow. The church elders allowed as how her profession was forbidden by the Bible and fortunetellers were as bad as witches—let alone a colored fortuneteller—and they didn't care to have such goings on so close to their place of worship. Gloria was a child when they came to the house that Sunday evening after working themselves up into a righteous lather, but she vividly recalled A.T. standing on his front porch and listening to their petition. He heard them out and then calmly told them he had no intention of removing a tenant who paid her rent on time and never made a bit of trouble for him. When they objected, A.T. reminded the preacher that he'd bought him the first suit of clothes the man had ever owned, that one of the deacons still owed him for twenty yards of dirt delivered years ago, that another of their number had never paid him back for bailing his worthless son out of jail, that he had a drawer full of bad checks from a prominent member of their communion of saints, and that he had stood by when the preacher's brother-in-law had sold A.T. a beater car but returned soon after to remove the ten gallons of moonshine hidden in its trunk. (A.T. once gave me a Mason jar of shine, explaining that it was good stuff since it didn't have any hair or detergent in it.) At any rate, the church fathers had enough, finally, and withdrew, and Princess Little Dove stayed.

Princess Little Dove's being black wouldn't have bothered A.T. at all. He was, of course, a racist, but I never heard him express malice or hatred toward African-Americans. The word *nigger* was perfectly natural to him, but he used it in a descriptive rather than a pejorative sense. Blacks addressed A.T. as Captain Boone and gave him the same fake respect and deference they pretended for whites in general, but I had the feeling they considered that he dealt with them fairly. I was somewhat troubled by the case of Essie Lee, the family's black housekeeper who also helped with the cooking. She and her old hound dog named "Hangover" lived rent-free in one of A.T.'s houses. She ate most of her meals in his kitchen, had access to his account at a grocery store, and when she needed a doctor, A.T. would pay for the visit. Trouble was, he paid Essie Lee very little salary at all. I once suggested to my mother-in-law that the arrangement was reminiscent of an older era in the South, and she simply said, "Essie Lee can leave any time she wants to." Of course, Essie Lee didn't have a car, and I was drafted once to take her to the doctor. Sweetly and with dignity, she refused get in the front seat but insisted on riding in the back. I think of my chauffeuring experience as "Driving Miss Essie." She insisted on calling me "Mistah Clark."

I went into the kitchen one afternoon to find the source of a wonderful aroma laced with bay leaf and thyme. A huge stock pot was steaming on the stove. Essie Lee watched as I lifted the lid and looked down at the skull of a hog looking back at me with his empty eye sockets. She was boiling the meat off the head to make Brunswick stew, a tasty concoction of stewed pork, okra, corn, and butter beans, with shreds of chicken when squirrel wasn't available. Coming from a background of beef and potatoes, I began to appreciate Georgia cuisine—especially the vegetables, small yellow squash and zucchini or fresh green snap beans and sweet onions cooked slam to death in a liquor bubbling with fatback and what they called streak-o-lean. Nearly everything was fried—pork chops, catfish, salty country ham, Gulf shrimp, and, best of all, tender chicken fried in lard in a huge black iron skillet—fried at such high heat that the delicate flour batter was always brown and crispy but never greasy. They served a sort of flat crisp bread made by frying white corn meal that I have never been able to duplicate—though I have learned to fry chicken. I came to love grits and red-eye gravy and fresh eggs scrambled in butter, but I resisted their iced tea, which they loaded up with both saccharine and sugar. I never got used to the Georgia sweet tooth. Someone gave A.T. a bottle of seven-year-old hundred proof Black Jack Daniels Tennessee whiskey, and I nearly gagged when I watched him pour it into a glass of Pepsi and add a spoonful of sugar for good measure. Essie Lee told me she would bake me a chocolate cake, and I looked forward to it all day. But when she sliced it, it was only yellow cake with chocolate icing. It was explained to me that what I had in mind was called "devil's-food" cake. One day, craving red meat, I brought home a magnificent beef roast. To my horror, Essie Lee boiled it on the stove in her hog's head stock pot.

As the summer continued, I began to settle into my new environment—pretending to work for A.T., hunting occasionally with Bubba—when we came back with some rabbits one day, Gloria suggested we shoot the little kittens playing in the den, since they too were soft and furry. I enjoyed driving out to fish camps for cold beer and flounder and crisp cole slaw, or picking up a little Civil War history and geography— Sandersville's claim to fame was that it had been burned by Sherman on his way to Savannah from Atlanta. We made a trip to Milledgeville and tried unsuccessfully to locate the survivors of Flannery O'Connor's peacock flock.

More than once, I thought of that great writer. I had thought the gothic South in her stories was pure imagination, but after a while, I realized she wasn't exaggerating.

Once a man came into A.T.'s office furious and indignant because he'd not been seated on the jury set to try a black man for raping his employer's white daughter. "They asked me did I believe in insanity as a defense, and I said I did but not in this case, and they dismissed me!" I had wanted to witness this trial, but it was over, jury selection and all, in one morning and afternoon. The defendant was apparently clearly insane but was sentenced to death anyway. From time to time, A.T.'s tenants would come to his house to borrow his telephone. One evening, a woman holding one tow-headed toddler on her hip and dragging another behind her used the phone to call the Justice of the Peace in order to get a restraining order on her husband. I gasped when I heard her say, "I thought it was going to be all right until Buddy thowed the baby at me." No one else was fazed. "Oh, that Buddy, he's a case." Once we went to the hospital to visit Mary's hairdresser. The young woman had met a man at a local tonk, and they were on their way to his trailer when she jumped from his speeding truck, breaking both legs and both hands. He had told her he was going to eat her until she hollered uncle, and she feared she was going to be cannibalized.

Very few people called on A.T. socially. One of the few was Little Bit—a man around thirty, who must have weighed over three hundred pounds. On the occasions when he worked, Little Bit drove a taxi in Milledgeville. The sheriff had been irritated by Little Bit a few years before and had gotten a local prostitute to lie and say Little Bit had tried to rape her. While he was in prison, Little Bit had assembled a lamp made entirely of Popsicle sticks. He brought it to A.T. when he got out. I wondered if he had had to eat all those Popsicles but my mother-in-law assured me they were "clean sticks."

Around the Fourth of July, Little Bit invited me to sit in on a poker game, and I took him up on it. Archie Bunker once suggested that hijackings could be eliminated if passengers were issued pistols as they boarded the plane, reasoning that then "everybody would be afraid to make a move." Archie had a point. When you're playing poker in a stinking shed cobbled together with two-by-fours and sheets of corrugated iron and everyone is drinking pretty steadily and smoking non-stop in spite of the gasoline-soaked rags and disassembled carburetors scattered all about, when you're in a situation like that, it is amazing how controlled tempers can be and how mild-mannered the players are, regardless of winning or losing, and then you realize that everybody in the place is armed, which, rather than increasing the level of barbarity, has the effect of putting everyone on his best behavior.

This was a good thing because my poker buddies were a pretty scruffy lot of crusty-fingered grimeys, bony skulls beneath homemade haircuts, gobs of Redman tobacco and clear glass jars for spit cups, wads of dirty twenties for table stakes, narrow squinty pale splintered eyes checking me out, accents so thick and mush-mouthed Little Bit had to translate their bets for me. It looked like a casting call for "Deliverance." One dangerous-looking individual had come straight to the game from jail. Some of these guys clearly couldn't afford to lose much, and for once the cards wouldn't quit coming my way—seven-card stud with three raises on five bets and no limits, and I'd have a pair down nearly every hand and usually match them. I was ahead at least two hundred dollars and desperate to quit, but there was no way I would be allowed to leave the game. Around midnight, a slack-jawed idiot with an obvious flush raised me forty bucks, all he had from the looks of it, and I had to call since I had a pair of kings down and two showing. He watched me take his money and then stumbled outside, on his way home I hoped. But he'd only gone out to his truck where he retrieved a Roman candle and fired its contents horizontally into the shed, ending the game and sending the rest of us scrambling for the exit. Mercifully, there were no explosions or injuries.

Such diversions were rare, however, and I settled into the slow pace of Southern life, avoiding the sweet tea and trying to ignore the casual racist language. But having spent most of my life in cities, one thing I could not become accustomed to was the darkness of the rural Georgia nights.

Driving after sundown on the narrow country roads was like driving into a lightless cave, just pure blackness ahead, behind, and all around. The darkness seemed thick, as if the headlights could reach only a small distance ahead of the car. There was nothing but blackness beyond the blackness. Often there were no yellow dividing lines on the roads, and white lines at the shoulders were uncommon. Sometimes the car's lights would strike gashes of red clay that marked the ditches, or else walls of pine trees would faintly reflect our headlights. Whenever I came upon a vehicle ahead of me, I was grateful because its tail lights would at least indicate the curves of the highway. Even the headlights of approaching cars were somewhat helpful, but traffic was sparse, especially if the hour was late. There really wasn't anywhere to go in central Georgia after sundown in 1966 anyway, at least nowhere for people not intent on trouble. One night, I was to find just how far into deepest, darkest Georgia I had come.

When the car passed us, I was relieved to get its obnoxious headlights out of my rearview mirror. Besides, I was also glad to have its taillights now as a guide to the curves of the dark and unfamiliar two-lane highway. The speed limit was only 55, but given the condition of the winding, mostly unmarked road, I was content to poke along as the car in front put more and more distance between us until it was finally out of sight. I was a little surprised a short time later when I realized that not only could I see it once more up ahead but we were gaining on it rapidly. It was as if the car were waiting for us to catch up. I slowed to its speed, around forty, keeping several car lengths between us, and as soon as it was safe to do so, I passed the car and maintained passing speed for a while to put some distance between us.

A little later, I noticed high-beam headlights in my mirror, and they were coming up fast. Soon, the interior of our car was full of bright light. Whoever it was was right on my bumper. When the road straightened and I could see the path ahead was clear, I dropped speed and moved as far to the right side of the narrow road as I could to let the jerk who was tailgating me go around. As he roared past us, I was a little surprised to recognize the car as the one I had just passed myself and which had first passed me five minutes before. I try to avoid little games on the highway, so I was gratified to see the other car move ahead of us at a high speed and finally disappear.

Gloria and I were returning to Sandersville from Macon, where we had been to visit her mother in the hospital where she was recovering from cancer surgery. The highway barely qualified as a red-line road, and the trip usually took well over an hour. It was around eleven o'clock on a Saturday night, and we had the road nearly to ourselves, so we had been making good time when the other car passed us the first time. We were probably half an hour from home when he passed us again. A few minutes later, I found myself closing rapidly on some faint taillights up ahead. My heart sank when I realized we were once more behind the car that had just passed us and that he was once again slowing down to the point that he would force me to pass him again. He dropped his speed so much and so quickly, in fact, that it was obvious to Gloria and me that we were being messed with. There was nothing to do, however, but go ahead and pass him a second time

42

and hope that the teenagers or whoever they were would get bored with the game.

The other car was moving no faster than thirty-five when we went around it. We could see that there were two people in the dark Crown Victoria, and as we went by we exchanged stares. Our playmates were grown white men, and, amazingly, they were wearing neckties! For a second, considering their Crown Victoria, it crossed my mind that they might be police, not necessarily a good thing in central Georgia in the summer of 1966. No telling whose side they might be on. Times were very tense. Medgar Evers had been shot down three summers before. Goodman, Schwerner, and Cheney had been murdered and buried in an earthen dam in Mississippi only two summers before for their crime of trying to register black voters. In fact, we had driven from Memphis to Georgia on the same highway and on the same day in early June that James Meredith was shot during his so-called "March Against Fear." Civil rights workers in the South of that era could not depend on local law enforcement for protection, knowing that the same man who is sheriff by day could also be a torch-lit Klansman by night. Besides, my haircut or lack of it had already drawn some stares from the good old boys.

In case these guys were cops, I didn't want to give them a pretext for stopping us, so I slowed down to just above the speed limit after I was safely past them. But in no time, here they came. We were beginning to establish a routine. They tailgated me dangerously close, blinding me with their high beams. I slowed down and moved slightly towards the berm, giving them ample opportunity to pass. They did so, then sped up the highway a mile or so until they decided to wait for me again. I decided to stay farther back, but when they slowed to thirty, it was impossible not to soon be back where they apparently wanted me, trailing along behind them, glad for the absence of other traffic—considering the target the rear of my car would make to someone speeding along a curve behind us—but wishing there were other cars around because the situation had become more than creepy.

Gloria urged me to pass the bastards and then burn up the road as fast as I could until we got to Tennille, where there was a police station of sorts. Built on the little town's square, it was a kiosk-like affair—rather like a one-hour photo place—that was large enough to accommodate a telephone, a police radio, and a cop or two. I decided my wife was right. We were probably only ten miles from Tennille, so it wouldn't take long for my Cutlass to get to the square and reach what at least purported to be the enforcers of law and order. When the road ahead seemed straight enough and clear of traffic, I started around the Ford. But this time there was a change in the script—before I could get past them, they accelerated, and we barreled down the road side by side going seventy before I yielded the race and dropped back, not feeling particularly like James Bond or Junior Johnson and also alarmed by the way the Ford had edged over the center line, crowding me, threatening to run us off the road. Once again, my antagonist slowed, this time moving to the center to block me and then moving back, taunting me. We could see the passenger leaning over the back of his seat watching us.

"Give me the gun," I said, not believing I had said it. Gloria took the .38 from the glove box and handed it to me. I set it in my lap. For a minute, I had time to appreciate the absurdity of the circumstances. What was I doing playing tag on a midnight highway in Georgia with a loaded gun between my legs? It occurred to me that the men in the Ford were bound to be armed, too. If they opened fire, would I be able to aim and shoot with my left hand while steering with my right? About a mile outside of Tennille, the other car suddenly accelerated, leaving us behind. Gloria memorized the Ford's license plate number before they were out of sight.

44

In a second, we were in the little town, and handing the gun to Gloria to return to the glove box, I pulled up next to a county squad car parked by the little police hut. There were three lawmen there: a sheriff's deputy, a federal tax agent—a.k.a. revenuer—and the grizzled old top cop of Tennille, Officer Manning. They weren't much interested in our adventure at first, but they perked up when they recognized Gloria as A.T. Boone's daughter. We got out of the car and were still telling our tale when the Ford pulled up and the two men got out. Both in their late twenties—one dark and scrawny and one redheaded and fat—they were dressed in white short-sleeved shirts and wearing ties, looking for all the world like Mormon missionaries. They immediately began to claim that *we* had tried to run *them* off the highway. "We figure them for freedom riders with that long hair on him and those Yankee plates," the scrawny one said. Yankee plates? Arkansas?

Officer Manning said he wanted to hear my wife's version of what happened, but the redhead kept interrupting and calling her a liar. "I know you!" she exclaimed. "You're Red Salter!" "And you're a lying bitch," Red said. Officer Manning had had enough, and reaching for his handcuffs, he stepped in front of Red. Manning was in his sixties, and though he was a tall man, he didn't seem to be a match for Red, who I now realized was built more like a tackle than a fat man. "Put out your hands," Manning said as he reached for Red's wrists. Red jerked his arms back, and Manning struck him hard in the side of his head with a huge fist. The deputy had opened the back door of the police car, and Manning shoved the startled giant backwards into the rear seat, managing to crack Red's head solidly against the edge of the roof of the car. The revenuer, who was carrying a metal flashlight at least a foot long, rushed into the other side of the backseat. We couldn't see what was going on in the squad car, but the sounds of blows and gasps of pain were clear enough. Then they dragged Salter out of the car and propped him against a fender. His shirt and tie were missing, and his face and chest were covered with bright blood. Manning asked us whether we wanted to press charges. My wife said yes, but I said no. As far as I could see, this had worked out pretty well. Why complicate matters? It turned out that our tormentors were "policy men," purveyors of cheap burial insurance sold to poor whites and blacks. Red was arrested for resisting arrest, and the driver, Red's boss, was released and told to go home to Augusta.

We drove the two miles to A.T.'s house. I could hardly wait to tell him how well I had handled things—no one hurt except Red Salter, no shots fired, A.T.'s daughter safe and sound. I was wrong. A.T. was angry when he discovered that I hadn't fired my gun. "I'd at least of put a couple of rounds in his gas tank to remember me by!" And when he found out the Augusta man had been released, he was on the phone to the sheriff's office insisting they cut him off before he could get out of the county. Then he piled Gloria and me into his car to go to Tennille where we would press charges.

When we pulled up at the little square, what looked like two dozen rednecks were already there, milling around and drinking beer. It was like a grade B movie, some kind of pickup truck epic. A.T. got out of the car, but when I opened my door, I found it blocked halfway by Officer Manning. "Why don't you just stay in the car for a little while?" he said softly, explaining that those assembled were all Red's relatives or friends, and they most likely would be upset with my freedom-riding Yankee self for causing all this ruckus. My wife explained to me that the Salters were a large Snopes-like clan and that the man with the huge beer belly talking to A.T. was their patriarch. A.T. and this individual seemed calm enough, but I wasn't so sure about the rest of the Jukes and Kallicaks who were gawking at us, trying to get a look at me.

46

I was happy to remain in the car. Through the half-opened door, Officer Manning inquired whether I had a gun. Not on me, I replied. How about a permit? No sir. Manning allowed that it might be a good idea for me to take the gun with me when I traveled in Washington County. "Just keep it on the passenger seat in plain view," he said. "And if you have to get out of the car, put it in your belt so people can see it."

It was nearly dawn before we finally went home. The Augusta man had been apprehended, and somehow it was arranged that he and Red would spend the night in jail and that we would drop the charges the next day. A.T. was content that his honor had been satisfied, along with mine and his daughter's, and the Salter tribe was also mollified, though as they dispersed they seemed to me to be a little disappointed that things were concluded in such a peaceful manner.

A.T. let everyone know that Red and his boss were damned lucky, because his son-in-law was a crack shot but also had a cool head, and the Salters assured A.T. that Red would never had done what he did if he had known A.T.'s daughter was in the car with the Yankee plates.

For the rest of the summer, I carried my .38 lemon-squeezer wherever I went. It felt a little odd at first to walk into the service station for cigarettes or into the hardware store for ammo with the pistol's handle protruding from the waist of my jeans, but no one seemed to take much notice, and after a while I kind of got to like the feeling. Gloria kiddingly predicted I would probably manage to blow my manhood off, but I never left the house unarmed. I would see Red from time to time. He rented a little house trailer from A.T. and had to drive by our place to get to his. A.T. later kicked Red off his land, but not because he had terrorized me and his daughter but because A.T. found out that Red had destroyed a dog by first shooting it in its legs before finally delivering the blow of grace to its head. No excuse for cruelty to a dog.

As for me, I could tell that A.T. thought I had let him down by not starting a firefight on the highway. Gloria assured me that no one could live up to her father's expectations and that I shouldn't let it worry me. But what rankled most was that I had come to like the old S.O.B. so much that I didn't want to disappoint him. I realized then that I had been in the South long enough.

The rest of the summer passed without incident, and as soon as my mother-in-law had recovered from her surgery, Gloria and I started back to Arkansas. We took the southern route, headed for Tupelo on our way to Memphis. Just the other side of Birmingham, Alabama, we passed a white van. Stenciled on its side in green letters were the words, "Knights of the Green Forest—KKK." The van stayed behind us all the way to the Mississippi line. But I wasn't too concerned. After all, I still had my trusty lemon-squeezer, and I was now willing to demonstrate that I knew how to use it.

C. D. ALBIN

Cicero Jack, Farmer,
Rues the Ruin of an Ozark River

They may as well track mud on my grandmother's
Persian rug—beer-swilling week-enders
down from Kansas City or St. Louis,
hell-bent to float a clear stream where they swear

litter laws don't apply and local accents
prove inbreeding. Yesterday I watched one fool
stand and whiz till he flipped his hooting friends
face-first into the current, their new aluminum

canoe upended while they waded, wobbling
and cursing, toward the nearest bank.
Watch for moccasins I called to one drunk
sloshing beneath limbs, but he stared back

like I'd sprouted a horn from my forehead.
That's when I turned, left them to serpents
as their natural kin. But later, truck-stalled
in the middle of Brixey Bridge, I spotted

their stone-stoved canoe adrift in swift water.
My heart kicked like the time I met a riderless
 horse down Devil's Backbone, and old as I am
I shinnied the bank to rescue what I could.

The canoe cradled nothing but tennis shoes,
an Orvis cap, and empties of Coors and Busch.
Knee-deep or better, river rock rolling
beneath my feet, I wrestled the whole mess

to dry ground, scanned noon-bright surface
until hyena giggles and belly laughs carried
over the water to tell me they'd survived,
would return to weekday suits, striped ties.

BRUCE WEST

Photographs from *Landscapes*

Shady Acres, Missouri

The Woods Behind the Houses, Missouri, #4

Fallen Sycamore, Missouri

Strawberry Net, Missouri

Goodman's Garden, Missouri

My Backyard, Missouri

The Chats, Missouri, #6

JESSICA GLOVER

On My Way to Heaven, Stockton, Missouri 2005

Itinerants on the shore have taken off their shirts this morning
to reveal the raw glow their flesh holds. The deck hands shout
in an ancient cadence, release a reefed sheet, and hoist it aloft.
I watch their rituals with religious devotion. One man, shoulders
broad as the flag above, stands near the mizzen, blacks out the sun.
Both boots planted on the polished planks, he rocks back, cups hands
across brow, spits—I think how he could bend two ropes around
my bed frame, trade this heart for a terracotta pot, then steal away.
I watch him climb atop the sailboat's mast. He sways above me,
lifts his hands toward the sun, and falls back with complete faith
that the harness around his waist will hold. Below, I am laid out flat
on a freshly-scrubbed deck. My skin as white as those new sails
taking their first breath after the winter months. The wind catches,
and I watch the top half of his body swing back and forth freely
against the May sky. You're going to die, I yell with a nervous laugh.
He pauses. Ospry circle the ripples for a shadow darting just beneath
the surface. The sailors pour another round on the dock. The boat rocks
gently. I finally relax and spend the afternoon thinking of an answer
after he yells back down to me: Can you imagine a more beautiful way?

Jessica Glover

Sky Lanterns

Wild children bound across a cut wheat field
with painted bamboo cages to light candles, release
a hundred ballooned flames for the October horizon.
The oiled rice papers expand, slowly ascend
over the rows of upturned faces. She imagines
each luminescence—an eviscerated soul
floating like jellyfish from a bleached coral
to the water's surface. Her thoughts drift along
the hilltops with them. By dusk they will crash
against a telephone pole or a building's window
in the nearest city. The hoi-polloi shuffling over
the remains as they hurry along to a luncheon.
Maybe one will make it to the border, settle briefly
on a stream's alluvial sediment before it succumbs.

Jessica Glover

Babushka Dolls

Barely able to stand, she cooks the family breakfast. Scrapes the butter from the wrapper. Wipes the butter from the knife onto the edge of the iron skillet. Then folds the wrapper neatly, corner to corner, and files it in the back of a drawer. *Because sometimes all you have is the butter on the wrapper.* She turns back to the stove. The butter has slid down the side of the skillet and now sizzles away. But I've never heard her say those words. Only heard you, Father, tell your seventh-male-child-version of grandmother's lessons of poverty, of lack, of depression. I remember a painting in her dining room. You remember too. Frame still hanging on the same nail, in the same wall, since we were both children old enough to blush over the voluptuous bathing women but still too young to understand their curves, their power. Does she know I want it when she dies? That I pray her death is as peaceful as her Sunday morning ritual. The family eats breakfast on the couches, talks about the preacher on channel five. *After this man is another man. Then a black and white western.* It's always black and white on Sundays. I slip from the conversation, pass the painting of those waiting women, and creak down into the basement. I read for hours from her granny novels, those paper backs with the front cover lovers, yellow and creased. The words so seductive page and page. She had a cousin I've never met build special-sized plywood shelves to hold them all. Spines line one full wall round the corner to the middle of the far side where they stop at an old bed piled with empty shoe boxes, dusty plastic flowers, babushka dolls she collected when grandfather was stationed overseas. His clothes still hang on rods around the room. His uniforms stand at attention. Beside them, his daily clothes slouch on their hangers. Neutral styles from a harder life, too dated for the cousins to steal. Rough overalls. Scratchy, square-cut jeans. A pair of old boots, still muddy. Would he even wear them if he finally came home after his long battle? What would he say to his widow sitting in her recliner watching the gospel channel? Would he laugh: *Woman, why you kept all this crap so many years?* Twenty-five? No, closer to thirty now? Does it even matter? Your mother doesn't wear her wedding band anymore. When I suggest we should have the ring re-sized because it's too small for her finger, my mother, who prattles around aimlessly trying to fit herself, shakes her head. *No, she's not been able to go down there for many years now.* Her voice catches and drifts back towards the basement where I gather the painted babushka dolls, crack each woman like an egg, and dig the identical, smaller version out of its dark home. No arms to reach out for the other, I line them up. Each a stair step ending in the baby lathed from a single piece of wood. Father, I have known pleasure, known her missing double buckled platforms, but I cannot picture my grandmother as any doll but the matryona that holds everyone safe inside her. I don't know how she came to own a fresco of twenty naked women in the goddess' bathhouse. Tell me how she felt crossing back over the Pacific alone, the power of the liquid earth heaving and sighing. Did she breathe the salty air? Store it deep inside, knowing she would never leave her house again. Father, did she ever rise in the middle of the night to stare at those majestic women, and then walk through her consecrated home, naked and hovering through the remains?

JESSICA GLOVER

Baby Jandolyn

I.

They left this town after the accident.
My truck met their bull chewing its cud.
When I didn't see Ed weaving the wire
back in place I headed over. The heifers
suffered most. Stood spraddle-legged,
balking in their stalls when I arrived,
udders engorged to veiny white globes.
Heard them even before I turned down
the dirt drive. Three days gone I figured.
Must have stolen out in the dead of the night.
Up and left. Probably couldn't handle
the town's talk. The way I see it though,
at some point, all fifteen year olds fuck up.

II.

We couldn't stay after the accident.
Finding the baby that way got to Bobby.
The mineral-rich water preserved the body;
coroner said the black marks on her neck
matched the final story her mother told.
It doesn't seem natural what that girl did.
Mothers, even young ones, don't do that.
They don't let their babies slip through holes.
Mothers don't let their babies float for days
in some well while the family's searching
all hours, hollering over the hills and praying.

Mothers pray. Mothers protect their children.
We had to leave that town and not look back.

III.
Been around the dead on this job, but that
changes you. Wife turns off the lights—I see
that bundle materialize from the dark.
Until I can see even the wet hairs on her
limp arms. Took over an hour to pull her up.
Everyone just standing around, staring,
waiting for something. I expected her to cry
when I flipped back the swaddling blanket
with blue giraffes dancing with pink hippos.
Fear will make a person do crazy things.
That mom didn't think, merely reacted.
Saw her baby dangling and panicked.
Plucked her up and tore off through the woods.

IV.
Twisted dandelions. Jandolyn laughs
when I pop their heads off and the blossoms fly
across the blanket spread under the Oak.
She rocks back in her swing. Leans forward.
A phone rings in the house. She rocks back.
From the window I see the infant swing.
She laughs. Throws her body forward and laughs.
I lick the milk from my wrist and heat the bottle.

The screen door slaps shut.
I see her from the porch, from the front steps.
I see her from the edge of the blanket.

V.
Truth is I was going to marry Jules.
I bought her an ice cream cone and she cried.

Never took a lick; let the cream run down
her arm and drip off her elbow. I watched
as ants crawled around the mess, turned white.
She was stunning and tragic all at once.
I told her we could leave, that I'd take care
of her—and the baby—she kept crying.
I swear I would have stolen my dad's truck
and took off. We'd sing country songs.
She'd prop her feet on the dash, fall asleep.
We'd drive away until the eddy,
a rivulet, turned into an ocean.

SARAH WANGLER

Cows Eat Their Afterbirth #1

We were born: we don't know when.
I played a country song so Garth would sing
To me. Calving heifer lowed, stood & turned
& wondered what the parasite in her
Belly was kicking for, while he squirmed his way
Into her canal. Barn cat thought it was bedtime,
Curled in straw next to me & my body heat,
Purring with fleas. In her pen my heifer's
Eyes showed white—like a new mother—& she
Sniffed for a place to bleed on piss & pie
Covered straw. She paced the birthing pen.
I'd led her here when I saw her wink at me
This afternoon, pink under tail. I knew
To look there when colostrum filled her bags,
Udders dripped, anticipating. She lay
On kicked-over grain pail—why think of food
Then? Just push. Nobody would moo that so
She let the calf take over. He knocked
At her cervix & I tied her head,
Reached in to check. Felt tail, no hooves to hold,
A breech birth no cow could calve alone.
Afraid she'd smash baby's head in contraction,
I stuck in a second hand to pull. She screamed
Over Reba, none of us fancy enough—
I held her calf on my lap & wished
It weren't snowing, that Dr. Risley were there
Covered in viscera, to tear hooves
From placenta. I ripped that sack, let him breathe:
We were born & our blood is clean.

Benjamin Pfeiffer

When the Heavens Are Bright

How often at night,
When the Heavens are Bright
With the light from the glittering stars,
Have I stood there amazed,
And asked as I gazed,
If their glory exceeds that of ours.

—Dr. Brewster Higley, 1876
"My Western Home on the Range"

My cousin Robbie fell through the ice on Thanksgiving Day at my granduncle and grandaunt's farm in Western Kansas. We were in the woods, the less usable part of the farmland, with my Mom's cousin, Oscar, and my Mom's brother, Logan. The men had set up dirty mason jars on the polished ice of the catfish pond, a gunmetal disc ringed by trees and snow. They were practicing their marksmanship. When they fired, the reports from the rifles made me flinch. In between rounds Robbie and I gathered up the broken glass, crusted with preservatives. The ice was inches thick but also speckled with bullet holes. As we moved, our sneakers left partial footprints in the dust-dry snow, and coal-colored water seeped through cracks where the ice was weak. Three or four times we set up the shooting gallery while Logan and Oscar watched us from the shore, laughing and talking, exhaling clouds of steam, smoking hand-rolled cigarettes and drinking beer. Each man carried a relative's rifle. Logan, for example, had Granduncle Jack's antique Karabiner 98 Kurz—the Wehrmacht's Kar98k—a German bolt-action rifle Old Jack had smuggled back from Europe during the Second World War.

Old Jack had joined up before America entered the war by traveling north to Ottawa and volunteering for the 3rd Canadian Infantry. He served as a medic in the army and, when he returned home, became a traveling physician until he retired. Old Jack's wife was half-Jewish, he told us, God rest her soul, a first-generation immigrant, and among the Jewish expatriate circles everybody knew exactly what the fuck Hitler was up to, and they didn't like it. Even if other Americans were ambivalent about the Jews and the negroes and the queers, his generation wasn't going to stand by and let some goddamn dictator exterminate innocent people. He told us the story of the war the same way he told stories of Red Riding Hood, Hansel and Gretel, or Rumpelstiltskin. So, Old Jack would say, as we sat in a circle around his overstuffed chair, what was a man to do? Get his goddamn gun, that's what, and get to Europe.

The old man had a scar on his left side from the invasion at Juno Beach in 1944 where a bullet—fired from a Sturmgewehr 44 assault rifle—punched through his flak jacket. That wound had ended his tour of duty. He talked about it in medical terms, alternating storytelling gestures with pulls on his pipe, which glowed orange, mirroring on a miniature scale the dying fire in the hearth. In the next room, our parents laughed, and drank another Budweiser while they watched the football game on television. Outside the prairie stretched for miles, gently rising and falling, like the chest of a person sleeping, sloping glens and highlands thick with wheat. The ballistic trauma caused hypovolemic shock, Old Jack said. I lost pints of blood, whole pints bleeding out, my very life mixed in the English Channel. Cold stops the process of death, he added, tapping the bowl of his pipe against the bricks, scattering the ashes into the fireplace. Death is a process. It can be reversed, even if some doctors don't think so. Sometimes Old Jack let us see the faded scar from the wound, and, if he was feeling vulnerable, he let us touch it, too, where the flesh was white and puckered after sixty years of healing.

"Get some more jars, boy," Oscar said. "Set 'em up. The fuck you waiting for?"

My mom's cousin had lank hair, red in color, and a patchy beard that failed to cover his weak chin. The last time he sent Robbie out on the ice, he said, "Set it more toward the middle, boy," and flicked his cigar toward us. The stub landed closer to Robbie than it did to me. My cousin looked at me, and I think he saw that I was nervous, because he shook his head slightly and turned away. Robbie was four years older than me, fifteen years old, I think, quicker, funnier, and tougher. He had scarred-up knuckles from fighting at school, he smoked pot behind the barn with his brother, Todd, when their stepmother was inside, and he had french kissed a girl— or so he claimed—and had fondled her bare tits, too.

"I'll do it," I said.

"No, it's getting dark," Robbie said. "I'll just set up a few."

"OK."

"Hurry up!" Oscar called.

My sister, Danya, wasn't around when Robbie went out to set up the shooting gallery for the last time. She was only four years old, afraid of loud noises, with enormous blue eyes that made her look like a cartoon. She disliked Oscar and Logan because they were rowdy and ill-mannered, and because they stank like tobacco and cologne. Granduncle Jack's property stretched over one hundred and fifty-five acres, probably, and Danya could have been anywhere in all that space. She had a knack for vanishing in those days, even for escaping our watchful mother, a special kind of magic that made her invisible to grown-ups. She rarely spoke to people, but she did speak to animals. Sometimes I discovered her talking to squirrels or dogs or frogs or birds in a spooky, professorial voice.

So if Danya was anywhere near when Robbie fell through the ice she was probably behind the tractor shed—wide-eyed, trudging through the snow, bundled in her florescent pink coat and mittens—on her way to pass the time with Granduncle Jack's basset hound, Lila. She usually climbed the woodpile, gripped the chickenwire fence, and clumsily lowered herself into the dog's pen. Then she'd crawl into Lila's doghouse and curl up in the straw. She'd let the puppy lick her face until Grandaunt Audrey called us for dinner.

Robbie died under the ice. At least, his heart stopped, his breathing stopped. A quiet crunch as the ice gave way, like a porcelain dish broken inside a pillowcase, and he was gone. His feet and legs disappeared first, then his hips and chest, and finally his head. Icy water—opaque with grit and broken twigs and bits of crumbled-up leaves—darkened his jeans and his flannel shirt and rushed into his mouth as he was yelling in surprise. He vanished so suddenly, and so completely, that for a moment it seemed surreal, or implausible, like a magic trick you see on television and assume—because you don't know any better—that it must have been faked.

When the ice broke, fractures spread across the surface. In the shallows, I lost my balance, and fell hard on my tailbone, with enough force to make my eyes water and to send out another spiderwebbed crack in all directions. One of the glass fragments I was holding sliced a moon-shaped cut into the palm of my hand.

Logan reacted first. Immediately he slid down the hill to the water's edge on his ass, ignoring the broken branches, and also ignoring the muck around the rim of the pond, where his foot got stuck. He flung himself out onto the ice on his stomach. Old Jack's rifle clattered out of his fingers and came to rest at the edge of the hole where Robbie had vanished. The force of Logan's jump pulled the boot from his foot. He rushed across the ice with one of his wool socks sticking to the surface of the pond. My uncle moved quick for his size, which was considerable—Logan had a double chin and a sagging gut from the endless beer and junk food he consumed late at night in my grandparents' basement. He worked nights at a manufacturing plant, attaching the electrodes on car batteries, and mostly he slept during daylight hours.

Logan plunged the rifle into the water like a broom handle. "Grab hold!" he shouted. "Grab on!" A whole minute and a half passed like this. Not knowing what else to do, I crawled back to the shore on my hands and knees. The ice burned my fingertips. I stumbled over to Logan's boot, stuck in the mud, and I began to wrestle with it. As I tried to work the boot free, the clay worked its way under my fingernails, into the creases around my knuckles. The cut burned on my hand.

"He ain't grabbing," Oscar yelled. "Break the ice!"

Logan lurched drunkenly to his feet, bringing the rifle over his head like a club, and began to swing it up and down like a sledgehammer. Crack, crack, crack. The hole widened, broke away. My uncle lay down, ignoring his own safety, and buried both his arms in the water up to his armpits. He thrashed around—water sprayed into his face, soaking his beard.

Oscar reached down, holding onto a tree for balance, and gripped a fistful of my sweatshirt. He hauled me onto the hillock. His skin looked tallow, the color of an old candle. Oscar had a genetic condition, a hereditary immunodeficiency, which made him sickly, unable to do much physical labor. Plus, as a treatment for the condition, he received blood transfusions at the hospital, St. Boniface's, blood transfusions that could have contained HIV. Although he couldn't prove it, Old Jack—a physician who was almost never wrong when he made a diagnosis—suspected Oscar had caught the virus and now suffered from full-blown AIDS.

I only weighed eighty-four pounds, maybe more with the water and mud clinging to my clothes, but the effort of lifting me onto the hillock made Oscar pant. I started to cry. Oscar cuffed me on the back of the head hard enough to double my vision. I noticed his knuckles were scabbed, probably from working on farm machinery.

"Quit it," he said. When he spoke, he sprayed spittle on my cheek. He lowered his nose until it was inches from mine and I could smell the hops on his breath, see the scum on his teeth. "The fuck's wrong with you? Run back to the house and call the ambulance."

Terrified, I ran—more to escape Oscar, I think, than to save Robbie's life—and halfway to the farmhouse I tripped over a rock and hurt my ankle.

Granduncle Jack's farmhouse was built in the 1840s by a family of Scottish immigrants. The masons used limestone for the foundations; oak for the frame, support beams, wraparound porch, and everything else. The land and house offered endless possibilities for visiting children. Every year, Robbie and I played cowboys and bandits on that porch and in the surrounding yard during holiday gatherings. We used rubber-band guns made with clothespins, dented costume hats, our father's old boots. The cowboys—always Robbie, and Todd, if he joined us—wore tin-plated sheriff's stars pinned to their jackets. I, as the bandit, wore a red-and-white bandana wrapped around my nose and mouth to hide my face. They always won these games, except for once, when I ambushed Robbie by backtracking through the kitchen, then caught him on the porch, drinking lemonade. Todd got me afterward, though, and—unlike any time before—they slapped me in irons and walked me to the cottonwood tree to be hanged.

"This is just the way it has to be," Robbie had explained. He and Todd fashioned a noose from their shoelaces, tightened it around my neck, fixing a slipknot to pull apart when they kicked the bucket out from under me. "You shot a lawman. Now you got to pay the price."

When I burst into the farmhouse kitchen calling for help, breathlessly trying to explain what had happened to Robbie, my lungs filled with heat from the fireplace and also with the smells of Thanksgiving: walnuts, cranberries, pecans, roast turkey, creamed corn, and pumpkin pie. I was completely disoriented. I tripped on a ceramic gnome who stood guard over the foyer. When I lost my balance, I banged the side of my head on an iron-banded trunk, and I lay on the floor, senseless, spread-eagled on the floral-print linoleum.

The conversation ended. All the adults, even those glued to the football game in the den, gathered to see what had happened.

Danya walked over to me and toed me in the ribs. She was carrying the cat, Waffles, a fat old Siamese with a crumpled ear and blue eyes—irises, in fact, like hers.

She might drop the cat on me, I thought, stupidly. Waffles had all his claws.

"Geramie," she said. "Why are you on the floor?"

"Where's Jack?"

"You tracked mud in the kitchen."

"It's all right, Danya," Old Jack said. I smelled his Aqua Velva aftershave before I saw him towering over my sister. He put his pipe in his teeth, held it by clenching his jaw, and with his hands free he gently lifted Danya—Waffles folded in her arms—and set her to one side.

"Your brother's bumped his head."

I told him about Robbie. Also about Logan and Oscar shooting mason jars on the pond. I mumbled, blurring my words together, and I could tell I wasn't making much sense. "We were helping," I finished, trying to sit up.

"I'm sure you were."

Old Jack stayed calm for a few more seconds. He fished out his penlight, shone it in my right eye, then my left. He cupped his hands around my eyes, too, looking into them, checking to see if the pupils dilated. "I don't think you have a concussion," he said. Calloused fingers parted my hair, examined my skull for soft spots. "Your head's OK." He rapped his knuckles on my forehead. The rest of the family, including my parents, pressed their bodies together in the doorway, trying to investigate the commotion. Old Jack pried the fingers of my left hand open and studied the moon-shaped cut.

"Robbie—" I said.

"Hush." Old Jack stood and turned to address the crowd of parents, cousins, and in-laws. "Everyone stay calm. There's been an accident. Robbie fell in the pond. Todd—" he pointed to Robbie's brother "—bring me the cordless phone. How far's the range on this thing? Will it pick up a signal in the driveway? We need to meet Logan and Oscar outside. Right now."

I stood with Old Jack's help. His hands shook, a slight palsy he always had. When I was on my feet, Old Jack disappeared into the dusk, slamming the screen door, not bothering to put on a coat over his flannel shirt. The adults, including my mother and father, followed him out to the driveway.

Danya whispered something to Waffles, set him down, and came over. She held both arms up to me, opening and closing her fingers. My head ached and I felt dizzy, and she was getting bigger every day, harder to carry for long distances, but I picked her up anyway and let her put her arms around my neck. She touched the purple welt rising near my left temple. "I'm OK," I told her. Together we followed Old Jack outside into the yard.

Night had fallen, and overhead we saw pinpricks of watery starlight, already five million years dead, ghostlights traveling to Kansas from across our galaxy. A black sky held the forest, the fields, the barn and grain silo. The horizon was clear, no hint of bad weather, although the ground was blanketed in snowdrifts. Old Jack talked into the cordless phone. He pulled on his pipe when he wasn't talking. The orange glow illuminated his face slightly, just another star in the blackest night. "It'll help reduce the risk of the ischemic injury to tissue," he told someone on the phone. Probably, I realized later, a colleague who worked at St. Boniface's. "Send a helicopter, goddamnit. We're flying him to Pennsylvania. Don't argue with me." He waited a moment. "I swear to God—No, listen. Tell them to land in the fucking wheatfield."

Danya giggled. Old Jack turned around, shook his head at me, and waved his gnarled old hand, saying, I thought, take her back inside, don't let her see this, don't let her see Robbie when they carry his body out of the forest.

"I see them," my mother said. "Oscar's carrying him."

Under the stars, Robbie's skin was a pale, cerulean blue. All of the world's colors looked wrong somehow, including Oscar's hair, which looked orange, and Danya's coat, which now looked almost scarlet. Granduncle Jack wheezed when he saw them. The old man handed the phone to my mother, who fumbled it and dropped it into the snow, and he took off to meet them. His movement broke they spell over our family. We followed him. Danya buried her face in my coat as I ran, bouncing her against my chest.

"We need to warm him up," Oscar said. "Get blankets!"

"No, no, no," Old Jack said. "In the *snow*."

Old Jack put the pipe back between his teeth, but most of the ashes had spilled out when he ran across the yard, lurching and wheeling off balance, and the pipe's bowl was dark. I had forgotten, I think, just how elderly he was. When Oscar laid Robbie on the ground, Old Jack rolled up my cousin's sleeves, the coat and shirt and thermal underwear, and he plunged Robbie's wrists into a snowbank. "We have to keep him cold," he muttered, and when Oscar started to say something, Old Jack added, "Do as I say, boy."

Old Jack unbuttoned the throat of Robbie's jacket and began to scoop snow inside by the handful. He opened Robbie's jaws just enough to fit two of his fingers inside, and with his free hand he passed snow through the opening. The adults formed a circle. Watching. Waiting. My mother and father came to stand with Danya and I, although they said nothing. Grandaunt Audrey covered her mouth with her hand and made choking noises. Oscar put his arms around her shoulders and folded her into his arms. Tom—who had just turned eighteen—cried and wiped tears from his cheeks to keep them from freezing. Old Jack placed his hands over Robbie's heart, one over the other. He pushed the heel of his hand down, again and again, forcing the blood through Robbie's circulatory system, and as I watched him I thought of how he would sit in his recliner, telling stories about the war, lifting his shirt just enough that we could see the scar from the wound he got on Juno Beach, and I thought about pressing my thumb to that scar, the fibrous tissue that had never quite healed. And, as I touched his ribcage, Old Jack said to me, Death is reversible, Death is a process, I know because I lived it.

When my granduncle finally crawled away from Robbie, I thought he was going to die, too. His hair was disheveled, his pipe lost in the snow. He looked gray and wasted and exhausted. The old man slouched down, steadied by Logan, and sat with his legs crossed, spine pressed against the oversized tires of his Ford pickup. My uncle handed him the Kar98k and the old man laid it across his lap. Then he tilted his head back. He squinted. At first I thought he was looking at the stars, or praying intently for God to save Robbie, and maybe he was, but then I realized he was also straining to see the medevac. I looked up, too, and regretted it right away. One hundred billion stars, revolving and orbiting an outer spiral arm of the Milky Way unconnected—as far as I still know—to any worldly anchor. Nauseated, I set Danya down in the snow, because I couldn't hold her anymore, and before I could corral her again she toddled over to the old man. She plopped down beside him, although he didn't look at her, and she folded her arms like his and molded her face into a facsimile of his scowl. When he ignored her, she reached over, and put her index finger, small and white, into the rifle barrel on the Kar98k, and she said, in a child's baritone, "Tell them to land in the fucking wheatfield, boy."

I stumbled over to the toolshed, pressed my palms against the moss-covered wood, and began to retch. Vomiting, the emergency room doctors told me later, means a concussion, or it can, a warning sign for anyone with a head injury. I lay down in the grass and let the world rotate around me. No one paid attention, not even my parents. They stayed away, gathered around Robbie. No one spoke. Danya took her finger out of the old man's rifle. She wandered over to me and lay down beside me on the grass. I closed my eyes and tried to remember the moment Robbie had fallen through the ice, the look on his face, something, anything, but for some reason the images I conjured didn't seem right, exactly—Robbie's mouth was too wide, his eyes too white, a reenactment of the disaster playing over and over like a melodrama in my mind's-eye. Danya lifted her arm, and pointed first to one star, and then to another, connecting the dots like in one of her coloring books. After a while I heard the whirring thump of rotors, the helicopter speeding toward us, flying low over the prairie, creating a space against the black sky, a darker void through which even the brightest stars could never shine.

TRAVIS MOSOTTI

Surgery

For my wife

I. *Notes on the Waiting Room*

Then fluorescent lights tongue the sleepers.
Then the rigged puppet things get stuck

in revolving doors. Then sterile doesn't
have a smell—lymph node, duct work,

broken clavicle, fresh coat of paint
for the all night benders. *The whites*

are in a row, clattered the nurses.

II. *Letter for Safe Return*

Dear Regina,

Once they put you under, they'll start
pulling in other directions like
your head was fixed to rails. Let
the stars unfasten and wander
from their constellations;
let the luminous things hold and
guide you; yes, let them go out
ahead and coax you from the fog.

Swamp trails, tiny buttery rivulets,
parked cars blistered with rain,
a pinch of Nicaraguan tobacco.
These will smell new when you
come back, rediscovered, mediocre.
You'll ache again for the cold
curve of needle under your skin.
You'll listen harder for the soft
places between guitar strings
that used to hide you so well.

The hospital will quiet tonight
to a morphine drip, loose
gowns, loading dock cigarette
breaks, jaundiced newborns,
bedpans, obstetric clamps,
gurneys near the fresh linens,
morgue freezer, little chapel,
loved ones bent in awkward prayer.

MEG WORDEN

An Amputated Limb

It was late afternoon by the time I was herded from that stark-white holding cell underneath the courthouse, shackled and driven in a van to the county jail, undressed, deloused and led up several flights of dingy stairs to the women's unit and deposited in front of an imposing desk manned by a petite officer with slick, blond curling-iron curls and shiny lip gloss—a juxtaposition to her combat boots and severe uniform, its collar cinched at the neck with a slender black tie.

"Go get a boat; you're on the floor in seven," she instructed without looking up from her *People Magazine* word-search, a french-tipped index finger pointing past and behind me.

I turned to look in the direction of her finger and saw women, all in green canvas uniforms, sitting around on chairs watching me, some braiding each other's hair, or talking quietly. Ever since the gavel had hit the sound block that morning, the flow of tears had not waned. They only increased at her cryptic instruction.

"I'm sorry, but I don't know what that means." I cried, rather noisily now. "I've never been to jail before."

Even though I could feel the eyes of the women in the room, I was past feeling self-conscious. I hugged my bag of bedding a little closer to my chest, the hard cup inside the bag sticking sharp into my ribs. The little cup they issued for meals. With a spork. I couldn't stop shivering.

Maybe she really was surprised that I had never been there before, with the proverbial revolving door and all, but she looked up. Her voice even softened a little. She came out from behind the desk and led me past the women with their watching eyes and across the room to a door that led to a storage room where plastic cots were stacked against the wall. Above the stack a piece of masking tape stuck to the wall that said BOATS. They actually did resemble canoes more than cots, except they were flat. These "boats" were meant to lie on the floor and give a couple of inches space between a body and the concrete.

"Why are you crying?" she asked, pulling one down off the stack and handing it to me.

This question struck me as too odd to even answer. *Isn't it obvious?* It just made me cry harder.

"Take your boat to your room and stay there. I'm calling Psych."

No problem. I had no other plans.

That plastic boat hit the concrete floor in cell number seven (A metal bunk bed, a tiny stainless steel table with a round stool bolted to the floor, a little sink, and a toilet) with a hollow thwack. I sank down on it, dejected and demoralized, but finally able to sit. Nowhere else to go. For now. It smelled like ammonia or pee, or both, in there. My bed was on the floor in the only available space. Right in front of the toilet.

"I'm Ruby. This your first time here?" asked the thin woman with a head full of red braids from up on the top bunk. She was writing with what looked like the ink cartridge of a ballpoint pen. Not a pen, just the cartridge. Later she would show me how to unpeel the labels from shampoo bottles, and wrap them around the cartridge to make it easier to write. So it was a little thicker, so it didn't bend so much in your hand. Later she would explain why we weren't allowed to have the whole pen, too dangerous. I guess you can make a shank out of a pen. I wouldn't have thought of that.

One of her legs hung over the edge of the thin pad atop her bunk. A mat-tress without the tress. I could see scabs on her bare ankle, her arms and her face, scabs and the tiny white scars of previous scabs. Her toenails were yellowed and her fingernails were long and slightly curved. She pulled her legs up, crossed them, leaned her elbows on her knees and gave a sideways grin, baring teeth, black and broken between dry white lips.

"Hey," I said weakly, "I'm Meg. Yes, it's my first time. I have a little boy and I don't know what I'm going to do."

"Aww, Sweetie, it ain't that bad. You be back to yer kid in no time. When you get out?"

"I don't know. The Federal Marshalls will be here to pick me up sometime. I don't know when. Probably after Christmas. Then I have to go to prison. Two years."

"Federal Prison!? What the hell did you do? Holy shit, girl, you look like you never done a thing."

Now, I knew I hadn't been a saint, but I guess it never occurred to me exactly how unsullied I would appear against this gritty backdrop. I wasn't sure whether I felt relief or more isolated in the face of her observation. It was too much to ponder.

"Sold ecstasy. You?"

"Me and my old man run a meth house. I'm his cook. I cook the best shit around, for real. We got all kinds of people working for us. God, I miss him. I was jus writing him a letter. He here too. Probably gonna do some time at MDC. That's for Missouri Department of Corrections," she added helpfully. "State prison. It's awful. You lucky you get to go with the feds."

Her rotting smile widened when she started talking. She seemed proud of her job, her big house full of folks cleaning and cooking like servants, for free drugs, proud of her story, like it was a real success, like she had really made it.

It was nice of her to reassure me. To call me lucky.

Ashamed, horrified, regretful? Yes.

Lucky? Not so much.

"Do you have kids?" I asked with no small measure of trepidation after hearing about her home life.

"Yeah, I got two, but I ain't allowed to see em. State took em away when me and my old man got back together. Said I'd have to stay away from him to keep em and I ain't about to do that. He's gonna marry me."

When the small intercom sounded from the wall, "THIBODEAUX TO THE OFFICER'S DESK!" I was startled, but grateful not to have to respond to this Ruby, who just told me that she chose her meth dealing boyfriend over custody of her children like she had made the obvious choice. Like she was just mulling over a menu and thought the mozzarella sticks sounded tastier than the side of brussels sprouts.

A square man with round glasses and a wrinkled oxford shirt stood in front of the big desk, a clipboard and a couple of manila folders in the crook of his arm. His chinos were a little too short and I could see black socks between his hem and his loafers. He looked light for his heavy frame. Inflatable, like a balloon man, untethered from his parade float and blown into this place with a gust of leaves. A gust of please-can-I-leaves.

"Are you Ms. Thibodeaux?" he asked. "I need to check your wristband."

"Yes." I nodded while holding up the plastic I.D. bracelet on my left arm.

"Let's have a seat. Talk a bit."

He led the way to an empty table in the common area, a rectangular room with five tables on one side, a TV and chairs on the other, a phone bank with five red metal phones and, the heavy gray steel doors to each cell lining three walls, a number painted on each one, ten in all. Three walls had cells, and the fourth wall had open showers. Open showers right off of the common area facing the officer's desk. Facing the whole room. In fact, one was running, and in it a woman, was soaping up as carefully as she could, trying to keep herself from being exposed to this man who was now sitting down at a table with me.

"So I hear you're pretty upset. Do you want to tell me what's wrong?"

Again with the obvious questions from these people. I can imagine nothing but my baby's tears and that I'm not there to wipe them away. And I have been relegated to a cell with a woman only too happy to give her children away to strangers in exchange for methamphetamines. What's wrong with ME? Why aren't you asking her what the hell is wrong?

"I miss my son, and I'm scared," I managed.

"Well, do you plan on committing suicide?"

"No."

"That's good news."

He smiled, and he sighed and he leaned back into his chair, clicking the top of his pen in and out. Click-click. Click click. The wrinkled shirt untucked a little more as his belly expanded up and back and his tone-of-voice slid down an arc of relief and satisfaction. Relieved of the extra paperwork involved, satisfied that our two-minute chat had gone so swimmingly. He had determined that I was okay.

"We would have to lock you in segregation and put you on twenty-four-hour surveillance, if you were."

He nodded toward the cell door closest to the guard's desk, indicating the room I would have to live in. The bare room full of cameras.

The little square window of the cell door framed a face. A face with darty eyes that disappeared as quickly as they lit on mine. In fact, the face just vanished as if it was never there.

For a second there was nothing but glass.

And then something red was on the window. A sponge maybe? Paint? But why would she have paint . . . and then I got it.

A bloody maxi pad was smearing across the gruesome little window. And then the face re-appeared and it, too, was now smeared with thick, red clots of blood. I stared open mouthed, shocked.

"Well, it looks like I need to go," the psychologist said, clearly distracted.

"Yeah," I said, now dying to get back to the safety of my little corner of concrete.

I assumed the woman sitting with Ruby back in cell seven was the resident of the bottom bunk. She was tall and her long hair was only blond on the bottom half, her dull hazel eyes twitched under invisible eyelashes, her asymmetrical face bluish and translucent, like she hadn't seen the sun in awhile. The little stool twisted and squeaked underneath her.

"Paula, this is Meg." Ruby pointed at me. "She in here for the first time, and she Federal. Can you believe that shit? Look at her."

Paula's hands kept flying up and moving through her hair, sort of swishing it away from her face, then again, before it could escape. Then again. And again. That hair didn't stand a chance with those acrobatic hands around. Her right knee bounced over the front part of her foot, the ball of her foot and the toes pressing into the sole of her torn plastic shoe, the raised heel peddling the floor. Paula moved constantly. *Bounce bounce swish, bounce bounce swish.*

"Aw hell no," she said, her voice raspy and low. "That's crazy. Least you get outta here soon. I got a year in this shithole. Done seven months already. County time is the hardest time they is. The hell d'you do?"

Maybe I was tired. Yes, I was definitely tired. Insanely tired. Maybe I was overcome by a weird motivation to prove that I was worthy of incarceration. Try and fit in. The isolation, at that moment, too unbearable an alternative. Probably I couldn't hold it in, hold it together for another second. I sort of vomited it out in one big rush. I told them my whole story, and once I started, I couldn't stop talking. It felt so good, their nods, their supportive comments. Fourteen months of holding it together. Fourteen months of *tell no one*. Ruby and Paula listened and didn't seem to care at all how much I cried, how I looked, sitting there all bedraggled with stringy, wet hair, limp over my eyes, my bare cold feet. They were the first people in a very long time that had the remotest idea of how this all felt. Their empathy was catharsis.

They were glad just to have someone else around to talk to. They had both been here several times before and knew the drill. They explained how things worked. How we would get fifteen minutes to eat each meal. How breakfast was served at four a.m., toilet paper was rationed and how the lights never went off. Ever. They showed me how they wrapped their faces in their sports bra before they went to sleep. I looked from the silver toilet up at the industrial fluorescent lights over my boat-bed and wondered how I would ever be able to sleep in this place.

But I did sleep there. An angular, blackout kind of sleep. Dreamless and dark. Like they say about death, this sleep was a *going-to-a-better-place-sleep,* and days ran into nights under these bright bulbs. Everything ran together in this thick fog of time, spread thin and covering everything. Time tinted the days a pale surreal and globbed up sticky and thick in the corners of the night. We each had our very own ration of time.

On the phones that only dialed out collect, I called the farm and talked into Aidan's ear. *I'll be back, little man. I promise. I'll come back.*

The nicer guards let us have an hour in "rec" once in awhile. Rec happened in a square room with one wall of vents to let in the fresh air. No windows. Just vents, like a pet carrier. The walls and the vents were covered with thick layers of dirt. In it, fingertips had carved out messages for their people who were locked up on other units here. Dirt hearts pierced by dirt arrows. *Hey Big D, Patty luvs you.*

I took off my floppy shoes and walked circles around the room. Tried doing lunges, jumping jacks, pushups. Anything to move while I had the chance. Some of the women did the same. Others sat around the floor; backs to the wall, trying to one-up each other's tragedy. Sensationalize their pain. These conversations could get pretty unnerving, and I found out the hard way that I preferred the torture of lunges to listening in. Hearing a mother talk about selling her kids' bodies for crack is the kind of thing that leaves indelible scars, makes you forget that there is anything good left in the world. Hearing those things made the ache for my son, the need to protect him, even more intense. A powerful ache that would blow through my nervous system like bullets.

Then the hour is up before you know it, and the door back into the common area opens with a bzzzclank and then closes behind us with a SLAMbzzzclank. That's the defining sound of jail. Locking and unlocking and locking again. The slamming of steel on steel and its echo, ringing in your ears long after. It's the sound of Final. It's the sound of an exclamation point.

The majority of our time was spent locked in our cell where I learned that big farms are ideal for stealing tanks of anhydrous, the dangerous chemical fertilizer used in crystal meth production. I also practiced some modified yoga poses

84

confined to the space of a folded blanket, wrote letters and drew pictures for Aidan with my sticker-wrapped pen cartridge and brushed my teeth with my "anti-shank toothbrush" (that is the official product name for a toothbrush that is only three inches long). The marathon stretches of time left plenty of room to feel the loss of so many things, including, but most certainly not limited to, reading. The library was home to little more than pulp style romance novels of the fundamentalist sort. In lay terms, bad writing, no sex. One without the other, okay. But the inclusion of neither good writing nor graphic sex scenes should be illegal. The author of the one I did read, about the bonnet-clad schoolteacher who falls in love with the town doc, should really have to do time.

We took turns pressing our faces into the glass slits in the wall that posed as windows. You could fit one eye in to look out at the passing traffic, at the Christmas lights on the visible corner of the building across the street, the row of blinking neon signs. *Bail Bonds 24 Hours.* We also took turns pushing our noses in to these cold slits, two of us at a time, while the other one tried to empty her bowels in the toilet. The toilet right by my boat bed.

Paula taught me how to courtesy flush. "You keep your hand on the lever and start flushing while it's coming out." Paula explained with a rushing of water. "That way nobody has to smell yer shit." Another flush.

On Christmas Day a church group came in, and we were all *required* to sit in rows of metal folding chairs while they sang carols with smiles too big for their faces. Those oversized smiles made their forehead skin wrinkle and just amplified the apprehension in their eyes, made them look obvious. I imagined them getting back home after they left us. Pulling in to the smell of stuffed turkey and pumpkin pie, congratulated by friends and family for their embodiment of the real spirit of giving. It would be permission to eat as much as they could, to tear the wrapping off of their gaming systems with self-satisfied gluttony. I pulled my feet onto the chair and sobbed into my knees while they sang. I was in no mood to sanctify their efforts with gratitude. I felt like I was on display. Like I was the stuffed turkey. Forced to be reminded of what I was missing when I just wanted to hide. Those big empty smiles left big empty spaces.

A year later, a few of us in prison, would coin the term "Mandatory Merriment" for Christmas incarcerated. How we were forced to endure these charitable events. Forced to act grateful. *Don't embarrass the institution.* It reminded me of the way parents get so uncomfortable when their shy kids don't want to talk to strangers in the checkout line at the supermarket. "Tell the nice man how old you are, Little Johnny." And "Gosh, I'm so sorry, I don't know *what's* gotten into him, he's usually such a chatterbox." As if our kids should be required to talk to every stranger who talks to them. As if we inmates should be required to be grateful to anyone who chose us as their good deed of the day.

But, to their credit, in addition to spaces . . . they also left socks. A pair of white athletic socks for each inmate. I was still freezing after two days barefoot, in short sleeves. Those socks were like an electric blanket. I could have done well enough without "Joyful and Triumphant," but the socks, that was really a charitable act. Probably the best Christmas present I have, in fact, *ever* received. See, not just the unit, but the distance between me and my boy was so cold, I thought I just might freeze to death.

My mom sent a photo of Aidan. One of the ones that now hangs in my locker here in prison. The photo I had taken of him with Santa just weeks before all of this happened, with his face scrunched up, about to cry. He agreed to sit a few feet away from, but definitely not on, Santa. He wore a red turtleneck shirt in the photo and a scrunched up face with quivering pink lips, pursed into a little o. Like O, *the things we thought were so important.* When it came in the mail, I couldn't even look at it. When I called my mom and said please send a picture, I thought it would help. I thought that maybe if I had a photo, I could stare at it and it would help ease this awful hurting. But I couldn't look. Not without the nausea. Not without the torrid phantom pain of an amputated limb.

Before I slid it back into the envelope, I showed the picture to Ruby. She reached for it with one hand while she pulled a piece of pound cake out of her bra with the other. Fifteen minutes was never enough time to eat and our hunger was about so much more than food. If you didn't finish it, you had to throw it away or steal it. We were all hungry, but the meth addicts were the hungriest. Begged for seconds, ate like they hadn't eaten in years. *Hey, are you gonna eat your cornbread? Can I get it if you don't?* When commissary opened back up after Christmas, we had a little more to eat. The women with money in their accounts could get chips and candy. A favorite meal was one of those individually packaged giant dill pickles, pulled apart into little chunks and dumped—juice and all—into a bag of Fritos. But even if you can get enough to eat, you never get full.

"He's really cute, Meg. Looks just like you. I can't wait to see my family. I get out in a week."

"Hey, that's great. Who's picking you up?"

"My dad's coming."

"Is he going to take you somewhere special to eat when you leave here?"

"What?" Ruby lifted her face in a laugh, baring her gums, remnants of tooth enamel and pieces of poundcake. "He's not taking me anywhere but home. I have to start cooking."

"Wow," I said. I was puzzled. "Seems like they would take you out for one meal before rushing you home to cook for them."

Again she chuckled at my ignorance. "No, not food silly. I don't cook food. I have to cook the meth. We're so behind since me and my old man have been locked up, our customers are gonna find another source! Besides, I'm the best cook around. They gotta get me home."

"OOOOOh." I drew out the syllable and nodded as if I understood completely now that it had been fully explained. "I didn't realize it was a family business."

See . . . now that's the kind of hungry I'm talking about.

The Federal Marshalls finally came for me on a Tuesday afternoon, after I had been in County for three weeks. Twenty-one of the longest days in the history of days. Ruby was long gone by then, and Paula had moved to a different room. I had a bottom bunk now and could face the wall and get a little darkness when I was trying to sleep. Mostly, like that afternoon, I just lay awake, lying on my back, eyes swollen, gums sore and body drained of impetus. The graffiti scrawled underneath the bed above me said: *Get funky with your bunky, even if she's chunky*.

I looked over at my new roommate, Claire, at the steel desk, squeezing the ink from a pen cartridge into her drinking cup. She'd collected the used soap slivers from the showers and was using her spork to mash them up with the ink, the white soap taking on a purplish gray tint. She was utterly transfixed. A little basket sat in front of her, she had unravelled the cardboard from her tampon applicators and woven the strips into this little bowl shape. She told me that she was going to hand mold the inky soap mush into, "Guest soaps. You know, seashells and shit . . . for guests."

Even if I had the energy to remind her that we had no plans to entertain, wouldn't be throwing a New Year's Eve fete here in our cell, it was a moot point. I was watching her working feverishly on her guest soap project when the little intercom on the wall of our cell piped up again. It said: "THIBODEAUX! PACK YOUR SHIT!" Just when I felt as transparent and fragile as glass. Full of hairline cracks. It was time to go.

MILLER MANTOOTH AND LEE BUSBY

Interview with Ted Kooser

Many wonderful, interesting and otherwise flattering things can be justly said about American poet Ted Kooser, his achievements and the consequent accolades bestowed upon him as a poet (two-term U.S. Poet Laureate 2004-2006, 2004 Pulitzer Prize for Delights & Shadows, *etc.), his lifelong dedication to the art of poetry, his personal and near-tireless professional dedication to publishing and promoting poetry (both his own and that of others) throughout the country, and so on. Rest assured, however, they have already been said elsewhere, time and again, at a length and detail we don't wish to imitate. (We do encourage those who are interested in such information, though, to visit his official website:* www.tedkooser.net.*)*

In lieu of that, we would like to offer a single observation about Mr. Kooser that we had the distinct pleasure of making when he visited the Missouri State University campus in April of 2009 to perform a reading of his own work. Namely, despite his obvious talent and celebrated stature within the world of contemporary American poetry, Mr. Kooser is a gracious and refreshingly humble human being who enjoys talking poetry over a good dinner at a local Mexican restaurant as much as we do. (Disclaimer, the following interview took place on campus, after said dinner, but the latter observation is nonetheless true.)

MM: Lee and I have both read *Poetry Home Repair Manual* and other interviews and background pieces, but we are still interested in what you might have to say about any formal influences that drew you into poetry. You have discussed

89

elsewhere how, as a young man, you thought of poetry as a good way to meet girls, which makes sense to us [laughter], but at that point, what kinds of formal influences had you had?

TK: You know, it's been so long ago since I was in middle school and high school that I can't remember everything we had read. I do remember in the 8th grade having to memorize a big passage from [Sir Walter Scott's] *The Lady of the Lake* and some things like that, and I do think those kinds of things have an effect on you. So I had a sense of poetry that was kind of pleasurable to carry around in your head and recite. That kind of thing. Then in high school, I had an English teacher, Mary McNally, who was very encouraging. At that time, I was writing some sort of short lyrical essays that were very much like poems. And then, when I got to college at Iowa State, there was a poet there on the faculty who taught beginning creative writing. His name was Will Jumper, and he had been a student of Yvor Winters at Stanford. He got his PhD quite late. He had been in the Navy so he didn't get his PhD until he was almost 50, but he taught poetry writing from the point of view of a formalist. Our very first assignment was to write thirty lines of natural description in closed iambic couplets. Then we went on and wrote through all the other forms. I learned an immense amount from that. He was a very strict prosodist. He would say, "You can substitute in the first foot or the third foot but never twice in the same line." It was all very mechanical. But I had that kind of influence behind me. The books I was reading at that time, our little newsstand in my hometown carried a few poetry books. I remember one of the most influential ones was a book of May Swenson's called To Mix with Time. She was a poet who could do just about anything. She could write in any form and write beautifully. She was important at that time. Oh, I remember buying a Donald Finkel book in that

90

series and so on. And I was reading this and that and the other, reading the Beat poets, reading Randall Jarrell. I don't think I started reading Elizabeth Bishop until a little bit later on, but I read her pretty carefully, and so on.

MM: So even in the community where you grew up, which was rural . . .

TK: Ames, Iowa. Well, at that time, when I was there, it was a town of 40,000 people.

MM: We've talked a lot about the demise of poetry from popular culture, so would you say that, even at that place and time, poetry was more a part of the popular consciousness?

TK: No. No. I don't think, really. I mean, the people in my father's generation could recite Robert Service and knew a lot of limericks and things like that, but when I was a boy in the 1950s and early 1960s, by then Modernism had had its effect and by then there weren't a whole lot of readers of poetry. There are a lot more now than there were then.

LB: Since you brought up Modernism and the negative effect it perhaps had on poetry and readers of poetry, I was wondering if you think we have moved beyond that and what New Criticism did to poetry.

TK: Well, this is a very simplistic way of looking at it, and since I don't consider myself to be a literary scholar, but . . . at the same time that Pound and Eliot were putting forth their agenda for what poetry should be, which was that it should be learned and its audience should be learned, stating in effect that this was an art for an elite class of people. All this was happening at the same time the Armory show was being hung in New York City, and all those various movements

91

in the arts were moving forward, things were happening in music, and so on. The idea that Pound's emphasis on "make it new," everybody was trying to do something original and interesting and so on. But again, there were people like William Carlos Williams who, even though Williams was at times impressed by what Pound and Eliot had to say, and I've often thought that Williams's poem "Patterson" was an attempt to get himself into that group, but he really did stand for, as he said once, poems that dogs and cats can read. So he split off in one direction, and the Pound and Eliot people split off into another direction, and the Williams tree of American poetry, of which I am a part out there on the end, is still there and still vital, but it's been very much overshadowed by the tree that came off of Eliot and Pound, primarily because criticism has been focused on the Eliot-Pound side because critics are paid interpreters and they see in that kind of poetry an opportunity for interpretation and will follow it. Poets are not dumb. Poets have figured out that critics are attracted to the things they need to interpret, so they have written things that need to be interpreted, for the critics to interpret. And that is all part of this movement off to one side. It has extended and extended and extended for a century now so that we have poets whose names I won't mention who are out there on the extent of this who write work that is almost exclusively, if not designed, at least attractive to critics or interpreters. And when they publish a book, they get a great deal of attention from these critics because these critics love what they're doing to the exclusion of a lot of the people on the other side. I mean, a poet who writes clearly and accessibly, a critic does not see that as an opportunity. What is there to say: "He writes clearly and accessibly"? But if you write something that doesn't make sense to anyone, then you can write a whole volume of criticism about it. Again, I'm extremely simplistic about this, and there are all kinds of exceptions back and forth, that are not a part of this. I think I put [Wallace] Stevens in with Pound and Eliot, pretty much, although Stevens's work is much less calculating and more joyful and celebratory in a way. His work's full of color and light and motion and in a very playful way. But he is regarded by the critics as being part of that Eliot-Pound program, I think.

MM: This recalls to me what might be an ultimately apocryphal story about Eliot that I heard or read in which it was said that he would peruse the archives at Harvard and shake his head and laugh at all the dissertations that had been written about his work. Sometimes when reading Eliot and Pound and even Faulkner, I've wondered if they weren't on some level almost playing a game with the literary critics.

TK: Well, here's a Faulkner story that I've always loved. We had a man at the University of Nebraska by the name of Cater Chamblee who was there working on an advanced degree. Cater had gone to school at Oxford, Mississippi, and, as an undergraduate, they were assigned Faulkner's "The Bear," and at the end of studying it they were to write a take-home essay about it. So he and his friends were up in their dorm room, drinking wine apparently, it's like one in the morning, and they're trying to figure out how to answer the question. The question was this: Why does Boon Hogganbeck break the barrel of the gun over the stump? So here these young guys are, and they're getting kind of loaded, and one them says, Why don't we just call Faulkner and ask him? At the time Faulkner was living right there in Oxford, of course, so they rang him up and he answered the phone. He was awake and fairly cordial, so they told him they were students at the university and so on. Then one of them asked him, "Mr. Faulkner, could you tell us why Boon breaks the barrel of the gun at the end of 'The Bear'?" And Faulkner said, "I just thought it was a good way to end the story." [Laughter]. But that kind of thing probably happens all the time. I'm glad to hear Eliot would have had a sense of humor about it and laugh about it. I don't think Pound had a sense of humor at all. He took himself very seriously about everything.

MM: Going back to your analogy of the two trees, would you situate Pound strictly on the one side since he fostered the development of both Eliot and Williams?

TK: Pound's part of that would be the footnotes to *The Waste Land*. Not that Pound wrote the footnotes, but that's the character of Pound in that complex. He was encouraging a lot of poets at that time, but I'm just saying that he and Eliot are at the start of that. And you know, an example of someone who was sort of denigrated for writing outside of that tradition would be William Stafford. Stafford was never acceptable to the writers of the Pound and Eliot persuasion. He wasn't one of them, in that sense.

MM: He was made an outsider.

TK: Exactly.

MM: Kind of in line with that, but without asking you to pigeonhole yourself, would you say that you feel an affinity to any particular aesthetic school of poetry, in terms of your own work? You've mentioned William Carlos Williams as an influence, but do you think he identified himself as being an objectivist or an imagist?

TK: I doubt if Williams wanted to identify with a school. I think most of us don't want to. I do know that there can be benefits for people to be identified with a school. One of my friends who is a poet, Jared Carter, told me once that someone said to him, if you really want to be a famous poet, you ought to consider starting a school because people will pay attention to you. But no, I think Williams was interested in delivering babies. And I don't know that I fit anywhere particularly. I read the imagist poets and learned a great deal from them, and Williams has always been very important to me, so I sort of descend from the Williams tradition.

LB: In the *Poetry Home Repair Manual*, you quote Seamus Heaney to the effect that the aim of the poet and poetry is finally to be of service. I'm guessing that's the kind of category where you would place yourself. Your goal is to be of service by means of your poetry?

TK: Yeah. I believe in that, sure. To reach people, to provide language for people . . . It's very interesting that part of what happens to popular music is that lyrics provide people who are not adept with language provide language to them so that some young person right now is carrying around a song lyric in his head because it means so much to the way he's living his life. That's the kind of thing that poetry can do, too. It can offer language. I see them working a lot more closely together than the literary professionals would like to believe. There are song lyrics that I think are just absolutely marvelous, that any poet would . . . for instance, Kris Kristofferson has a song that has a line in it, "Maybe I'll never believe in forever again." Any poet would die for a line like that.

MM: Who are some of your favorite songwriters?

TK: Well, you know, when I was at the Library of Congress, I had John Prine come in and do that thing. Prine's one of my favorite songwriters because of the fact that he has so much fun with it. He's punning all the time, he's doing nonsense, just enjoying it immensely. Tom T. Hall has written some great songs. Kristofferson has written some great songs. I don't know whether Jerry Lee Lewis has actually written a lot of the lyrics to his songs or not, but the lyrics to a lot of his country songs are really wonderful. Well, of course, Willie Nelson is a great songwriter.

MM: What about a guy like Leonard Cohen?

TK: I never really particularly cared for Leonard Cohen's work, too much, but he was an example of that kind of a writer, a poet whose work was accessible.

LB: Going back to writing as a means of service to the community, would you say that you've read much of that kind of poetry from the last decade or so?

TK: No. I think there are few contemporary poems that are really of service to a broader community. You can find them. You know, in that newspaper column I have, I find one a week, anyway, that I can publish, that I think newspaper readers can use in that way. I can go through, looking for poems that I can show newspaper readers—now we're talking about people who are not in any way literary professionals, people just reading the daily paper—I can go through whole literary quarterlies and never find a poem that I think any newspaper reader would understand without having to take a course. Then there are other quarterlies in which, now and then, that kind of poem will appear. So we do find some.

MM: Changing directions just a bit, I was reading an interview with Jack Gilbert in *The Writer's Chronicle* recently in which he said (and I'll just read the quote here):

> It seems to me that a lot of people want to be poets. They want to be poets for a very human reason. They want to get recognition, and if there were no

recognition, I think there would be fewer poets. Some, perhaps, but not many. I hate to say it, but it's true, at these professional poetry workshops it's all about fixing up a poem so it will sell. There's no pressure today, it seems to me, to write poems that matter. Everybody wants to write poems that will be celebrated, but that doesn't mean they matter . . . I think this notion came about when poetry got mixed up with money and fame and so forth . . . There's a cheapness to so much poetry. I would like to see a moratorium on poetry for twenty-five years and see how many people are writing poems seriously. I think you would have about a dozen left.

His position is perhaps pessimistic in terms of his perception of the impulse that ultimately drives most contemporary poets to continue writing, but how and/or why would you agree or disagree with his particular stance?

TK: I don't know. There are lots and lots of people who feel that way with regard to the creative writing programs, and I think with some justification. On the other hand, I wouldn't want to run the risk of discouraging someone in any way who really is interested in writing. I was encouraged when I was 17 and 18 years old by good fortune, but I could've been discouraged. I wasn't writing all that well at that age. Somebody could've said, you shouldn't be a poet, you're never going to be any good at it, and so on. But, as to his statement about poems that matter, you have to think about "matter to whom?." If there are lots of poems that Jack Gilbert has written, and lots of poems that various poets have written, that don't matter to me but might matter to someone else. I think a finer distinction would be whether or not poems feel as if they are really necessary. I see an awful lot of poetry coming out of the creative writing programs that are simply exercises in language. Someone's got an idea to say, I wonder what it would be like to write twenty poems about Christmas tree ornaments? And then they write the twenty poems. And none of them have any kind of emotional impact. I mean, there may be someone out there to whom they matter, and they probably matter to the poet, but they aren't *necessary*. I think there's probably too much of that, but again, I'm not sure it would be such a bad world if everyone were trying to write poems. I think, what could be wrong with that? And sure, they're going to write a lot of poems that aren't any good and aren't going to matter and that aren't necessary, but I don't want people suggesting that it is an art limited to an elite cadre of people who are "poets." I have a friend who is a poet who would say exactly the same thing Gilbert says there. He said to me, "We cannot democratize the arts." In other words, we can't make the arts available to everyone. I'm not willing to go that far.

MM: I certainly wouldn't agree to that, either. I do wonder, though, how much of Gilbert's sentiment might also be directed towards writers whose primary impulse to write and publish is, or has become, too tied up with career concerns.

TK: Yeah, a lot of it is too tied up with career advancement. I had a graduate student at the University of Nebraska who I asked one day, "What are your goals?" And she said, "I'd like to get a couple of books of poetry published and get a really good teaching job." Well, in saying that, there's not even a moment's pause to think about whether or not those books are of any quality whatsoever. It's just that they are lines on a resume. They just go on the C.V. That can't be good. People need to understand that there are alternative ways of living your life. You don't have to be an English teacher to be a writer. It's gotten to the point that since 99% of the writers are in English departments, everybody thinks those two things go hand in hand. If you can find something to do that you can make a decent living at, and writing on the side, I think can be very good. I was made a better writer by having worked with ordinary people for years at a life insurance company. And my level of discourse was brought down to a level that was more accessible to them by the fact that I perceive them as being my community, whereas if you are in an English department, they're your community, and you're writing poems that are going to please those guys in the coffee room.

MM: My test for my own poems is to ask myself whether or not my grandmother, who has no advanced formal education and has never studied poetry, can read and enjoy this poem even if she doesn't know that it's mine.

TK: I think you're probably better off with your grandmother as your imaginary reader than you are with the chair of the English department, for that reason.

LB: When considering a PhD creative writing program or a low-residency MFA program, do you see one as having a greater benefit for aspiring writers over the other? It seems to me that a low-residency program is more like an apprenticeship that emphasizes the writing, whereas a PhD program is more traditionally rooted in the lectures and course work of academia.

TK: The advantage of a program like we have [at the University of Nebraska-Lincoln] is that we really are training professors of creative writing there. We are not training creative writers. The people who walk away with a PhD with a creative dissertation, they also have a lot of academic work behind them. Those people are getting jobs. We've been pretty lucky with our graduates getting jobs. So if that's the objective, it works for those people, and I'm glad they've got jobs. As far as getting help with your writing to just be a writer, I think the MFA programs, the best ones, are the full-time in-residency ones, and the non-resident, extended ones are good, too. The objective is to find someone who will read your work intelligently and comment on it. And you can also find that outside of the institution. I did that with my dear late friend, Leonard Nathan. I wrote him a letter in 1970 or '71, complimenting him on a poem of his I'd seen in the New Republic, and we began to correspond and for 35 years we wrote letters back and forth and looked at each other's work. He was my MFA program, really. That can be as good, too. Although, I think there comes a time when, as a young writer just starting out, it really is stimulating to be in a community of young writers where you can sit around and drink coffee and drink beer and talk about writing and writers. That can be fun. Then there's a time later on in your life when you're really not doing that much. You're really just writing.

MM: With regard to your poetry, it's pretty clear to those who have read your work and who have heard you read that you have a distinct voice, something that tells us this is a Ted Kooser poem. At what point in your writing did you realize you had established your poetic voice, and was there a conscious attempt to do so?

TK: No. I think it's all about finding yourself. There's a point at which you set all your influences aside and figure out who you are and how you're going to carry yourself forward. If you look at my first book, you could very easily go through there and say, "Well, here's the Edward Arlington Robinson poem, and here's the William Carlos Williams poem, and here's the John Crowe Ransom poem, all those influences. And then maybe twenty years after that, those influences, although they're still present, they are so occluded by all the other influences that you start becoming yourself, in a way. You can never escape your influences, but you can assimilate them so broadly that you no longer appear to be copying anyone or imitating anyone or doing that kind of thing. I think that's the natural development, the way that it happens. There was a level of—I hate to use the word confessionalism, so I probably shouldn't—I had to come to terms at some point with how much I was going to tell people about my feelings. Initially, my work, for half of my career, avoided that completely. Any expression of feeling I set aside completely. And that comes from the old admonition of the Moderns against sentimentality and so on. Then I came to understand, I really am a kind of sentimental guy, so maybe it'd be okay to express some feelings in these poems. And so I started doing more of that. Now I do more of that, although I still use restraint. That book of mine, *Winter Morning Walks*, is really exceptional in that way because I really am talking about how I'm feeling in that. I'm sick. I'm getting well, but I'm sick. I'm using poetry as an instrument to express my feelings about that, which was pretty new to me, generally.

MM: Well, that sort of bears on an idea that we were wondering about when Lee and I were discussing some of your poems in *Sure Signs* and *Delights and Shadows*. We were pondering to what extent you're willing to negotiate, if at all, the actual facts of a personal experience that you may use as the impetus, or inspiration, for a poem. Are you more interested in remaining faithful to the material reality of the person or observed object, or are you more interested in trying to serve the poem as an accessible piece?

TK: The imaginative act of writing the poem is already at one step abstracted from the real thing, so there's been some sorting that goes on there, and then there might be additional sorting. In *The Poetry Home Repair Manual*, I tell the story about this poet Don Jones. I told him that in this line of verse—he had a line "the cans of pop I bought her"—and I said to him, if you use the "bottles of pop I bought her," you'd have a better sounding line, and he said, "I can't do that because they were real cans." Well, I wouldn't hesitate to change a can to a bottle, but I won't mess with the truth or fabricate anything that I think affects the central truth of a poem. But details can certainly be manipulated to some degree.

LB: I know a lot of your poems are more lyrical as opposed to being strictly narrative, but almost every single poem has an implied narrative with regard to what's happening, even if it's one of your object poems. Like you said earlier, you're a descriptive writer, but then it always seems that there's a story being told within the description of the object. Is that something that you look for? I'm thinking of the poem "Uncle Adler" in *Sure Signs*, where we don't really see the man, but we see everything else around him, and the reaction to him, but we get his story from everything else that's going on.

TK: I've been thinking, the last few years, quite a bit about being a human being and how we relate in conversation and so on. There are a lot of things you can learn about overhearing people in conversation: number one is that, in a personal anecdote, nearly every anecdote you ever hear or overhear, begins with setting. You will say to me "I got up the other morning and it was raining, and I went outside and the grass was wet." We set the setting up in every one of these things, so that's a natural thing with us, I think. My guess is that when people were sitting at the mouths of caves in France 15,000 years ago, that's how they started stories. That's a part of it. Also, that little bit I gave you there, had some narrative to it, and we exchange information in narrative form. "You know, the other day I was on my way to the drug store, and I saw a three-legged dog." You know, that kind of thing. You've got that sequence going, so I think both of those things are so natural to human expression that poems tend to follow that, in a way, or can, because a poem, in a sense, as I see it, is sort of a refined, one-sided conversation with somebody, looking for a reader on the other side of the table.

MM: In the composition process, when you're trying to formulate lines, in the articulation, are you thinking in that sense, that "I'm talking to somebody"? Not that you necessarily have a specific person in mind every time, but . . .

TK: I always have an imaginary reader in mind. I mean, I don't consciously say to myself, *Hey, you need to do this*, but I always have someone that's out there, and most often it's my mother who's been dead for ten years. But it's a person like Mother who had a couple years of college and liked to read books, but does not have a PhD in English. So that's part of my starting point, addressing a poem that someone else can understand, and it turns out that that seems to be a very natural thing to do. But a lot of people see that as being very controversial. A lot of writers would say you shouldn't pay any attention to anybody, that you shouldn't be writing for anybody.

MM: I don't really understand that point of view, because I think, especially as teachers of introductory poetry classes, it seems like when we ask somebody, "Who or what is this for?" the student, who, granted is new to this, most usually says, "I don't know. I'm just writing this poem for me." And the minute that you tell them to try imagining that they are writing this to anybody, for whoever you want, someone that's intimate to you, and you want to communicate with on a clear level, in revising the poem, it instantly gets better, at that level. So I don't understand the argument that you can write for nobody. I don't even know that that's a real thing, in a way.

TK: I think it may be something that happens in middle school, or something like that, in the way that poetry is taught. That somehow or other, we get the idea that it's not for that other person, really, but it is.

LB: I believe that's something you said in *The Poetry Home Repair Manual*, that we need to get away from the idea of self-expression and look at poetry more as communication between two people.

TK: I had a phone call the other day from Russell Chatham, who's a very well known Western landscape painter, and he'd just finished reading that book, and he said, "What you said here about communication applies to visual art as well."

MM: I think that's very true. The idea that, especially early on in a semester with new students, so much of their entire conception of what a poem is, is reflected in the way that they try to write a poem, which is, "Here's what I'm thinking," instead of trying to communicate with someone.

TK: Also, they say, "I'm going to write a poem that's going to look like other poems I've seen, and if the one that I've seen is scattered all over the page, then that's what I'm going to do with mine."

MM: It seems that a lot of students want to write poems that, as I believe you've put it before, "*announce* themselves as poems," rather than relying on that intimate communication between two people.

We were wondering, when putting together a manuscript, do you have a particular logic, like in *Delights & Shadows*, for instance?

TK: I can tell you what happened there. I usually don't think that I'm even approaching a book until I have at least fifty poems that have been in literary magazines, so that they've had that test first. If some editors liked them enough to publish them, then I think that that's a good sign. So let's say that I got 50-55 poems like that, and then some other ones that I think are equivalent. Every one of my books I've done this way, I just simply get into a room with plenty of carpet space and start moving them around on the floor, trying to balance them and seeing if I can see anything. In *Delights & Shadows*, there are four sections, and I began to see a possibility of grouping: some family poems here, some poems about *things* here, and that sort of stuff, so that they're sort of just general sections. The biggest advantage of having sections in your book is that it takes up four pages, so you don't have to stick in four bad poems. But I've never sat and thought that about writing a book of poems, that's just too big of a thing.

MM: That was going to be my follow up question: When you're composing a poem, is there any sort of thought at all as to where this poem might appear in a book?

TK: No, no. Once in a while, it dawns on me that I'm doing something that relates to something that I've done before and that maybe those things can work together. I've been thinking about another book in which, and if I had a working title I'd say it'd be called *Together*, because I have some poems that deal with the way two and three people relate to one another, that I've observed. I've got a poem I'm probably going to read tonight about a couple of men I saw in a car repair shop who had gone there together, one had drove the other there. There's a poem in my valentine book called "Splitting an Order" about watching an old couple cutting a sandwich in half. That kind of thing. I seem to be writing about those things, and that maybe together that would be a category. But it's way too early for me to even be thinking about it, because, towards a new book, I might have 15 to 16 poems that I really like. I have a couple hundred that have been in magazines that I don't want to collect, because I don't think that they're quite right. Frankly, part of the problem is that, once you get some sort of recognition, it's too easy to publish. We have poets who have achieved some recognition, and then they all of a sudden put out book after book, and that's the way the books feel.

MM: Do you find yourself sort of questioning sometimes, when you submit poems—I mean, obviously you think they're good enough to submit, but at this point, 'Ted Kooser' becomes a product almost . . .

TK: I'm being really careful about what I send out. I don't send out anything that I don't think is really the best that I could possibly do, and as a result, I'm not sending out a lot of stuff. And I can't get completely far enough away from my own work to completely tell whether or not it is as good as I can do. You know, I think it is. I don't know of anything else to do to make it better, but I know that there are a lot of them that fall a little short. Another thing, and I don't know whether you guys have had this experience or not, but you get five poems that you think make a pretty good looking submission, and among those is one that you think is really as good as it gets, and you send them out and somebody takes one of the other poems and sends your best one back. It gives you an idea of how wrong you can be.

MM: You have a rather vast body of work at this point. How do you pick out which poems you're going to read, like at the reading tonight?

TK: There are things that readings lead you into, I think. One of those is longer poems. Really short poems don't work well at readings, and I like to write short poems, so I tend to avoid really short ones. I heard Robert Bly say, "I'll read that one again," which is one way of doing it, but generally the short ones go by the audience too quickly, and the audience likes longer poems, poems with narrative. It's very interesting, and I didn't realize this until fairly recently, that poems that don't have people in them are not quite as attractive to people as poems with people in them. A description of an object that does not, that is in no way associated with human life, even though it was very well done, is not very interesting to audiences because audiences want to identify with people, I think. So I tend to read kind of the same poems wherever I go, with variations, because those are the ones that I've watched the audience respond to, and they like them. Katherine Anne Porter said—and she was a notorious liar, so we don't know whether she did this or not—she said that she recited all of her stories, or told all of her short stories, to people for years before she wrote them down, so that she could see how the audience was responding to the various details, and then that would help her shape the story. Carol Bly, who died last year, did the same thing with short stories. I've been to readings where she simply told a story. And this'll happen to you too. You do a reading and you pick out two or three people in the audience to refer to as the reading goes along to see how they're doing with it. I had an experience once that was really interesting. This was 25 years ago. I did a reading in Ithaca, New York, at the public library, and there was a farmer in the back row, a bald farmer in a pair of bib overalls and a plaid shirt, and I thought this is the kind of guy that could respond to some of these poems. So I kind of referred to him, looked at him as I was reading, and he seemed to be with it and everything. So I got to the end of the reading and he got up out of his seat and came right up the aisle and shook my hand and said, "I'm Archie Ammons." It was A.R. Ammons.

MM: That's amazing!

LB: I agree, that's a great story.

Dana Gioia has quoted you at one time saying that poems belong on a page and not in an auditorium. Do you feel that about poetry in general? That's it's best served to the audience as something they can experience one-on-one, alone with the book?

TK: I think the standard ought to be, for me, that they stand up on the page first. If they're good on the page then they're going to be okay in the reading. I just don't want to write a poem that is okay in the reading and doesn't work on the page. That is just simply dramatic, and I also would like to think that my poems will stand alone without me being present. Now that we have so many interesting poetry readings around the country, we have poets of national repute who are so closely identified with their poems through performance that I think they have become inseparable in a way, so that when one of those poets dies, all of their work is going to go down with them, because they're no longer going to be there to perform their poems for the public. And in a way that happened to Dylan Thomas. He was known for that beautiful voice and that deep, resonant reading, and also for the persona of this brawling Welsh poet and being drunk and his woman chasing, and all that stuff that went along with him. But when Thomas died, I mean the poems are still there and some of them are quite beautiful, but who reads Dylan Thomas today? Not many. Maybe people on campuses are reading Thomas, but I think his poems were too closely attached to him, and we've got people among us who are going to have the same problem. But I do like to read poems and have people appreciate them, and come up to me afterwards and tell me that they were moved by this, that or the other. I mean, you have to like that, but I don't want to write any poems with that as my goal.

LB: What is the change in mindset that you go through when sitting down to write poems as opposed to writing *Local Wonders*? Is there a prose-to-poetry switch you undergo?

TK: It just depends on what I get started on that day. In my morning writing, if I start to write something that looks like prose, then that's where I go with it. *Local Wonders* was a collection of a lot of prose scraps that I'd written that way, and they just all came together as a book. I never knew that I was writing a book. One day, I had been reading a book by Hal Borland, who's a nature columnist, and I was reading his book *Sundial of the Seasons*, in which he had taken his newspaper columns and had arranged them over the course of a year. And I thought, since I have setting in all the things I write, somehow or another, that what I had written in all of these scraps would divide up into four categories, like the seasons. And sure enough, they did, and there was the book. It had just accumulated while I wasn't paying any attention.

LB: I know earlier, in the Q & A, you had said that when you write you sort of get into a trance, and you don't think about where you're going. I don't usually think of prose being done that way. Is there perhaps a set objective that you're trying to achieve with prose as opposed to poetry?

TK: If I was writing a book review or something that had some sort of an end in mind, then that's a different thing; but as for lyrical prose, I write it the same way that I write poetry.

MM: Last question: Who are the five best poets that we've never read?

TK: Connie Wanek. Joseph Stroud. Jared Carter. Nancy Willard. And Jay Meek.

TED KOOSER

T'ang Poem for Midwinter

The gravel lane is locked in ice
from thawing and freezing snows,
the colors of its pebbles rich
as if they were wet, deep reds,
warm yellows lit from inside.
Walking with care in my slippers,
my old robe covered with dog hair,
I carry the mail from the tin box
out by the road, a handful of bills
and a letter from an aspiring poet
wondering how to get started.

II. Direct From Moon City

KEVIN BROCKMEIER

Moon City Review Short Story Competition, Adjudication

WINNING STORY: "Chapel Bluff" by Liz Breazeale

I admire "Chapel Bluff" for its many accomplishments of description and vision, the sympathy and care with which it investigates the lives of its characters, and the way the landscape not only punctuates but seems to absorb and then release the action of the story. The color and consistency of the narrative voice and the occasional shifts Breazeale incorporates into the stream of observation made me feel I was following the motions of a truly living mind. Her prose is full of grace notes, and while the *Moon City Review* contest attracted a number of compelling entries, none of them equaled hers in either ambition or achievement.

—Kevin Brockmeier, Final Judge

FINALISTS:

"Dying of the Edge of the Great Midwest" by Anthony Bradley
"Hard Times" by Matt Kimberlin
"Every Color There Was" by Sarah Marino
"The Starshine" by Andy Myers
"Pineapple Upside Down Boy" by Rob Pickering
"Mark Twain Versus the Drug Ape" by Mathew Reinig
"Naked American" by James Rives
"Trash" by Patrick Steward
"Cassandra" by Laura Underwood

LIZ BREAZEALE

Chapel Bluff

Everybody in Sikes knows my brother killed a man.

Eighteen years he spent payin' for it, 'til the day he died. Which was five days ago, accordin' to the letter I got day 'fore yesterday. When Mary Ann first got here she checked the mail and gave me this letter from the state of Missouri saying Ricky was dead. I knew I was his only survivin' relative, but . . . shit, that ain't exactly something a sister expects to hear about her older brother. I didn't, at least. Weren't even anything violent that killed him. It says he got hit with pneumonia, and I guess he just wasted away, then he gave up. I reckon that rage he had, it didn't make much of a motivator after a lifetime. Probably he felt he didn't have anything much to come back to. I bet he wondered if he ever did at all. Reckon I was all he had at one point but I don't guess that's true anymore.

It's here in my lap, that letter. The edges are thick and rough on my fingers; I've ran my hands over 'em so many times in three days, my hands are cross-stitched with thin, lacy-white paper cuts. From where I'm sittin' by the window, the sleet looks like it's colored everything dull grey. The tree branches ain't anything more than stiff, dead arms.

It's a lie to say Ricky's my brother; he was only my stepbrother. I never knew my mama, and Daddy only kept one picture of her out. Never saw it again when we moved to Sikes to live with Regina and Ricky. Daddy kept it on the kitchen counter in a painted gold frame still with the Walmart price sticker on the back, all faded and peeled and

115

yellowed. Mama was smiling in the picture. When I look at myself in the mirror, every time I remember that smile, and even though she wasn't a model or anything, I look at my dull brown hair, long nose and muddy eyes, and I don't know if I've ever grinned as big or beautiful as her in my life, besides when Mary Ann was born.

Even before we moved to Sikes, I never had many friends. I rode the bus home after school and I'd go over to Cotton and Mary Ray's place down the road, 'cause they were the closest to grandparents I ever had. Daddy worked all the time, at the sale barn in Urbana, running cow auctions and horse sales. He drank at work. They all did there. Most nights he'd come home and I'd be in my room reading. Every now and then he'd come to my door and just stand. Used to think maybe he was checkin' in on me. Lookin' back, I think he just needed somewhere to lean. As he sloped away, I'd hear him talking to himself, sayin' something like, Ain't she do nothin' but read?

Cotton said once, "Yore daddy, he used ta be a good man. Dunno what it is. Maybe was yer mama that was good all 'long." I dunno. If my mama was so good, why is it she married him? Why is it Regina married him?

But just 'cause I'm a natural introvert, I think that's the right word, that don't mean I didn't hear. Everyone'd talk. They'd see me reading, always reading. About the universe, usually. I used to think the stars and planets, black holes and the like, were all so fascinating. The universe was all so full. Full of billions of things we ain't ever gonna know about, and I figured that was kind of like earth. Billions of people out there I'll never know about, and they'll never know about me.

I check that letter one more time, and my gut feels like a screw gets twisted in it. I gotta look out the window, see if Mary Ann's car's come up the drive. She's supposed to be here soon.

116

She's a good girl, my daughter. I worried for a long time she'd turn out like her daddy. I suppose she ain't got much good genes to work with from either of us, but I'd rather her be like me than him. She's prettier than me. Long curly hair and a curvy frame. I look more like a pencil. Sometimes I look at those blue eyes of hers, and it just takes me back to the bluff, to thick green weeds overhanging the cliff, reaching up and droppin' off from the sky.

Goddamn. Mary Ann's got no idea. No idea what her uncle did. No idea what I been rememberin', and I wanna tell her. God, I wanted to tell her since before I got this damn letter, but I just—Jesus, it don't seem right to drop all that on her, just so I can feel better.

She ain't here yet. Sleet's still falling, but the only place it sticks is on the trees and the bush right outside the window.

It was barren winter when we moved to Sikes. All small towns are alike: they're desperate and cramped with talk and have an undertow of sadness that'll carry you away, so it wasn't hard for me to leave Urbana. I musta been in second grade then. Maybe third. No, it was second, because when we moved, I remember Ricky was in third grade, and he's a year older than me. Was. The trailer Ricky and his mama lived in was pale tan, and knocked off to the side of a wild gravel road out past Chapel Bluff, with a mailbox sitting crooked on a wood post, circled by a tire. The roof sagged towards the house front a bit, and there were always leaves in the gutter and on the shingles. 'Twasn't unkept, I guess, 'cause Ricky must've mowed and all; it just looked old, like everything in Sikes. I slunk out of Daddy's truck with an old carpet bag over my shoulder, and when I walked up to the porch, a ratty gray and white cat scrambled out from under the stairs and ran off screeching. It could've run for awhile before findin' another house.

Ricky helped me lug my stuff in. He just glared at Daddy. First time we all had dinner together, must've been months before, when Daddy and Regina started dating, he asked Ricky if he ever saw his old man. Regina got flustered. Ricky slammed his chair into the table and stalked off yelling.

Ricky's old man was in jail. I think he beat Ricky's mama.

After we brought all our stuff inside, I sat in my room on the carpet, readin'. That was my unpacking, taking a book out of the flimsy cardboard box holding them and flippin' through them. Probably that old encyclopedia of the universe. I heard the door creak, cause everything in that house made some kinda noise. I jumped off the floor so fast the book looked like it leaped out of my hands of its own accord, but it wasn't Daddy standing there in the doorway. It was Ricky, and if the shades weren't drawn crooked over my window so there wasn't any light comin in, I bet he woulda made a shadow over me.

I don't have but one picture of Ricky, and that's in a yearbook. Don't remember where that's at, now. That was one of the only things I kept when I got outta Sikes. Kept it 'cause I thought, maybe, maybe, maybe; but maybe ain't no use to a guilty conscience.

He had scraggly brown hair that went past his ears. When we got older, I'd cut it for him, but I never trusted him to cut mine. His eyes were dark, like shark eyes, deep and covered over with something sharp and angry, some primal anger left over from some old wrong, coming from his daddy. That day he wore an old camo coat, a size too big for him that made him look like a scarecrow with old hand me downs hung on it. His nails were short but never dirty. His lips were always vergin' on scarlet, chapped from wind and probably bitin' 'em as much as he did. He was restless, but not in a skittish way. He moved so violent, any move he made punched him forward. I always thought that's what a wolverine would move like.

118

He stood in the doorway and looked surprised by how hard the door slammed. He just stood. And stared. I was still breathing heavy, but I managed a soft, "What?"

He blinked, real slow, and then said, "I was here first. Not you." He shoved two fists down into his coat pockets and sullenly said, "Was here first. They made me move rooms fer you. I used to sleep in here. 'S cramped in the office." He thought for a long minute, then he said, " 'S fine, I guess. You live here. I ain't alone now." When he got older, his voice was almost a growl.

Looking at him kinda scared me, but he seemed so all alone it didn't matter to me how I felt. "You—you wanna read?" I said. "I got some dinosaur books. You like dinosaurs?" Tryin' to make up for ruining his life a bit.

Ricky's fists came up out of his pockets just a little bit and his caves of eyes got a little wider. "Well . . . well, I guess. Mama says I don't read enough." I handed him the book and hoped he didn't mess it up, and we sat together and read 'til Daddy and Regina got back.

I feel like there're some things I remember in real time, just as they happened. Others fly by thick and fast, like a record on the wrong speed, or the sleet fallin' outside. I hope Mary Ann drives slow. And I hope she's been flossing. 'Cause with college girls, you can't be sure about anything. Don't know from personal experience myself, just from the parent side. Mary Ann, she surprised the hell outta me, with goin' to college. Considering how she came to be. Goddamn. I can't lose her. I can't tell her. She's all I got left.

I guess this letter I'm holdin' is the most proof I'll ever need that she'll be the best of her family. Makes me sick to think of how appalled she'd be to learn.

For a minute after Daddy and Regina got married I thought things would change, but Daddy was still workin' at the sale barn except now he had to drive for longer to get to work, and when he got home sometimes he'd still be drunk.

Whether he was drunk or not he'd sit in the living room and turn on the tv and just watch, anything that was on. Ricky and I'd hear him flipping through the channels, sometimes just changing it and changing it and changing it like he was playing Russian Roulette. We'd go outside most of the time when he was home, no matter if it were nine or ninety nine degrees. If we were inside Daddy'd give Ricky the worst time. Ricky'd say something like, "He's drunk again; your daddy's no better than—"

"What you say, boy? 'Choo say to me?" Daddy'd shoot back, 'cause Ricky'd say it loud enough he knew Daddy'd hear.

And Ricky'd snarl, "You heard. You heard me."

Sometimes he'd let me drag him outside, 'cause I couldn't stand to have them fight because of me. Others I'd stand and watch it almost come to blows. It was probably my fault; that's the way I felt. Shoulda kept 'em apart, or stood up for someone. I dunno. Daddy was an angry drunk, and Ricky was just angry.

Something thuds and snaps on the window, and it starts me out of memory. I leap up, and I look out the window. There's nothing there, just wind shakin' the icy buildup on the tree branches and sleet still slammin' down. But down on the ground there's a bird twitchin' and trying to roll. His red breast just looks like an autumn leaf bein' blown about. Maybe he'll make it.

Mary Ann should be here by now. I won't call her, don't wanna bother her any.

The robin red breast's got up now, his wing looks kinda messed up, and when he hops about, he shakes his head and looks befuddled. I tap on the window; maybe that'll help him on his way. He bounces under the thickest part of the bush.

Reminds me of Ricky's first fight. He tackled Jacob Butcher in the cafeteria in sixth grade for sayin' something

120

about me. Ain't important now what it was. All's important is the blood that poured from both their faces onto their shirts.

Here in the present I can still see flashes of red through the mesh of leaves and twigs, inside the bush. Mary Ann always did like animals. She breezed through every book about horses she could find, and now look at her. She wants to be a vet.

High school made Ricky's temper worse. Don't even know if you could call it a temper, just 'cause it wasn't something that flared up. It was like a disease, one like malaria or whatever, that never goes away.

There was a bonfire one night during junior year. And I wish to God we'd never gone, Ricky and I, but it was just up the road at Chapel Bluff, where Steve Parson lived. Even though I didn't care much about Steve Parson, I loved Chapel Bluff. From the top of the cliff you could see the trees dip down low over the river, and it was like they wanted to steal some of the life from the water as the light from the sun leaped and sparkled on the surface. The hay fields spread out below were peaceful in the winter, and sometimes the rock cliffs under you would rattle with the echoes from somebody out hunting. The sky hung like a church ceiling over you, whether it was night or day, spring or fall. A view like that, it could break your heart.

Ricky knew I always had a soft spot for Chapel Bluff, as he's the first person that took me up there, and he said, "C'mon, Charity. Let's go, you ain't been to a bonfire since you moved here."

I mumbled, "Ricky, you know ain't nobody at that school cares whether you take me or not."

His grin made him look like he was baring his teeth. "Charity, c'mon. You need ta have some fun. We're goin'." So he pulled me to the truck, and I knew I'd just end up drinking all the more 'cause I wouldn't have anyone to talk to besides the odd drunk boy who'd meander up.

I stood as close to the edge of the bluff as I could without leaving the ring of light from the fire. Ricky'd come by to give me a Keystone or a Coors every few minutes, and every time he did I'd think to ask him if we could leave, but the more I had, the harder it was for me to try and get the words out. "Rickyyy . . . don't you think . . . I dunno, you know? Should—"

I remember it kinda fuzzy; I think he said, "Charity, it's a'right." He put his arm around me and squeezed tight. He was real warm. Each beer I had made the stars group closer together.

At a point after that, I remember Jacob Butcher coming over to me and whispering something about the view in my ear, then putting his arm around me and taking me to his truck.

There's only bits and pieces. And those jumble up and speed past.

Hitting my head on the truck door. Red t-shirt on the seat. Hands under my shirt. Mumble words. Sharp, and pain, and then pumping. I might've laughed, I might've said yes or no or a million other words that I couldn't separate anymore. And then next I remember the door falling open and my head flopping out while a hand ripped me out by my arm, and I couldn't walk, so I slammed into the ground.

There was mud on my jeans. I threw up out the window of the truck I don't remember getting into. Blood somewhere.

As soon as I woke up, I was sore everywhere, and there was blood and mud on my clothes. I puked in my trash can and Ricky came in.

"What the fuck," he growled. He shook the bed when he threw himself down on it, and it made pain shiver up my body. "What the fuck. Last night. What the fuck. You know, you fuckin' know I hate him. I hate him, and you in there, fuckin' him—" He slammed his fist into the mattress, and

122

his face contorted, his dark eyebrows standin' out against his pale skin.

I could barely breathe I was so sick, and that just made me feel worse, and it was all my fault he was so mad, all my fault, I shouldn't've drank all that much, I shouldn't've let Jacob take me back to the truck. "Ricky, Ricky, I was so Goddamn drunk. 'M sorry!" He grabbed my wrist and it was such a deep pain that my stomach heaved. "Ricky, ow, you're hurting—"

He whipped back. He stood up with his eyes wide, an unbroke colt. I looked at my arm, I saw the bracelet of bruises around my wrist. Last night.

"I—I—" he stuttered, something I never seen him do. He moaned, soft, "I fucked him up. Bad. Threw him outta the car an'—an' we was both just punchin' everywhere." And he reeled around and ran out. I puked. Then I laid back down, and the last I remember before falling asleep again is running my fingers around and around my wrist, like what was colored on it would protect me.

On Monday at school in the hall Johnny Dixon shouted at me, "Hey, Charity! Heard 'bout you an' Jacob last weekend—how 'bout you 'n I head up to Chapel Bluff an'—" But Johnny never had a chance to finish because Ricky shoved me outta the way and slugged him dead in the face. He punched him two more times, and every time sounded like he was slamming a mallet into a slab of ribeye steak with the bone still in it, and I know he'd'a kept tearing into him if the counselor hadn't ripped him away so hard his back crashed into the rusty lockers behind him. He dragged him down the hall, twisting and screaming, "You ever talk to her again, and I'll kill you! You son bitch, I'll kill you!" He was fighting so fiercely they looked like he were dancing right into the lockers on both sides of the hallway, but I doubt anyone noticed the dents they left.

Johnny hopped up and wiped his mouth and his nose, blood smeared everywhere, even in the spaces between his teeth and he screamed back, "You just try, you piece a trash! You ain't even good enough to share a cell with your daddy!" He sprayed gritty red blood dots on everyone around him and when he threw himself past me, he made sure he said, "Only reason any guy here ever talks to you is 'cause you'll give it to 'em good in the back of their car." I might've slapped him myself after that, but Ricky was already in the shit 'cause of me anyhow.

Ricky and I laid out on the trailer roof that night so he could avoid Daddy when he came home. Ricky and me, we laid out on that roof for hours and hours, I think Regina'd told Daddy she didn't know where we were. We were just drinking beer we'd taken from Daddy's stash, cause that was standing up to him in some way. And I just watched the stars. I was always thinking about those damn stars. About how far away they were, not in the way people get sentimental about it, and see how insignificant they are in the universe. I guess that's just 'cause I always felt that way. I only thought about how far away they were while I felt close to Ricky, and I guess that's when I first got that niggling little thought, the idea that if we were the last two people on earth, ok, that'd . . . that'd be fine, if everybody else just melted away like the Nazis at the end of *Raiders of the Lost Ark*.

Ricky was laying on his side, watching me watch the stars, with a beer can in his hand. He whispered, "You ain't mad, are you? I just, I dunno, I just ain't gonna listen to him talk that shit anymore. All 'cause of—"

"Ricky, I said sorry." My last beer had left a bitter tang in my mouth, I remember still feeling awful 'cause Ricky'd been so mad, so jealous after the bonfire. "I—I dunno. He ain't more mad at you than me, though; you just take it too personal. You gotta just not think about it."

"Take what personal?" I could see his face pretty well in the light from the stars and the moon, and the shadows crossed over his face, and they made him older than eighteen somehow. He brushed his scraggly hair out of his eyes.

I said, "Everything." His eyes looked hooded. So I soothed him. "You need to let me cut your hair again." It made me feel like I could actually do something worthwhile, like I wasn't always in the way.

"I know. See, we look out for each other."

I thought about the bruises from Chapel Bluff. I remembered fifth grade and sixth and seventh and every year after when something would be wrong 'cause of me. Name calling on the playground 'cause of my shyness. Jokes about drunks, about a house of rejects. About gawky, bird-nosed, book-toting me. All my high school days, plain and quiet at lunch. Outcast. He got the blame for that, I thought right then. I counted every time, but suddenly it felt like there were too many, so I looked up at the stars, but that made it all seem worse, and my eyes blurred over with tears so I said, "You don't need t' do that. You don't." I'll never forget, even though I been trying for twenty years, what his eyes looked like in the night when the stars struck them and how it chilled me. Some people, I bet, get lovelier under moonlight. Ricky, he just looked like the first man who ever walked the earth; his cheekbones and his nose stood out, sharp, like weapons themselves. He was never big; he was tall, sure enough, but wiry. Sinewy.

" 'Course I got to. I gotta fight, you an' me . . ." He sat up sharp. I followed. The woods drew in around us, and the cicadas sawed on louder. The stink of cows got denser. And he said it quiet, but savage. "I'd kill any man that hurt you. Sure. I'd fuckin' kill 'im." And the thing that scared me the most wasn't that he said it, 'cause he threatened all day long. But it was scary 'cause I knew he meant it, and it was the first time I believed he could do it. Shit, he just got suspended for bashing Johnny's face in. He was hell-bent on making everyone pay for something gone wrong too long ago.

I noticed over the years that memories, they're like the Big Bang. For a bit, seems like there's nothin'. Nothin' at all. Then something triggers a mind, and everything flies out of control, and with no warning at all, there's everything all at once. Expanding forever, and you can't never reel it back in.

Ricky and I went up to Chapel Bluff one afternoon after the bonfire. Two months after. He was drunk. I wasn't, least not off alcohol.

Goddamn. Every time I think about what I did, what Ricky did, I can't even breathe, it stops me dead. I think about it 'most every hour of every day. Replay it. I cringe every time. My throat closes up.

When he asked me why I wasn't drinking, he was slurring. He stumbled and he took me down with him. Layin' on the ground with the blue cathedral ceiling opened up above, I panicked, I felt sick to my stomach and my gut was pounding so I choked on words. Scared as I was, something came over me and I had to say it or it'd keep making me sick. I thought I could trust him, right then, and I was so terrified, so nervous, I got a lurch in my stomach with every word I said. "Ricky," I said, stronger than I thought, "I ain't drinkin' 'cause, 'cause, 'cause I can't. I can't, Ricky," he turned his glazed over eyes on me. "I—I—Goddammit, I'm pregnant!" It was like I'd thrown up, but it didn't feel any better. I wish I could strangle myself, every time I play it back.

He didn't say a word. He moaned, he howled, he made some noise that ain't got a name. It was just animal. He leaped to his feet, and he scrambled to the truck. His muscly arms ripped the door open, and he launched his skinny body inside.

I begged, pleaded. I sobbed. I asked him not to leave. He snatched my arm and shoved me into the truck. I couldn't stop shakin', bawling and trying to talk. He was silent of any

126

human noise; the only thing he did was pound the steering wheel and snarl. I curled up like a shrimp. I cried harder.

Everything went fast but slow.

Jacob was fixing a fence when we got to his property. Drunk men usually can't fight worth shit but Ricky pounced out of the truck and screamed and then he and Jacob were on the ground tearing at each other. I never stopped screaming to stop, stop, stop, you have to stop—til Jacob reached for a hammer, and I launched forward to get it before him, and there was dust swirling about them both. Jacob stopped for a minute when I got the hammer, and Ricky jumped him again, except the fence post was behind him, and it didn't give, his neck just snapped.

"He ain't movin'!" I shrieked, I cried, I was gasping huge breaths so I wouldn't throw up, but I did, anyway. I stood there stock still, and I kept retching and retching so much that if you could throw up a baby, I would've right then.

Ricky grabbed me. He dragged me to the car, but I couldn't stop lookin' at Jacob's body, and I couldn't even be mad he done this to me; all I knew was nothing at all except Ricky'd just killed a boy, he'd killed a boy who was limp, still warm, layin' with his neck propped up on a fence post, like it was only a pillow.

I don't know how we got home.

The cops came. I cried so much my whole face was raw and red for days.

I got bigger while it seemed Ricky's life got smaller over the next few months.

Every time I'd look at Ricky I'd see hell in his eyes. They went on forever, with nothing but hate inside. Every time I looked at him I thought, he'll rot in jail. He'll die there. I'll burn forever. It was like I let that horrible, awful thing happen. He killed a boy. Sure, Jacob was mean. And I had his baby. But . . . Jesus Christ, how could I be in the same room with Ricky, knowing he done that? That he done it all for me.

I was gone from Sikes as soon's I could be after Mary Ann was born.

Ricky and I never had a grand farewell. Weren't any tears. I acted like I'd be seein' him again.

Ain't no room for anything sentimental in jail.

One day I was there. And the next we was just gone. I'd gotten a job while I was pregnant, at the diner. And I'd saved enough to last a bit 'til I found another job somewhere. Seems all those months, though, when it was me and little baby Mary Ann, they was the hardest. All days and nights stretchin' out into nothing. Infinity. By and by I decided I'd never mention Sikes. Not Sikes, never Regina, nor Daddy, or Mary Ann's own daddy, neither. If I ever told about anyone it'd be Ricky, but soon's I tried to say something, anything, the way his eyes looked that night on the roof, or the way we sat on the floor of the trailer the first day we moved in, whenever I tried to pick out those memories, all I could see was the blood on his face.

Sometimes I used to get restless, and my mind wandered. Around the country, out across the empty hay fields in the winter, listening to the cicadas and diving down Chapel Bluff, and then on through the woods and on to the city, where my brother was at, laying on a cot. Used to wonder if he'd think of me. How I abandoned him and how he gave up everything for me for no other reason than he loved me. I'd wonder if he still loved me. I'd pray that. But every part of me was sure he hated me with all the venom he had left. Now, well, 'til I got the letter at least, I sit and I imagine what it'd be like to go see him or even just call him and say, I'm sorry, I'm sorry, I only did it 'cause—but then that's as far as I get; even in my imagination I can't say how I wished my daughter had an uncle.

Anymore, I don't wonder like that. The tv in front of me, pictures of Mary Ann, the snow that comes in the winter; all those things, that's all I got. Can't go back, not to Chapel

128

Bluff, not the trailer roof, never looking up at the stars. Those old avenues closed to me twenty years ago, maybe more, maybe when I met Ricky or when Mama died, how could I know?

That robin, he ain't there anymore. And Mary Ann, she's clenching her coat to her while she's walking up my drive.

Don't know if I should stir it up by tellin' her. Or if should let it all die with Ricky, and flow away with his last breath, with the wind, on down the crumbling dirt edge of the bluff and past the glittering river and onto the tree-covered mountains, so tall their jaggedy edges scratch the sky.

BILLY CLEM

Dear C—

Dear C—

I hope this note finds you well
on the other side of the pond.
I've not heard from you since
our good meals and spending sprees,
our mutual kisses and sadness
for your necessary leaving.
I'm left to imagine you've made it
home, to hours and hours of work,
helping well beyond clock-time
after a long deserved break
in the relaxation of far way.

Here, we hear of more troubles
erupting in the North, Catholics
and Protestants fighting again
this centuries-old battle.
Are yours there safe? What
do they make of this once more?
Do they hide at night, refuse
communion in the daylight?
We get only the most titillating
bits, of course, bombs, the dead
police, bullets, the same scene.
Please, share what you know,

tell me about you, what you feel
again returning to non-news, a reel
replaying itself, an idiot gyre.
You are safe, I pray, in your flat
where no home-made bombs
wait for another summer's fires,
where ne'er-do-wells dare
not come round for help.

My friend, may you be buried
under stacks of late reports,
full voice-mail, e-mail ignored,
tea and biscuits, some brown
bread and butter with friends,
and a love understood by few.

Love, B—

BILLY CLEM

The Neighbor's Cat

The neighbor's cat, I call her Princess,
dines out nightly, not on natural delicacies
of local birds or squirrels or baby possum.

She comes to my place, instead, a garden-
apartment, ground-level windows always open
early spring to fall, through which we talk.

How was work today? "The usual.
And you? Anything new, Princess?"
I woke up. I ate. I napped. I ate. I've come here.

That's my cue to say, "Have a seat, Princess.
I'll be right back" with a bowl of cool water
and some treats my friends often ask about,

You don't have cats. What are these? Cat treats?
You eat them yourself? You're allergic to cats,
always sneezing and wheezing around ours.

Princess laps up the water, eats her dessert,
tuna or chicken or turkey flavors preferred.
When she's finished, our chat ends. She goes
home, full. I floss, brush, gurgle, and go to bed.

SATARAH WHEELER

After the Wings Tore Through

There's a girl down the street
who never takes down her
Christmas lights.
Mouth like an oil slick,
shining and expansive.
Her hair, like
the contaminated marine life,
floats black about her shoulders.
Blades sharp and penetrating
in her cotton dresses.

After the wings tore through,
surely they never looked the same
again, I think.

Sometimes I catch her sleeping
on the porch—her skirt,
her hair a quiet pond.

Sometimes, when I'm not thinking
about her, memories rush in
like tides of her dancing
in the city with a red mouth
and torn stockings,

of her white teeth
clinking against

a shot glass,
of her arm
tied and pinched,
my mouth on her
collarbones,
the waxy taste of lipstick.

I think of her bare feet crossed
beneath her on the tiny porch
when I feel like dying.
It's always the small tears in her
shoulder blades that stop me.

I think of her when I'm drowning,
her hands folded like letters say
are you a Believer?
She wears a single silvers angel's wing
on a chain around her neck and I think
maybe, maybe.

SATARAH WHEELER

New Jersey

Near the most honest seas, the grayest seas,
ruffled and yawning upon not beaches, but shores,
I dream that I march from the ash sand and into it,
right up to my neck and then over my head and inhale.
The water is dirty and it stings like exposed electrical wires
and my lungs bulge with it. I am the bluefish, and the seaweed,
the popcorn box half digested by sea salt. I am the reflection
of the Ferris wheel bones and the muffled shrieks of
marine children building sand castles in their natural habitat.
Behind rows and rows of boathouses and miles of land, years
above sea level and on two legs, I long for this seafaring existence.
I dream of undertow and never seeing the surface again.
Dissolving into sea particles and washing up near a metal
garbage bin, hot and buzzing under the pier.

BEN BOGART

Sundays

On Sundays I move in slow circles around the house
    filing complaints with the dogs,
    dodging work for the week,
commanding my two-strong army of slippers
    against the gravity of Saturday,
    finding morals and missing energy in everything.

Matt says his is the Church of *Meet the Press*
    and, baffled, the Baptists leave his porch
    only to find mine and my wild hair
and me, shouting accusations at the cat who can't
    tell the difference between this day
    and the last. Wouldn't God have told him?

I make biscuits not from scratch but from *whoosh*,
    the sound made as I smack the seams
    of blue Pillsbury tubes across the countertop.
Marmalade makes the hangover go away
    and I stare into the Bible-black eyes
    of Audrey Hepburn on the Fox Movie Channel.

I'm never quite happy
    with a Sunday, which crawls and meanders
    like a limp and trivial fuse.
I take my weekly holidays quietly,
    wishing I had a cigarette,
    that Sundays had more time,
    were something for me and not just everyone
    else.

SHERI GABBERT

The Music of These Worn Down Ozark Mountains

Summer nights we sat in a lawn chair circle,
the pickers together, the rest of us
on either side. We sang inherited harmonies
as we told the stories of generations
lived in the Ozark Mountains.

I could hear those voices singing as she bid farewell to me
Far across the fields of cotton my old hopes I could see
As the moon rose in its glory, then I told my oldest story
Of that girl I left in sunny Tennessee

and songs from the War Between the States,
but never damned Yankee tunes, and songs
the old folks grew up with or danced to while
they fell in love and the music stories of the
Big War and the one that followed which was
even bigger and more terrible. The old folks
told once again how their brother, Tom, was
awarded a silver star for taking charge of his
platoon on one of Normandy's beaches when
his commander panicked at the carnage, weeping
over what remained of a soldier's torso.

We sang history as August heat lingered
long after Missouri breeze had gone to bed,
cicadas and lightening bugs and an army of
crickets repeated every note, each summer's

symphony performed by that night's orchestral
insects as if Fall and Winter did not exist,
as if the music belonged to them, not us,
genetic coding of an ancestral past, the unconscious
collective memory of bugs and mountain families.

How many August evenings I have sat alone listening
to the past and wishing just one more time to be
in that circle, the chairs all filled.

LORA KNIGHT

Poacher's Moon

Geese fly south for the winter || everyone knows this except
for the geese who fly || over my house any old time ||
pausing only in the flat dead heat of July || going in any
direction || likewise the moon || does not light merely the
night sky as appointed but rises anytime || harvest moon,
poacher's moon || blue moon || what am I to call this
lace doily in broad daylight || tramping out mid-afternoon
on a Tuesday? || it reminds me of my daughter || who
was pulled out like a wave like a flood || while I crashed in
around her || I've always wanted to feel the full-on crazy
|| that waitresses and E.R. techs can attest to || wanted to
look full into that fat scarred face || and howl or cry || the
geese ignore the doily || drift down only for the full glow ||
my daughter was moved without ever seeing the man in the
moon || last night I saw him || blindfold by a cirrus cloud
|| eyes bandaged like some cosmic war wound || God
bless him || he's as hapless and helpless || as I am.

One, Acquainted with the Night

I met an exorcist at Waffle House,
once. While I waited there to be cast out
into the world, debris washed in,

drawn by the sign *OPEN ALL NIGHT!*
He specialized in small demons,
like the cigarette winding down

in my ashtray and my prolonged unwillingness
to sleep. I have his business card still,
black & white: *Exorcist.* I questioned him

about other demons, the more traditional kind—
graveyards and chains, drowned pigs.
I wonder what he thought of the swine flu,

where the tables appeared briefly to be turned.
I could call him, I suppose, and ask. I would insist
on telling him that I exorcize nothing:

not Styles who had been someone
once and now leaned in too close
whispery and stale. Not Lola,

who drank too much always
and one night stole the *Pay Checks Here*
sign and gave it to a trucker, claiming

he snored. Not the execrable coffee,
or the night, or the town, or Diane,
who read handwriting and knew the names

of every president in order, the way
I know the names of the short-order
cooks. And certainly not

the wearied-eyed exorcist
who wayfared in with his calling card
from I-44, forked his hash browns,
and bedeviled no one.

Jenn Velasco-Cafagña

For the Dead Who Hang Out at Anton's

After Edna St. Vincent-Millay

To be an adult is to sit in coffee shops next to people
    who have died and really hate the taste of coffee,
and do not offer to buy you a cup. You ask

them about today's breakfast special, what they tell
    the former English professor who comes here every day.
But they say nothing.

So you throw packets of Sweet and Low at them, force
    them out of their well-worn chairs by their stiff
and moldy raincoat collars, and shake the hell out

of them; but they are not lucid anymore. They are not even
    a part of the undead world, and so you scream and stomp
behind their black stools at the counter.

When the waitress serves you your long-awaited coffee,
    she glares at the cup as she struggles to hold the pot's handle.
You decide to leave just before she loses her grip,
    and the dead you thought were gone are now waiting for you.
The one with colorless eyes fixed upon you, holds the door open wide.

Jenn Velasco-Cafagña

Visiting My Brother at the State Hospital

He looked down, then backed away
and sat in a chair designed to make
someone else comfortable.
I was nine the year
my mother had my brother committed
to the Nevada State Hospital.

My mother talked to his doctor
while I waited in the car with my grandmother,
and when she asked me
what flavor of ice cream I wanted
one of the other patients came up to my window
and smiled like he had just heard
the funniest story in the world.
He waved to me before the orderlies
walked him back inside.

None of us spoke at the Dairy Queen
or during the ride home.
I was trying to figure out
why my brother was home one day,
watching television with me
or drawing pictures as I read to him,
then living in a place that reminded me
of the roller coaster ride that scared us
at the county fair,
the one we used to ride over and over.

Shannon Wooden

Superhero

The first one was an accident. Alone in her classroom with the autistic boy avoiding the "mainstreamed" cafeteria, the one who couldn't stay out of the bullies' way because it just didn't make the right kind of sense to do so, Victoria maybe wasn't choking so much as gagging on that apple slice. But it didn't matter anymore once the reporters came, once the interview went viral, once the awkward child believed in his ability, his courage, his destined greatness. He was a superhero. She could see it in his eyes that he'd never retreat from that lesson and would know, now, always, that he could help others, even these strange, inferior others whom he would never fully understand. She saw him embracing his outsider status like Kal-el, finding a blooming empathy rooted firmly in his very isolation. He'd ably performed the Heimlich. But she had saved his life.

After that, she began to develop a sort of *awareness*—she didn't know how else to put it—a sort of tingling spidey-sense when she was near a child silently trudging down a path toward despair. She could see, somehow, their terrible presents and terrifying futures. The knowledge, of course, became oppressive: tormented with their lives, she could find no joy in her own. Even the tiniest moments of beauty began to seem gaudy, even cruel, in the face of such potential pain. But one Tuesday, waiting at the bus stop in front of the school, she had a flash of lucidity. Taking a silent breath, saying a silent prayer, and stepping directly in front of the oncoming bus, she gave herself to the child standing beside her, whose life she knew would otherwise bring only perversion and struggle. As he pulled her back onto the curb, he unconsciously repudiated the self-loathing of his future and conquered what would become the chronic disappointment of his aggressively heterosexual father. She could see his triumph. Celebrated as a hero in his class, at the all-school assembly, and in the letter she later wrote to the editor of the local paper, he knew, at least momentarily, his great capacity for becoming, and he would grow to honor and nurture it.

They weren't all so dramatic. Sometimes, it was as simple as leaving a wallet on the concession counter at the movies so that the boy behind her whose date was two hours away from breaking his heart could prove his genuine worth, his vast superiority to the punk on whom she would otherwise waste so much time. A moment of perspective: for him, or her, or both. Delayed, perhaps, but real, and right here in a world where nearly nothing else was. Only once had she misjudged (she was too late), but even that, Victoria thought, might have saved the girl (already learning to see her own riches in the terms of the hormonal boys who passed her around like money) from a boy who wouldn't even return someone's kid pictures. He'd hit her someday—anyone could see that now. But maybe the girl would protect herself, armed with this glimpse into his forming character. To Victoria, that was easily worth the price of the wallet, the Christmas card portraits of nieces and nephews, and the eleven bucks inside.

Her moments of *awareness* took a hiatus for a while—a few months, when she tried to carry the future inside of herself instead—but after another lost pregnancy, she decided that her contribution to the children would have to be just this: she could give them these invisible moments of strength, the opportunity to rewrite their tragic futures, the blossoming knowledge of their own heroic selves in the great and terrible Gotham of this world. So she slipped on stairs and let the bullied catch her. She draped her smock through the candle on her desk and let the misfit throw a fire blanket around her waist. She kicked over the stepladder, stranding herself atop the shelves in the supply closet, so that the paralytically shy could call security. She left her emergency brake off and let the masochistic (future anorexic, maybe cutter) rescue not only her car but every child on the playground at the bottom of the hill. Once, after watching a mother berate her son for being afraid to put his face in the water—*you'll never get to go off the diving board like a big boy* and *do you see any of the other children crying?*—she caught her swimsuit strap on the bottom of the pool ladder, underwater, and let him dive in to unhook it.

Her husband never knew. It wouldn't have been enough for him. The potential dying inside her again and again—her great cosmic failure—finally drove him away, as she knew it would eventually. It is okay. The world needs her in other ways. This afternoon, Victoria has become aware of the girl at the bus stop. There are bruises hidden under her skirt and she thinks she deserves them, she thinks this is what love must feel like to a woman, she thinks she should run away— or stay—and whatever choice she makes, a treacherous path of self-destruction is laid out before her. Victoria assesses which way everyone in the little crowd is looking and knows that if she chooses her moment just right, with one simple step she can arrest this girl's destiny. By Friday, the mayor will be declaring her a hero. She will know what it means to be proud, to feel necessary. She will bask in love and adoration and appreciation, and she will never let go of the conviction that she deserves these things. She will someday do something great. The downtown bus is coming—it doesn't stop here—but anyone would believe it an easy mistake to expect it to. Victoria's heart is filled with love as she steps into the intersection.

146

Lee Busby

Marriage Counseling

I came this close to falling down, just now standing
still in my living room. My legs went weak. My dog
talks nonsense, corrals me to where he wants me to be.
The sun shines bright and looks damn hot from the couch,
but the snow outside don't melt. I've poured myself three
glasses of ice tea—extra sugar, a little vodka, no lemon, please.
Earlier I took the hedge trimmer to the lilac bush outside
the bay window. I worry about the bay window.
I shouldn't be allowed to be alone by myself. I've picked up
the phone twice and sat it back down on the edge, the very edge,
of my coffee table ($29.95 from LTD Commodities). I went to
the mailbox, came back and spread the newspaper all over
the place: front page on the back of the couch; want ads
on the floor next to the trashcan; sports page, of course,
in the bathroom between the sinks; obituaries in the spot
of sun that manages to spear the heart of the family room.
My dog whines to be let out, goes out, comes back in. It's easy
to feel righteous right now. I open the door, he goes back
out, turns a circle, comes back and I let him in.
It's the dance of the lonely. I make him sit on the couch
and show him the personals: Man with 30 acres of farm outside
of town seeks woman who wants to get away. Away from what?

LEE BUSBY

Hammer to Nail

The symmetry of my wooden fence is off
in the back corner, it has sagged and buckled
and my mangy dog shits there too much
for me to go stand there and fix it now.

I've finally caved in and taken up drinking
coffee because it seemed the right thing
to do while standing on my back porch
staring at my crooked fence. It tastes awful

and bitter, but I drink it because I made it.
I stare at my fence because I made it too.
I stare at my dog and throw small rocks
to scare him out of the back corner, but damn

if he isn't more stubborn than I expected.
His regularity has upset my equilibrium. If I sit
in my chair, he lays on my feet. Lonely, I suppose.
And tired. I scratch my head and he scratches his.

I get up to go in, he follows at my heel. I've learned
to make us both a good dinner; an extra burger,
one dog-size, on the stove, and he doesn't mind
the grease. I see how this could be a problem.

But we've been on our own now for two months.
We agreed to keep things in order, but he

doesn't listen to me. I keep thinking back
to seven weeks ago when I swung hammer to nail,

dug the claw end into the ground to ditch out a path
straight along my property line, sweating myself
into my dirt, trying to understand the boundaries
of what one man can ever hope to own or fix.

Banner Leaves the Filling Station

Why he hugged Kent just then
Banner don't rightly know. The man's
been pumping his gas since the flames
streaking his pickup weren't but a spark
of rust on one fender, and that's a while.
Barely more than a shit-howdy between them
all that time, but what's done is done.
Banner spits a stream of chew juice
and sunflower shells straight as a hawk
piss out the window. *Fucking Kent,*
he says to the dog he wishes were on the seat
beside him. Banner don't recall ever hugging
another man, not even his old daddy who loved
him dearly. He considers mentioning the matter
to Sadie, then remembers her old man's home
from his long haul to Cheyenne and that
trouble don't need a hand finding him. Big Sky
country they call it up there, but Banner
reckons the sky here is plenty big enough
to feature dreams that never quite come true.
Bigger just means easier to lose the little things.
Banner checks his gauge, figures he'll need
another half a tank day after next. Maybe sooner
if he drives a while and don't keep his foot
out of it. Could be Kent's been to Montana.
Could be Kent's been waiting for somebody
to ask him about that very thing. Could be

Kent could use a friendly ear to hear
his tales of adventuring generally. The man
aint been pumping gas his whole life, has he?
Banner downshifts. He reaches over, scratches
the air behind its ears. These old back roads
got 300 miles of gravel to turn over, and Banner
aims to overturn a good stretch of it by opening time.

MILLER MANTOOTH

Storm Siren

Due to the simple fact that she has a tornado
tattoo that funnels from her pale shoulder
down almost to the bend of her slender arm

while considering also the grace of her angular
momentum as she deftly twists her way through
turbulence generated by the collision of beer

specials and televised baseball but without
failing to mention the electrical tension
contained within the wall cloud of her eyes

I leave the bar without so much as saying to her
a single word, without even saying goodbye
to my friends, without finishing my drink

or paying my tab or taking a last look back
and I high-tail it home where I know my wife
will take me in, shelter me with the calm warmth
of her presence like a cellar door always open to me.

Lanette Cadle

Spring Comes to Kansas

I-70 in the long, roomy stretch across grasslands
that is Kansas was made for hydroplaning, a sport

inflicted on unsuspecting drivers whose main aim
is to get to Colorado ASAP. They don't know

the history, the dark humor that weather inspires here,
and if they did, well, not everyone finds stories that end

"and then they all died" amusing, but Kansans do
and mark seasons by disasters. My father

bulled his way out of Walmart, pushed by
the high-pitched teens slamming the locks

and walked slowly through the sideways rain
just in time for a fine view of a funnel cloud

that destroyed a block or two on the other side
of the tree line. He brushed the pebbled safety glass

off the driver's seat and drove home. Insanity has
different forms. This one is acceptable in certain

circles. He made it home. That's what makes it
a story, what makes it amusing. None of us

are immune. We all have a story. Mine is this:
I saw the yellow-tinged clouds and drove

through the drive-through anyway, heard the girl
shriek that they were all going into the cooler

and what was I, crazy to take kids out in this, but
here is my defense: the front was in Towanda,

Towanda! And we were in El Dorado. We drove off
without ice cream and sat on the porch, watched

the clouds roll in, and breathed the ozone tinge in the air.
My arms felt flecks of water, the beginnings that form

between low clouds and rain and relaxed in the glory
of a good storm, a real gullywasher. It's a story

that doesn't translate past state lines. I know that.
But I tell it anyway, and think of spring.

LANETTE CADLE

Constructing a Past

At five a.m. he would sit down to a light
breakfast with the four-year-old me, a charming
family portrait with Rice Krispies, scissored
into an even square and placed in his pocket
to remember as the day transferred
to work and fuselages, an aeronautical warning

of life constructed outside the hanger, a warning
that cold metal bends, then breaks but lighter
elements should combine and grow, a transfer
of energies called my child, my charming
red-haired girl with carrots in her pocket
in case she needs to be Bugs Bunny. But scissors

are never in the drawer. The endless scissor
fight, that call to put them back gives a warning,
an echo that sinks guilt in the corner pocket
every time. I try to be different, lighter
with my own children, who grow up charming
and orderly despite the chaos. The transfer

from unimportant to important, a transfer
done invisibly rends or heals, like the new scissors
my mother would put in the drawer, a charming,
secret that she never admitted to anyone, warning
me that good acts need to hide from the light
of day if they are to keep their luster. A pocket

of grief no one understands, a pocket
of dead batteries saved in the drawer and transferred
into something usable: building blocks or doll lights,
a small gift from mother to daughter that scissors
holes through our memories and gives fair warning
that truth, although desirable for Plato, is rarely charming

in the morning when it's time to fess up. The charm
remains for memories of rivets rattling in my pocket
while handing them over when he works, warning
me to mind the airgun, a love for machinery that transferred
true yet mixed with a love for words, the two scissored
together tight, like woven-paper pot holders held lightly

in larger hands, their slight unevenness charming
and the missing scissors forgotten until, hand to pocket,
they transfer from hand to drawer, without warning.

LANETTE CADLE

Provenance

My pearls were bought at my uncle's jewelry store
in Ludington, Michigan for my mother's
sixteenth birthday and passed down to me
for high school graduation, the me

in sandals and india cotton who was dumbfounded
at the concept of cotillion and debutantes
and couldn't see a time when they would feel right
around my neck. My uncle's store is gone.

So is my uncle. True midwesterners
give directions by what isn't there. The pearls
need skin to keep their patina and we
find our way by landmarks that hover

at a flicker of an eyelid, but aren't there
for outsiders who need road signs. Turn
left at the corner where the IGA used to be
that turned into Mike's Apple Market, the one

that got torn down for the hospital annex.
The present has no part in this. The building that exists
has no reality until people make it so. The house
you buy is the Johnson house, five families removed

and no Johnsons in sight, but they were,
and the toy car my daughter digs up planting marigolds

was rubbed to bare metal by tiny fingers, preserved
by the natural oils left by their hands, proof

that they were and each pebble knows it, forms
a provenance more powerful than any landmark.
I wear pearls now, but not the ones my mother gave me.
My daughter has those and adds one more line

in the provenance, a line that may read, worn with jeans
and given by her mother along with a patina of stubbornness
that needs no sense of direction or landmarks, a purposefulness
that coats these pearls with the oil, the warmth of living flesh.

CHAD WOODY

Our Daughter Rhymes with Silver

She never lived but in our minds
and in those things I warned you not
to buy: pastel flea-market finds,
cartoon decals for open spots

on walls only you had reserved
as nursery. You studied her
every stage, tracing growth from dot
to pea. Each week the sacred clot

approached new needs: a name, a day,
a crib. Then your insides shrugged, gone
to feeling sick a different way.
You seemed to know it was done.

Two days you cramped, letting go
one piece at a time, all that you
could part with. What we buried showed
no human trait, was never true.

Just before I laid down the stone,
you pressed a flower on the ground—
a little purple trumpet-cone
pronouncing loss without a sound.

Other people's children hurt you now,
toddling ghosts of what could have been.

We cauterize with jokes. We know
living has no fairness written in.

The tourniquet of now cranks down,
narrowing both past and future.
Even if our every stork has flown,
we'll sponge each other's bitter sutures.

CHAD WOODY

Old Men & Pity

No one taking notes in our marginal lives
marks the transit of our vigor, the slow tap
that drains a vessel down. Our mothers trace
our hands and write the dates of our firsts—
smiles, steps and words—but that day a man
first holds the handrail out of wretched awe
for a pitiless gauntlet of concrete steps
falls into obscurity, no mother to take notes.

They wanted to see the old house,
one more time before it sold or didn't.
I fished out keys and let them in,
swallowing my stride to orbit
their waltz of shuffle and waddle.

I knew he'd had a stroke but still
I couldn't stand the way she led him
like a foundering horse, talking to him
too loud and too simply, using his name
too much, to the near-gibberish point.

At the center of the house, he stuttered
and stopped, peeing down his leg
onto the carpet, looking not down but ahead,
as if trying to calculate something—
the cost of asking for help, perhaps,

or the price of a Coke in 1955 Texas,
which might be what he's tasting now,
lost in the sweaty distance of some
county fair replayed in the haywired
loops of his post-stroke brainpan.

I sprinkled baking soda on the rug,
pulled the door shut as she drove him away.
He stared out the Cadillac window
at the trees, which behaved now
just as they had when he was a boy—
branching, leafing, shading, swaying—
brushing away the years he'd lost.

KRISTEN CYPRET

Silences
For Dad

His shoulders strain as he eases my boxes
onto the sidewalk outside the dorm. He stacks them
like pallets of shingles, spacing them a hand apart.

We're surrounded by dozens of carts and cars,
and we wait for a path to open, for the clouds
to shed some light on this darkening day.

I study him as he reaches for the last box.
It's my container of books, and buried
deep, is the only text he ever tried to read

to me: a burnt edition of the King James Bible.
It was hers when they moved to Arizona,
when they pumped their water from a well,

and lived without lights. How it survived a fire,
I will never know, but she taught him to read
a few lines of a chapter, and it ended there. It ended.

Here I am, on the doorstep of something new. I want
to be here, but tomorrow he'll be on a roof, working
for my dreams, not even wishing he could make his own.

SUSAN DUNN

Unfinished House and
Chicken Poem

Someone's been working on the big house for two years
and still the siding's not up and 2x4s are the pillars
of the grand wraparound porch. They look like crutches
for one who is struggling to stand upright, so that the porch,
being a good place for a summer dance,
could recover for the rest of a morning cup.

The house brings out the worst in me, like I've lost
the rest of my plans. It used to be
 a one story bungalow, cute enough, but old
and I was glad to see work trucks there until sundown
many summer evenings, after the lilac blooms had fallen
and the green leaves looked black. Now, not even a muscled up man
throws shingles to the clever one on the roof.

There are so many other ways to say how troubled I am.
Sometimes I'm still carrying two buckets for the chickens,
like my grandfather did twice a day for years,
a balance of thirty-five pounds of feed, and five gallons of water,
the first of many stops before the chopping block.

Now I can't stack up the good evenly with the evil
that has been piling up in my gut like scraps.
I want that house to be sealed up with grey siding,
and the curtains in the picture window pulled to.
I want the one man I love to be stronger than
the man I hate, whose claws have been scratching,
scratching away the dirt, in order to sit down
and suffocate me.

164

TITA FRENCH BAUMLIN

Evening of a Fawn

Driving home this evening near dusk from a six-month checkup at the oncologist's, I almost hit a fawn.

I'd turned off the highway and passed three of the five curves in the woods below our house on the hillside cul-de-sac when the tiny creature darted out from someone's front-yard shrubs and cut directly into my right front wheel. I screeched to a halt.

The fawn swiveled back to its right, untouched, then shot off into the trees. Luckily, I had been driving slowly: our neighborhood by the lake is a conservation area, and I expect wildlife on the roads. It's also hot midsummer; the does have been fawning since late spring, and every week brings new life into our quiet world—small as a terrier, clumsy, tottering on legs no bigger than the twiggy branches on our newly planted pink dogwood.

But this was no newborn. She—I like to think of this fawn as a "she"—already sported sturdy muscles in those delicate legs, strong enough to streak a lightning course into the shadowing forest. She had been as tall as my headlights, though her back was still woolly and dappled with white flecks of deer-youth, a testament to recent emergence from the dark womb.

I watched her go. She dashed a wild zigzag; tiny hooves kicked up little puffs of dirt with every zig, then a leap followed, so huge that she seemed a gazelle. She offered another zag, then an exuberant double spring and another zig. And then--she was airborne! A streak of white, a shooting star in suspended motion. A stainless blossoming of such innocence, such clarity, that even gravity had no dominion.

She left but a white brushstroke dashed across the darkening canvas of the woods. It faded at last. And I could breathe again.

My wits returned slowly, and with them a shocked fascination at what had happened. She hadn't ever seen me. No, she leaped away from my car not from fear, not even from instinctive avoidance of harm so near. Whether my wheel had been there or not, she would have leaped, rapt as she was in her own sheer joy of movement: new body, young muscles, brand-new sensations of blood pumping and hot summer wind. She cut away and skipped and leaped because she as yet knew no world beyond herself—no cars, no injury, no pain, no death—only her vibrant body and the life force rejoicing through it.

And the thought of that innocence, that fragile world of bliss she inhabited in her young and perfect flesh, held me motionless at the wheel, sitting still at the side of the road, captived, longing.

I heard it before I saw it: the engine's roar up ahead as it turned onto my road and the pedal gave it gas on the straightaway down the hill toward where I sat. The white Pontiac zoomed straight at me so swiftly that my hand flew up off the steering wheel in a mute gesture--*stop!*--and my eyes, as frantic, scoured the wood. I think I screamed aloud.

No matter. I don't think she ever saw me.

She drove with her pretty, teenaged face thrust into the rearview mirror, eyes focused on the lipstick she spread across her plump lips. She must have been hitting seventy.

The Pontiac weaved a little from side to side as it made its retreat past me, on down the road toward the highway.

166

And just as suddenly she was gone, a bright, deadly meteor trailing off into the gloom, leaving at last only a streak of blood in the night.

D. Gilson

Faith

[One]
They built an altar way back in the Ozarks forest where I
went to church camp, place filled with Pentecost, clearing in
the oaks, maples with rough-hewn benches, a small pulpit.
At the altar I prayed with a leader boy—he laid hands on my
heavy shoulders, asked me my troubles. Blond from the local
college, all sinewy muscle, I wanted to tell him he was my
troubles, that I wanted to be lain at this altar, for him to kiss
me, to press into me, some new sacrifice and I will call you
father, I will call you Abraham. I didn't—we just prayed for
the demons holding me to lessen their grip, to set me free,
for a near escape.

[Two]
Beside the urinal someone has graffitied *communion: look,
swirl, sniff, sip.* And yes, this is the bathroom of a dive bar,
and I haven't taken communion for years now and tonight
has been a night for vodka, but as I pee, heft my cock in one
hand, steady myself against the wall with the other, I enter a
new communion—of bartenders and peanut shells, hipster
youth and Pabst Blue Ribbon, of suicides (my brother, his
cousin, their lover), of roaches and track marks, of last call
and a grab for coats, for keys, for sex, morning. I zip up,
wash my hands, my body, which is given for you.

[Three]

Last night there was sweat. I met Benjamin under hot
July outside the yogurt shop on Forbes. We walked and in
front of his apartment building he asked *come up*. I knew
this, no question, and we kissed, pulled tshirts over heads
and groped, kicked shoes off and unbuckled belts, shoved
jeans to the ground and stepped out. We fell to the bed
and thumbed nipples, chests. Our bodies glided in the heat,
sweat everywhere from beginning to finish. After, he slept. I
thumbed his necklace, Star of David. How far we fall from
grace. How far we do not fall.

[Four]

This house always open for prayer. Quiet, please. A sign reads
outside St. Stephen's Episcopal in New Harmony, small town
on the Wabash, mystical place home to communal living, to
art galleries and antique stores, a honey emporium. I come
in for slight relief, this land humid by the stagnant, muddy
waters. I come in to sit, alone, the late afternoon sun casting
shadows through dark stained glass, ambers and violets,
blues, across the floor, across the pew, across my lap. I think
of Jesus and pray—father, please take this cup from me—
having forgotten how, or if, this works. Tornado sirens begin
to ring in the distance, sign that we never know if the thing
will bear down or just pass over.

D. GILSON

The Fly

There's a fly aflutter in the urinal,
one wing useless, the other
struggling to find a way out,
like my brother, lain out on the cheap,
brittle shag of his trailer's floor, a man
foaming at the mouth from taking
all those Ambien chased with Prozac
chased with moonshine, telling our mother
and his pastor Satan is chasing him
into the afterlife, demons did this
to him, but he's turning back.
I pause, consider the fly—how it rises
and falls, rises and falls.

Julie Henigan

Winter Funeral

It was cold when Uncle Virgil died,
mid-winter on the Kansas plains.
A keen wind added water
to the mourners' eyes,
as snow melted on the windshields
of their cars.

He had loved this land,
the priest reminded us—
had farmed it all his life,
his subtle laughter
never leaving him,
even in the hardest of years.
He had loved, he said,
his family, his animals,
and trains.

My aunt sat huddled in her coat,
while the priest cast
his aspergillum
like a fishing line,
as though baptizing
and reeling in at once
another soul for paradise.

Silence came,
and then the whistle

of a passing train;
not a harbinger of death,
but a salutation to a trusted friend.
We took our own leave then
and started back.
Depriving him of livestock,
family, and land,
we left him within earshot
of the tracks.

BRANDON FUNK

Negotiating Sleep

After Neruda

I give her the last hour of my night
on this night, and twenty-nine years
of nights I have yet to sleep.
                         I gladly hand
over like ransom my two good shoes
for her flowerbeds to tend, a peony,
and smooth rocks dusted with pollen.

In exchange for it I surrender
a glass of bourbon and a week's worth
of good mornings.
         But what for clean chinos,
jagged tin, the candle's smooth wax?

I can't say what I'd give,
     since,
at this hour,
all I own are sandman's rags
bound to a luckless corpse.

Therefore,
     I bid her grace, intuition,
wool for the mind's light, and words
piled like cordwood, for sleep.

Night Dancer

They were arguing about the ingredients for the birthday dessert, her father's favorite pineapple upside down cake. Her mother stood tall, elegant hands dusted with white flour, the effect echoed in her peppered hair, and Claire felt her toes slip on the floor which was wet in the way that happens while baking. Pineapple rinds spiked in half smiles on the counter.

"I have baked this cake for my husband for thirty-seven years," her mother said, her alto voice quiet, calm as always. When Claire was in trouble as a child, she had both feared and hoped for the moment her mother would lose her temper, maybe like how people watch a magician in a water chamber, waiting, waiting, and he always appears safe and dry, the applause one of relief and disappointment at the same time.

"Mom, I swear to you, I am reading the directions off the recipe you wrote me! Put the sugar in, I beg you—No, Sophie, not right now; Nana and I are baking a cake—" She struggled to untangle her tiny daughter from her legs.

"But Mommy . . ."

"Do not put that sugar in that bowl." Her mother's voice was firm.

The phone was ringing. Sophie climbed up onto the chair and dipped her fingers, dirty with pink sidewalk chalk, into the mixing bowl.

"No, Claire!" Nana smacked down hard on Sophie's tiny hands. The small girl looked up at Nana, her blue eyes wide

174

with unaccustomed pain and confusion of being called her mother's name. Claire could hear the scream quite clearly in the thick silence before it made its way through her daughter's body.

"No more sugar," Nana said in that small space.

When Sophie's wail finally emerged, it was a siren. Nana was now pouring the entire bag of sugar into the trash can, insurance that it would not be used. She wiped her hands on her apron, her gray eyes victorious.

A feeling Claire couldn't describe welled up from her stomach, moving to her heart and up her neck into her head where it throbbed and roared and she was blind with it. "In the car, please." She kept her voice quiet, too, and she found this empowering. She picked up Sophie with one arm and abandoned the kitchen. Nana followed, sighing, and Claire imagined the orphaned kitchen like one of those pictures they put in *Time Magazine* to humanize a natural disaster, where there's a partly folded pile of laundry on the couch or only one shoe. Claire directed her mother and daughter into the Volvo. The beach bag was already in the back; she always kept it there even though John said it made the trunk smell like dead seaweed.

But the drive to Malibu was sweet with the cherry smell of Sophie's fruit roll up. The sunroof open, wind whistled into the interior with the echoes of country and hip hop and mourning Mexican ballads from passing cars. Malibu Canyon wound through the steep mountains and the afternoon sun broke through the trees sporadically, shadows dancing on a dashboard stage of orange and shade. When she rounded the final curve, the ocean emerged from below and behind the steep mountainsides.

Seeing the wide expanse, Claire stepped on the gas and thought for a minute that maybe she understood why some people kept small models of cars on their office desks.

"I've always loved it here," Nana said to the window.

The sand felt hot, and they ran like pixies to the dark, cool area near the water. Everything glimmered brightly in the late afternoon sun, and Claire thought that the ocean was actually prettier on overcast days, when the glare is gone and you can see all the small ripples in the water, the foam and the splash of a fish or diving bird. Nana pointed out the rhythmic rise of a dolphin's curved fin somewhere in the distance and Claire said it with her, under her breath, "A dolphin, a sign of good luck." The three sat on the large blanket decorated with Dora the Explorer. *Vamos a la playa.*

Nana unearthed a wide hat from the beach bag and put it on. Sophie was struggling against Claire's attempts to put sunscreen on her nose, and Claire inhaled her daughter's cherry breath. Sophie ran to the edge of the water and dug for sand crabs, analyzing the sand intently as the wave crept back into itself, leaving small bubbles, trails left behind by the tiny animals washed in to shore. Watching her little girl, the still-chubby legs dusted with sand, Claire felt the familiar wash of love and fear so big, as big as the ocean and just as complicated in its mixture of beauty and terror. She closed her eyes.

"Sorry about the sugar, sweetheart. I just didn't want you to mess it up, you know how particular your father is." Nana's voice was practical.

"Yes, I know." They both knew it meant more. She sank her toes into the sand, playing casually with a rogue popsicle stick. They spoke in the typical style of beach conversation, sitting side by side, eyes not on each other but on the ocean in front of them, a communal understanding that it would be silly to look anywhere else while sitting at the edge of the earth.

"I'm sorry it has to be this way, Claire."

Claire wondered if her mother still looked at her in the same way she herself looked at Sophie, and found this unsettling. "You shouldn't be apologizing. Sometimes I have

176

hard time believing you married him. He's—" She found the word quicker than she wanted to. "Empty."

"Don't speak that way about your father."

"Why not?" Her mother's profile was a shaded silhouette against the fading sun. "He brings you in the middle of the night, pushing you at us like some kind of animal—'I can't handle this,' he says. This! He says it like—" She stopped, seeing her mother's shadow move slightly. "Oh, Mom, I'm sorry, I'm so sorry." The popsicle stick lodged in the sand, a flagless pole.

"He was being honest, Claire. He couldn't handle it. He knew you could. You could look at it as a compliment, maybe."

"Some handling it."

"You're handling it." This was generous, and they both knew that, too.

She looked over as Nana smiled out into the ocean, putting her hand atop her wide hat. She was so beautiful, like a movie star, and Claire remembered with a slight ache that her mother *was*, actually, a child actress in that black and white movie with Clark Gable about the 1906 San Francisco earthquake. She had always remembered something her mother said about that movie, about how people called it the San Francisco earthquake but that wasn't accurate at all, because people felt it all along the fault line, up and down the entire west coast from Los Angeles to Oregon.

"This is the motherload!" Sophie yelled, running back to the towel, the thick sand making her fall on her knees over and over as she ran, her cupped hands together, trying desperately to hold onto the sand crab before it wriggled free and burrowed back down into the deep, wet earth.

They sang "Happy Birthday" in off-key voices. The night was hot, or maybe it was the small sunburn, a souvenir from this afternoon.

Her father smiled and blew out his candle. Only one, so as not to disturb the pineapples strategically placed along the top of the cake. A ridiculous dessert, really, it was upside down for Christ's sake. Nana clapped her hands like a child.

"Thank you, this looks very nice," he said, and Claire was irritated when she found herself pleased by his approval.

Claire's husband John rolled his eyes behind him and Nana saw. She frowned. Claire bounced to the kitchen and announced loudly in her company voice, "Shall I get the ice cream?"

"Yes, please!" Sophie rang out, and Claire was grateful for her innocence.

Nana sat in silence. Claire watched from the kitchen, her heartbeat quickening as she saw Nana's mouth begin to twist back and forth. It was as if she were gnawing on a lemon.

Claire dropped the spoon and walked briskly to the table. "Mom, will you help me in the laundry room, please?"

Nana got up obediently and followed her into the small room. The heavy door made it impossible to hear what was going on. John affectionately called it, "The Tomb."

She slipped off her platform sandals and held her mother's head in her hands, looking deep into her gray eyes amidst the vanilla-lavender scent of dryer sheets. "Stay with me now, Mom. We just have to finish this up. He'll be out of here in a half hour. Can you make it?"

Nana was silent. Working on her lemon. The wrinkles around her mouth went deep and shallow and deep again, and the movie star on the beach was gone, gone.

"Please, Mom. I know you've had a rough day, but I need you to hang in there. Just stay by me, OK? Please?"

Nana was watching an ant crawl along the ceiling. They exited the tomb and walked into the dining room, where Sophie was trying to get her grandfather's attention by pinching his earlobe.

"Sophie, stop!" Claire snatched her up, causing her father's head to yank sideways as her daughter kept a small, painful grip on the flaky skin.

"Well, I think I'm going to leave early, if you don't mind." He put his knife down, carefully, blade out from the plate as he had taught, and she wondered at all the tiny ways he had made her who she was.

"Alright, Dad, I'll see you to the door."

He looked up, a little surprised that she had so readily agreed. He tried to say goodbye as she rushed him through the hallway.

". . . and Sophie's exhausted from the beach. We'll talk to you later, Happy Birthday."

The front door was closed and he stood on the porch, and when Claire glanced back through the small window at his thinning hair and his halting steps, she thought that it was as if she'd never seen him before. That if she had run into him anywhere else, it would be like he was a stranger.

Two nights later, Claire awoke in the deep stillness of one a.m. The air was slightly off, and she creaked out of bed, tiptoeing in her tank top and sweats. An animal cried, soft and distant. She walked down the stairs and pushed the lace curtains away from the door windows. The porch was clear except for the usual line of ants, marching as the world slept.

The elusive cries continued. She rubbed her eyes and yawned to clear her ears. The sounds stopped and another began. "Nan." Sophie's small voice was so quiet, she almost thought she imagined it.

The stairs blurred as she raced to the carpet on the second story and to her daughter's bedroom doorway. A low, guttural sound emerged from the room, a foreign sound, and she felt a tingle slip and slide down her body.

Her mother stood in the middle of the room, her naked body alien in the moonlight. She crouched and stood in rhythm as the blinds let through small lines of light which reflected, shifted on her smooth and sagging skin. Her buttocks wrinkled, and her hands clasped in front of her swaying breasts. She shook her head as her mouth worked that lemon, lips pursing and chewing.

Sophie sat still against her *Toy Story* sheets. Her eyes were large and bright. She was staring at her Nana and didn't seem to notice her mother in the room. Tears slipped down the small cheeks but she didn't move or seem to breathe. The air was hushed with panic, silence except for the ragged breath of the night dancer as she moved up and down, up and down, and in the nighttime she was colored light gray and dark gray, and everything beyond and in between.

Nana's toes were gripping the carpet like claws, and she swayed precariously every time she moved up, but steadily she crouched and stood, again, again. Finding herself at last, Claire moved carefully, putting her finger to her mouth as a message to her daughter to keep quiet. The tiny girl sat and watched, her mouth tipped just slightly. Claire waited and moved in towards her mother. She began to bend in a similar rhythm and put her hand lightly into her mother's. She found herself humming softly.

Nana's hand was cold and hard. In the moonlight she had looked soft, but close up she was tense and rigid, her muscles clenched and quivering. Her lips were sucking harder and the animal cries began again, emerging from her bowels. Sophie started to sniff, and Claire saw her small form bury itself in the covers and something inside her longed to do the same.

The movement alerted Nana and she began to moan louder. Claire felt rather than saw John run into the room. "What the hell's going on in . . ." she heard, then nothing.

"Get Sophie and go, please," she said, in that same calm and quiet voice, and she found no power in it.

Her mother's eyes seemed to look into her own, but no—she should have known, now, that the moonlight was

180

deceiving. She carefully lifted her mother from the hunched position and guided her to the bed. She wrapped the too-small blankets around her, moving slowly but deliberately. Nana whispered, "No, no, no, no, no" over and over until her eyes closed, and her head fell lightly onto Claire's shoulder, and a wet stain spread across cartooned piggy banks and cowboys. Claire thought that tomorrow she might find that old movie with Clark Gable and watch it with Sophie and John. They would see a different gray and white and black Nana, a little girl Nana in a jaunty hat rescued from a building on fire. She ran her fingers through her mother's wiry hair against her shoulder and wondered how it was to watch "San Francisco" under the chandelier in the movie theater on Castro Street, if people looked up from their seats, wary, and imagined it falling like shooting stars. How it was to watch it in Los Angeles where cliffs and houses on stilts made strange, gravity-defying triangles along the valley peaks, where people would tell their daughters and sons and remind their mothers, "We were there, we felt it, too. It's ours, too." How they were unable to say that a movie could never show what it felt like inside, could never explain what it meant to know that the earth beneath them wasn't solid after all.

ALLYS PAGE

My Mother's Mont Blanc

She decided we'd drive to Dallas
despite the weather man's warning,
a blizzard was coming and would split
Oklahoma straight in half with snow.
But we always left on Christmas day
and so left anyway. The sky turning grey
before we had hit Joplin. *We'll beat it.*
This storm can't follow us all the way south.
But things have a way of catching up
with my mother, and thirty miles
before we could gas up at the Big Cabin
exit it was on us. The black ice shook
the steering wheel and those last miles
to the blink of the yellow Super 8 sign
seemed suspended by the wind and ice.
We holed up there and ate a Christmas dinner
of cheese burgers, Dr. Pepper, greasy fries.
Paying the bill she realized somewhere
between the iced-over parking lot
and the warmth of the truck stop she'd dropped
her Mont Blanc, a last token of her Dallas days
before she was swept off to the backwoods,
set on a plot of land that stretched too far,
in all directions, for anyone to catch a glimpse
of her pretty face. We searched the white
mountains of snow drifts for the following days.
The roads by then clear, we continued on to Texas.

After New Years, on the way home, we stopped
there again to get gas, grab another burger.
She didn't mention it again, but I saw her eyes
searching the dry blacktop. As we crossed
back over to Missouri, I imagined a waitress
just off her shift walking back to her truck, her eyes
settling on black resin and gold, and not knowing
what she'd found would hand it over nightly,
clipped to receipts, the truckers, somehow,
impossibly compelled to dot their "i"s with hearts.

Gremian

To Vex

Delilah told me once she doesn't mind
riding her Harley in the rain.
Sure, she fears hydroplaning
and at high speeds the water
needles into her clavicle.
But she likes how she arrives,
highway grime on her chest
already washed away. The bugs
no longer plastered to her
black boots. I like to wait for her
in the corner booth, muse on the words
engraved on the walls, chairs, whatever will take
to the blade of a pocket knife, and watch out
the window as she kicks down the stand,
and rings the water from her ponytail
underneath the awning. And she'll
come in, water rolling down her legs
in ribbons. The clack of her boots
turning heads as she walks to my table,
and sometimes, I think I can hear
her chandelier earrings clang
against her neck. The sound akin
to the knell of a gremlin bell—
which warns, but promises
safety as it hangs from the handle
bars so small, unmindful of the danger,
the constant ring of it driving you crazy.

184

JESSIE ALEXANDER-EAST

Hazel

Never married, lone woman living
between the damp leaves of
southern Arkansas. Hazel Merl
had black hair, leathered skin and
a wide moustache. She always
wore a polyester nurses uniform,
though she never was a nurse.

Great-Aunt Hazel, those women
you befriended from their husbands,
took to your home for weekends
cloaked full with trees
resting by the small lake
to give an expression of love
more complete with hands, breast,
and tongue, how were they changed?

After she died, her brother,
Doodle Merl, found a journal
in her desk under stacks of
checks and reciepts.

I wish him a small hell.
Forever stuck in a drafty room
with a scratchy blanket on his lap
and an empty bottle of bourbon
on the floor and no noise ever
again other than the creeping
crackle of the pages flickering
out of his chimney.

ERICA WARREN

Fabric Section

In the Wal-Mart fabric section she stands
next to her daughter, short and blonde,
both of them, opening and closing
the drawers of embroidery floss.
The barred cart behind them is sparse
with jelly, cereal in bags, half gallon
of milk, white bread. She shows
her daughter the different colors,
matches a yellow from a dozen different
yellows to the straight spiked locks
of unkempt hair, the small hands grabbing
for a darker shade. She tugs at her mother
to lean down, holds up what she thinks
will be the same and they smile,
one first and then the other.

Her shirt is too small, stained
like her dirty face, and her mother knows
but has nothing else clean
but the cheap dish soap next to a swatch
of dollar-a-yard floral fabric. The girl
has collected a fistful of favorites;
the yellows and a green, a red,
a purple she held to the bruise
on the knee in front of her.

Her hand is flat, the strands splayed evenly.
They hang over the edge of the small width of palm
and her mother sees him come toward them,
Busch case in his grasp. The girl turns around
as he throws the beer in the cart,
smashing the end of the loaf, knocking over
the milk. He looks at the fabric and glares
at the woman, then down at the girl;
slaps the strings from her hand, tells her
she'll stain things she does not have.

JENNER SHAFFER

Do NOT Let Them In

What presents for a supposed angel. Marty cut his finger
to stitches trying to avoid cutting my ear. The dealer for The Dead
poured beer in my bottle. So did Elmer, at Shell Knob.
Dallas of the trumpet gave me a flippered-turtle.
Search, cut, and paste. Send. The glowing green monster
in the alley behind Munchies, kitchen-help all in on it;
a four-year-old watching something slowly rise from a Dumpster.
The Norwegian rockstar drew me a creature holding its own
severed head in one yellow hand, axe in the other.
The mountain of the native princess, Skyline Drive
where she leaped. Her face so fair, hazed in blue.
Bo wasn't 30 when smack tossed him in the grave.
Distant in the bar last I saw him, we recalled ollies
in a hospital parking garage under sterile lights,
taking food to runaways and frenching them
in a condemned house in the woods
by Alice-in-Wonderland Park, grounds of the mental hospital
other-worldly at night. The true world after-hours, watching
for security. Cracked seam of building and sidewalk full of life.
Virga, hail bouncing like ping pong balls on Cpt. Kangaroo,
the curse of sad faces at the window for streamers.
Small, intimate parties. Machinegun-fire from the medical center.
Yellow barrels being buried by a black-water pond.
Treelimbs brushing my hair, touch of a distracted mother,
mayapples—what are you trying to tell me? Meaning emerged
from the disparate must be contrived. In a theme of disunity,
words huddle in a corner, and will not look me in the eye.

ANDY EATON

Poem for Springfield, Missouri

Ozark accents hover past our window open to the dark, dusk rain. Where could they be going in the rain, boiling in puddles like holes in the world? Someone is cooking meth, someone else is eating down at a grocery store that used to be a furniture store and now is also an all you can eat bistro market, which sounds an awful lot like not knowing what you are talking about and talking about it anyway. Anyway, any way the seasons change the people change less, stuck on things that do not happen, even though some air floats in from Canada, gives a fix and leaves, still streets fill with Cider Days, friends burn bratwurst and brew Oktoberfests. When I first moved here we all obsessed over the fall, oil of leaves we learned the names of in gutters, apples were everywhere and there was love. Even though it does not come, we still pretend it does.

ANDY EATON

Center City

The mic barrel has the singer in its sights.
Even if she were dead on, no one listens.
This is a grocery store. It is somewhere else.

Why do we go places and do things there
we are not there to do? Quiet as chess kings
thin men display the signs they asked for

saying nothing from the corner while the cold
and plywood push into their fingers. Tonight
their women stand evenly between them.

In the street the beat goes on, eyes roll, heads cock
when they hear license plates rattle, crowds
at the Starbucks hold hot sugar in paper cups

and a woman with words on her butt
kneels at the edge of the road as if in prayer
while someone holds the funnel of her hair.

BRIAN SHAWVER

In a Cabin in the Woods

Anita is out on the porch, throwing up. I can hear her sharp retches, and then the vomit itself cascading onto the shrubbery. She wears her chinchilla and her deerskin gloves. Just minutes ago, she collected them from the closet with such purpose and deliberation that I supposed she was leaving on an errand. I should have known better—there really is nowhere to go, and Anita has always liked to throw up outside in the cold. It is comforting against the tears and the bile.

Anita is my wife of forty-one years. She doesn't vomit often, although she drinks to excess frequently enough. After what happened to us she could certainly be excused a few belts, but she would be drinking anyway, even if nothing had happened, even if we were at home, sedate and intact.

She finishes and returns to the cabin by way of the sliding glass doors of the den, which was not how she exited. She is confused to find herself in this room, and embarrassed to see me sitting here, my posture rigid, my hands gripping the chair arms, like a father waiting for a daughter who has missed curfew. She plays the analogous role, casting her eyes down, shuffling to the closet to put away her things. She then veers toward the bathroom to brush her teeth. As she moves down the hall she trails her fingers on the wainscoting to orient herself, like a blind person.

When it comes to liquor Anita believes in variety, though this is not the case when it comes to much else. She rarely drinks the same beverage twice in one evening. Tonight, for example, she has consumed a light beer, a glass of chardonnay, a shot of gin (she must have been out of ideas), and some sort of frozen fruity thing, among others. A rum and cola finished her off (it is tempting to make a joke about the straw that broke the camel's back in regard to Anita's ability to hold fluids). Although she is not truly finished off, she is merely purged, and ready now to begin anew.

Anita's drinking problem causes us no undue hardships. She has never led an ambitious life, so her stupors have little practical effect on anything but her own liver, and I have enough money to perpetuate her smorgasbord of booze. Furthermore, she is a somewhat charming drunk, never bitter or incoherent. She doesn't get picked up by the police, she doesn't embarrass me at office functions. At a New Year's Eve party I once heard her say to a boorish young man, "If you're going to be an alcoholic, you should learn how to be a good drunk," an epigram that could very well be carved on her tombstone. This is a blessing to us, the benign form her dipsomania takes.

When she began drinking heavily, twenty years ago, what disappointed me more than anything was the predictability of it, alcoholism being second only to pill-popping among the addiction clichés of wealthy white women of our generation. There was a time—after law school, before the partnership—when we both took pride in resisting certain demographic norms. I've never taken up golf, for example, or complained about the Mexican busboys at the country club (another cliché, the country club, but this one proved inescapable). For several years Anita also ignored the conventions of her peers, their topics of conversation and games of bridge, the way one tries not to memorize the melody of an annoying song. But the pressures of conformity are different for women, or at least they were in our time, in our town. In 1979 she hosted a Tupperware party. In 1984 she voted Republican. She now wears a thin scarf around her head when it rains and videotapes the soap operas when she is not home to watch them.

The idiosyncratic nature of her drinking is a vestige of our desire to remain separate, one that has been easy enough to keep while the others slipped away. At lunch, while her girlfriends run through martinis, Anita hops around the bar menu, littering the table with various forms of glassware (here it is tempting to say something of the Mexican busboys, but I resist). Although no one seems to notice, she must count it as a significant act of dissent.

I do not mean to make Anita sound insignificant or ordinary. She certainly is not. She is good and unique, and she is suffering.

We are away from home, in a three-room cabin in the southwestern part of the state, the Ozarks. A foreign-sounding word for a foreign-seeming place, in spite of the fact that the drive from Chesterfield takes barely three hours. The landscape introduces into our lives certain elements that do not exist at home—darkness, denseness, silence, a persistent chill. Though the stereotypes of hill folk are of course exaggerated, one does feel a presence in the woods, as if men and animals lurked in the shadows with a patience I will never know. Occasionally I hear the crack of a shotgun—quail and grouse season, I believe. Judging by the taxidermy on the walls, my uncle William hunted these and other species with terrific zeal before he died of pancreatic cancer and left the property to me. After his death, we spent three weekends cleaning and sorting and appraising. At one point Anita opened the refrigerator and found it stocked with nothing but white cheese. Having known my uncle hardly at all, I will never be able to explain this discovery.

Anita and I have talked about selling the cabin, but without much enthusiasm. I admit I like the idea of owning a house other than the one in St. Louis, though this too is a predictable aspect of a man in my demographic group.

We once owned a condominium in Colorado, but Anita came to realize that drinking in Steamboat Springs was no different than drinking at home. We finally sold it when Anita discovered that our son Dexter was sneaking in on weekends with college friends and doing God knows what. It is strange how easy it is, to mention my son so casually as that.

I do not belong in a cabin. I do not chew tobacco, or make wood carvings, or hunt pheasants. I do not wear plaid shirts, I do not build fires. I belong to places that I do not especially want to belong to—the suburbs of St. Louis, the firm of Benton and Nevers, the odious country club where I am made comfortable.

It would be agreeable to be a man who belongs in a cabin, I sometimes think. A solid, competent, rugged sort, a dependable figure, this quiet unshaven man in flannel. The image of him comes to me from a strange place, from a song I learned at summer camp when I was twelve or thirteen:

In a cabin in the woods
A little man by the window stood.
He saw a rabbit hopping by,
Knocking at his door.
"Help me! Help me! Help!" he said.
"Or the farmer will shoot me dead."
"Come little rabbit, come with me.
Happy we will always be."

When we sang it as boys, certain gestures accompanied the song, elaborate simulations of the farmer's theoretical killing of the rabbit and the creature's slow dramatic death. The song has stayed with me, the way certain odd things do, and I think about the man in the cabin and the vengeful farmer and the fearful rabbit and the way I think of them changes.

The man's benevolence struck me when I was young—his immediate acceptance of the rabbit, his strangely optimistic belief that being together would make them happy forever. It is an unexpected feature of the man, given his solitary nature, his decision to live as a recluse. None of the other boys paid attention to such implications, and I didn't bring it up—I was already known as the boy who thought too much. In my friends' gesticulations they focused on the farmer, whom they portrayed as hulking and well-armed. He hunted this rabbit like Ahab, he lived for its blood.

I suppose the other man's kindness affected me because at the time I had begun praying to God regularly, asking Him, in effect, to endow me with such goodness. Every night I ran through the prayer in my head, the words never changing, my mind's voice keeping the same intonations and inflections: *Dear God, please let me grow up to be a good man who does good things.* I would then say *Amen* aloud, believing that the spoken benediction would send the mental request heavenward. If anything went wrong, if I skipped over any word, I would start over. In my childish grasp of theology, I believed in the necessity of the ritual's perfection. I may as well have been a Catholic.

Although God never did grant my request—I truly do not think I am a good man, and I certainly haven't done many good things—I still believe in Him, I still pray to Him, and I still love Him, whatever that means. I suppose, if pressed, I could be made to admit that I love Jesus, though that phrase has always sounded tacky to me, like something a Baptist would put on a bumper sticker. I attend the Presbyterian church, the one in which Anita and I were married. She does not. This, I believe, points to an important aspect of Anita's greatness: she has garnered a large degree of admiration in the community without displaying the slightest sense of obligation to her Maker or her fellow man. She has rarely tried to put our wealth toward any use other than our own happiness (not that I have either, but as I've mentioned, God did not make me a good man). She feels no guilt for

195

our prosperity and our indifference, and people love her for this; they consider her delightful and eccentric. She does not receive awards from civic organizations, and the mayor does not name her to committees, but they all know her name, and they smile when they say it. She is a good woman, she just does not do good things.

I have changed my prayer over the years. I no longer say *amen* aloud, because Anita makes me feel anxious about my faith. But I still have a set composition, and I still do it over if anything goes wrong. Every night, at the age of sixty-eight, I say this to the Lord in my head:

> *Dear God, please do what you can to fix me. I don't believe I function the way you intended me to. Amen.*

It bothers me a little that the second sentence ends in a preposition, but it is a heartfelt prayer. Last week I added another sentence: *Please keep the soul of my son Dexter.*

I imagine Dexter's death may have turned Anita to prayer. She has spent a great deal of the past week silent, looking pensive and wondrous. At the funeral she listened to the minister's words with intensity. People often turn to God at such times, of course, and perhaps this will be true of my wife, predictable as she has become.

Police officers came to the house five days ago, when Anita was at a luncheon, and told me of my son's death. He perished in a skiing accident, of all things. Three terrible thoughts entered my head as the policemen stroked their hats and tried to quiet their breathing (they were both very fat police officers).

The first thought was this: *True irony—the one time Dexter got off his rear end and did something active, it killed him.*

The second was this: *When I tell Anita this awful news, I must look more stricken than I do now—these fat police officers seem disgusted with my lack of remorse.*

The third one was this: *Dear God, please do what you can to fix me. I don't believe I function the way you intended me to. Amen.*

It is a strange thing to grieve for, this incapacity for grief.

Dexter attended graduate school at a substandard university somewhere in Colorado, an institution constructed for the idle children of the wealthy who wish to live among terrific beauty, ignore their studies in favor of drug problems, and ski. Although, as I've implied, Dexter was never much for physical activity, and he never spoke to me about the splendor of his adopted home, he had a good-sized drug problem and he wasn't much of a scholar. At the age of thirty-four, he had never been out of college. From this devotion to Academe he had received a bachelor's degree in general studies and absolutely nothing else, though he always seemed about three hours and a thesis away from his master's. He studied Public Recreation, the name of an academic discipline I often see on the personal data graphics for college football players on television, along with how much they bench press.

As far as I can tell, Dexter never spent a dollar that was not rightfully mine. When he entered graduate school, we simply extended the arrangement we'd made for his college years: I fed his bank account, ravenous thing that it was, and he appreciated the gesture. During his lifetime I was often angry with myself for being used in such a way—as was Anita; she might have thought Dexter was blackmailing me somehow—but I am glad now that I kept him happy and idle.

We sometimes visited him in Colorado, and found him cheerful and affectionate, although he did not try to hide his drug use, which I found insulting. We never actually saw the stuff, but the smell of smoked herbs lingered like the reek of a dead body, and the artwork on the walls was of the sort that only exists to amuse those who are under the influence. On one shelf rested a collection of exotic pipes and hookahs, some of them quite delicate and beautiful, and I suspected they were expensive but never-used, like the antique nutcrackers we put out at Christmas. It bothered me that Dexter would not expect me to know what a hookah was. I'm not sure how I know, but damn it, a dope-using son should be respectfully paranoid of his father's worldliness.

At the funeral, several of Dexter's friends approached us and offered condolences. One of them touched me on the shoulder, told me he was very sorry, then broke into a smile and announced what a hell of a fun guy my son had been. I do not know how he expected this would make me feel. I suppose the young man did not think much (perhaps he was my son's classmate in the Public Recreation program). But I knew what he meant. Throughout my life I have appreciated and loved the boys and men I considered fun, those in college who drank absurd amounts of beer and vomited on important alumni, those in law school who flooded the dean's driveway in winter so that exams would be postponed, those at the country club who always know the latest joke about the Mexican busboys. Such men are at the core of my fondest recollections from carefree times. Yet it is disconcerting to find that your son is such a man.

Dexter's drug problem probably offered no immediate threat to his life. From what I saw of his apartment, he stuck with organic substances, and even I would have noticed if my money supported a cocaine habit. As such, I thought little about it, I did not claim it as my responsibility or even something I had a right to care about. Like Anita, Dexter was someone who could spend his days in the clutch of an addiction without causing the world to shudder at the loss. I wonder if he knew this was my attitude. I must have seemed to him and his friends like an oddly generous parent, if ever they thought about it. I cannot imagine the strength and will it would have taken for me to cut the boy off, to have demanded from him what our friends have extracted from

198

their equally spoiled children, when I knew, as I must have known, that I would not mourn his death when it came.

Coming to the cabin was my idea. *We will go there, Anita, to think and be silent. I will pray for Dexter's soul.* Anita, I believe, is able to cope with the tragedy well enough on her own terms. She will drink and rage as she pleases, wherever we are. But we hadn't been to the cabin in so long, and it somehow seemed a good place in which to respond to this unique event in our lives.

We need to get away for awhile, to be in a new place, I told my colleagues.

Of course Tom, of course, take as long as you need. A typical thing to say, but they meant it. Their eyes were wet and their hearts were heavy at my loss. It was true of Andrew Gant in particular; at the funeral he wept as if it had been his own son. I wonder if there is something in all this that explains why I have achieved such professional success, and why Andrew Gant is unlikely to make partner. He and others I could name tend to give in to passion and empathy and instinct. It's something to admire I suppose, yet the intensity of his emotion earns Andrew suspicion among some of our clients. No one is suspicious with me. This is like the white cheese in my Uncle William's refrigerator; I do not know what to do with the information.

I sit here now listening to the Ozarks winds, which cut through the bare woods that surround us. Anita has lain on the couch across the room from me, a new glass of a new drink resting on her chest. She is morose and graceful in her senior citizenship and her grief. Something occurs to her, and she tilts her head up to look at me, but she waits for several seconds before speaking.

"We didn't have dinner tonight," she says. She sounds unutterably confused by the fact. Her befuddlement is terrible to behold, impossible not to interpret as the first of many such moments to come, as alcohol and age conspire to addle her mind. At some point in our lives I will function as nothing more than an orientation device, like the wainscoting she touched in the hallway—someone to tell her whether she has had dinner or not, whether her son truly did die or whether that was a just dementia-fueled dream, whether she prefers vodka tonics or scotch-and-soda.

"No," I say, in an infallible voice, certainty being the only thing I can offer her. "We did not."

Dexter has cracked his head open on a rock in snowy Colorado. His body twitched, the fluids of his head coursed steaming into the cold air and earth. This is what has changed. I do not know what I will do with the money in his account, whatever is left. People in our demographic group typically start foundations when a loved one dies. I will probably write several checks to make this happen, at the prompting of someone at the club or one of Dexter's friends, or perhaps even Anita, if the death has changed her that much. Perhaps I will endow a scholarship in Public Recreation. Soon, I will change my prayer; it has grown stale and meaningless in my head.

It is bound to snow soon. The flames of our quaint fire reflect in the window, and behind them I see the swaying empty branches of walnut trees. It is a bad night to be outside. A bad night, it occurs to me with the embarrassing shiver of nostalgia, to be the farmer looking for rabbits.

Now that I know this cabin, this wilderness, this weather, I am not certain that the rabbit was correct. I am not certain that the farmer was going to shoot him dead. Perhaps he just wished to scare him off. A small frightened mammal is liable to exaggerate, especially if he is in search of shelter on such a night as this. But the fact changes nothing in regards to the man in the cabin. He was a good man, and he did a good thing.

ROLAND SODOWSKY

Revision

Again while the dog chased off cats and thieves,
this his thanks: they've locked him out in the snow.
He retreats to a manger in the shed
out of the wind, mousy straw to lie on,

curls up and sleeps, but in the night the ox,
who hates the dog for his wit and grace,
butts the manger, noses and chews loudly
at the rotten hay, which he has scorned for years.

The dog awakes, finds a herbivore eating
his bed and protests, but the ox bribes
a Greek fabler to call him spiteful, and thus
for twenty-five hundred years libels a dog

who bore the ox no ill will, though he relished
a shank bone come butchering time.

ROLAND SODOWSKY

November Hubris

In a corner of Kansas, an old man
shook his fist and shouted at the trees,
I will have your leaves, not every last one,
who gives a damn about every last,

but most of your deciduous detritus,
yours, redbud, who are decent enough
to shed early and completely, my thanks,
and yours, sugar maple snob, who grant them

with churlish ill will, as if treasures,
and yours, sycamore, pecan, and worst of all
oak, who sans wind and frost would clutch
every curled withered worthless flake of rot

till spring; I will have your phony jewels,
your fluttering rubbish, with Wind's help strip
you bare and ugly, expose your trashy
birds' nests, and you will be as dead for months,

you will wonder in your dense woody brains
if you will leaf again, and you might not,
by spring you might be posts, laths, shingles, stumps.
Witness now my rake, its progress: Tremble!

Michael Burns

Observations

When sunflowers droop dead
We say they are ugly.
Tell that to the birds.

I built a hoodoo trellis
And painted it purple.
Now we're both excited.

What's left of the garden
Is so heartbroken.
Look at these sad tomatoes.

Noon, it's too damn quiet.
I'd listen to a soap opera.
Open your window, neighbor!

Praying mantis, you creep
Me out. I know what you want,
Rubbing your hands together.

Old men peer into mirrors
And study their nose and ears.
Why do they keep growing?

I say to the little dog
Who came to our yard
Don't ever leave me.

Death kept calling here
With his blocked ID.
I've changed my number.

Ah, LOVE, the one who says
You are abstract never
Saw my wife rise from her bath.

Michael Burns

On a Photograph of Freud's Actual Office Couch

It's saved on my computer file
and I like it! I've made it my wallpaper.
It calls for me to come in and lie down.

Maybe I'm compelled by tapestries,
rust-red pattern as if what happens
is hip and hypnotized. I study busts

of esoteric kin graduated in sizes.
On the couch, raised by scroll and pad,
I lie in such a way I can feel them

study Freud, passing no judgment.
They probably ate hearts or carved lips,
proffering gods false sacrifice.

Me-patient, say with my shoes off,
am hidden from doctor, bewildered head
resting. Dream-knowledge-memory

leads pigs off cliffs into hysteria. Id.
Have you loved? Touched someone's
places, churches, funerals, hearing

vacation of summer springing
joy through walls? Pulled handfuls of self
and feathers from pillows? Now I need

to peel back Oriental throws, exposing
the plain and simple structure, to get a grip
and eat its ordinary, horse-hair stuffing.

MICHAEL BURNS

If She Would Only
Answer the Phone

On the grounds of the old Kentucky Military Institute

Last night I saw a giant white skunk
crossing the yard, as big as a small dog,
and I thought to myself, "This is God."
You get too close, you'll get sprayed.

Then this morning I found a white goose feather
that made me smile. It was down by the long-gone
tennis courts, where the net poles stand
like monuments. Listen. Can you hear
the bounce of the ball? Two dead soldiers
who lived here once are stuck in a deuce game.

And so I try to throw over her again
my emotional net, as if to catch a moth,
a hummingbird I cannot bear to watch
needling its own sweet nectar. I'm sober
here beneath the moon, at the Recovery House,
but sad tonight. I ride my rocking chair
and wait for the owl to hoot. Then I call.

Anthony Bradley

Rolling

If there was going to be a change, it needed to be now,
before winter rolled across the tractor trailer cabs
parked along the outer highway of the family plot.
This was when I was still set on walking backwards
in my father's boot prints, trying to grow sideburns
like his when he was still leaving at four a.m. to provide food.

I'd turned sixteen, old enough to run the haybine
in my father's opinion, across the Ozark hayfields,
built on rocks the size of a Colorado boulder.
It never occurred the family might lose a son
to farm accidents, rolling machinery and the like,
so I'd watch my brother ride a tractor sideways,
each bump knocking the axles with intent to tip.

My father had a saying when something went wrong,
when blood was shed and what not,
he'd say *What'd you do that for*, incredulous
as to whatever the situation was, be it accident or not.
When Oliver went down hard during the peak of the hay season,
my brother was left bleeding with a torn forearm.

My father said what was expected, but I glimpsed worry
on his face, hidden under the skin cancer scars and facial hair.
It wasn't enough, only the end of a long line of neglect,
so I headed out North to find something else,
leaving my brother to the mercy of my father's Midwest.

Anthony Bradley

Dying on the Edge
of the Great Midwest

I never knew my mother. She died shortly after I was born, in a window shopping accident. There aren't too many things that can go wrong in a window shopping situation, I know. Those popular internet videos, where the old person drives their Mazda through the store front of a fast food joint? That's what happened. Except my mother was standing in the way. And it wasn't a fast food joint, it was an art gallery.

My father dealt with her death the best he knew how, by beating me over the head with tips on how to handle women, making sure I had the goods since Mother wouldn't be around to teach me. He said every man needs to assess himself every five years. Well, it's been another five years, and I don't like what I see.

I resemble one of those old Western snapshots, the ones photographers use to take after you were shot full of holes, for whatever reason. Propped up against a handcrafted box, mouth set at a permanent crooked angle, shoulders pointy and high from rigor mortis. I'm not dead, but I sure look it. Can't say my insides are any better.

My girlfriend left me several weeks ago. *Girlfriend* being the term I was fond of using to describe her, despite her never personally using it. Truth was, we'd only been seeing each other once or twice a week for the last few months, just enough for a quick lay and maybe a movie. Not at all like the old days, when we didn't have to pretend to enjoy each other's company.

Our visits would always take place at my apartment, which I didn't mind. She would bring over a couple of joints with her if she had a good paycheck to last the week. Once in awhile, she would get angry after we had reduced them to ash, and ask me why I never felt the need to contribute.

"I don't have any connections," I'd say. Which was mostly true. I'd peddled back in high school, and all of my old friends were divorced pot heads. I never told her that, fearing she might look down on me. Smoking pot and selling it are two different things.

Naturally, I was able to find plenty after she left. *Plenty* turned out to be exactly what I needed, her leaving hitting me harder than I would've predicted. Although getting hooked on a woman had always come easy for me I'd tried my best to be indifferent to whoever I was sleeping with, just in case, but the strategy hardly ever worked. It wouldn't be long after a relationship ended that I would call on an escort to help substitute the time I'd spent loving these women.

When you pay a woman to spend time with you, you don't have to worry about letting her down. And you know when she's going to leave; it doesn't come as a surprise.

One of the unique aspects of hiring an escort is asking what to call her. You can always expect whatever name they tell you to be a complete fabrication. Lies are something easily spun by women, but at least with these girls you knew where to look for it. Names aside, everything else an escort gave you was the bare-assed truth.

Oh, and pimps? *Who cares?* I've never met one in all my encounters.

My last escort went by the name of Alisha. She was about twenty-three, petite, and African-American. My selection didn't have anything to do with her color, wasn't a curiosity thing, or a fetish, as some people oddly classify interracial sex. It was more along the lines of having an option, a choice. With escorts, you get what you ask for.

210

Alisha was cheap compared to the other local girls I'd had. She wore a do-rag over her hair, pressed tight against her scalp. She came into my bedroom, which was also my bathroom and my living room crammed into the same space, wearing grey sweatpants and a shirt proudly displaying a university logo that she probably never attended. This wasn't Vegas. I didn't expect her to come in with garter belts and specialty condoms. This was the Midwest. We like our girls plain.

This girl was eager to get to work. She lost the sweatpants as soon as she set foot in my living space. But that kind of tactic appeals to the crude clients with no sense of romance. I liked to make things more personal than that.

One of my high school friends once told me after the subject came up one night, "Always come to a hooker loaded—pot, blow, whatever. Then they'll do anything you want 'em to."

This turned out to be an accurate statement, as I found out over the years. I'd always made sure to have at least a quarter ready. I mean, I wanted them to like me. Unfortunately I couldn't roll a joint for no man's money, so I'd make the girls do it for me, which went a long way in making a better personal connection. The whole experience would then transcend into something completely unique, watching a girl you'd just met, naked, spreading out broken herbs across her thighs, using her tongue to wet the paper. It was almost better than the actual sex, and, in some cases, definitely was.

Alisha helped me roll one, and then produced a treat of her own. Out of her purse came an assortment of tools: some kind of copper-looking netting she picked up at the gas station on the way over, a pack of flavored cigarillos and a small bag of white powder. She laid them out carefully on my bed sheet.

"Give me some kinda poker," she said.

I dug out an old paper clip, one she proceeded to bend straight and use for some, as she put it, *Inspector Gadget shit*.

She asked for a spoon, and I was too embarrassed to tell her I only had one in the whole apartment. It was lying at the bottom of a pan filled with water and chicken noodle soup remains. I made sure to turn my back to her as I scrubbed it clean. When I brought it back over, she was eyeing my bookcase.

"I need a book to read," she said, taking the spoon from me without looking at it. "I ain't got nothing new to read."

I'd recently spent a small amount of cash on a plethora of true crime books, research for a possible essay or book attempt. It was a fascination picked up from my father, who had a large bookcase when I was a child, with everything from David Simon to Peter Capstick. He wouldn't let me read most of them, due specifically to the language contained within, not the subject matter. There were a couple of times he took an ballpoint pen and scratched out the explicit words, just so I could read about the trials of Leon "Whitey" Thompson or the scope-shattering adventures of Carlos Hathcock. Of course this show of patience by my father didn't keep me from nabbing the books I wasn't supposed to read, stashing them underneath my mattress until the chance to read them came along.

I'd recently heard about how Ted Bundy tried, mostly in vain, to involve himself in the Green River Killer case before his execution date came around, as a stalling tactic. The book containing his interviews was on my book pile, ready to read. Alisha picked it up, and gave it a once over.

"Bundy was a freak," she said, stressing the word *freak*. "Can I borrow this? I'll bring it back, sweetie."

It's hard to tell a girl no when she's not wearing any pants.

Admittedly, escorts occasionally made me nervous. Women in general, really. One of the reasons I'd tried so hard to have an actual girlfriend, as opposed to a working girl, was the intimacy factor. I couldn't always get it up for an escort, due to a variety of factors, but familiarity was the biggest reason. You don't want erectile problems when you just laid down three-hundred bucks for sex.

Alisha was easy to be around. She was genuinely sweet, and passive, which is a good thing for a first encounter. But she didn't want to kiss, or at least make a thing of it. I managed to get a few thorough kisses out of her, her tongue nice and spongy. I'd been inside her for about ten minutes before I lost it, and tried my best to save face. Embarrassed, I let her leave with my Bundy book, knowing I'd have to reorder it if I ever wanted to actually read it. Escorts may have a sweet side to them, but you sure as hell don't loan your belongings out to them.

My ex-girlfriend had known about my fascination with escorts. She didn't care who I had slept with in the past, as long as it was only her from here on out. And it was. I'd kept my promise. I'd spent years trying to find someone like her; the last thing I planned on was seeing anyone else. Then she went and left me.

Several weeks ago I became unemployed. My girlfriend didn't seem to care one way or another at the time, but after a long night of drinking I'd convinced myself this was the reason she had left. It didn't really have anything to do with me personally.

She'd stopped showing up on our *together* nights. She was always game for sex and dinner on Wednesday nights, but I'd been immersed in a novel I'd picked up at a dime store, and missed the fact that she hadn't shown. My body was stuck in the same rituals, and it wasn't until I became aroused near dusk that I noticed she wasn't anywhere around. In a desperate move, I used my last bit of funds to reconnect my cell phone, which had been shut off for about a week or so. Thirty minutes after dropping close to two-hundred dollars to reconnect, I received a text informing me where she was.

213

She was gone, and not coming back. The next morning I realized she had packed up all of her bathroom essentials, my sink cabinet left with nothing but a dust cover and glossy circles where her hair products had been. To say she left right under my nose would be an understatement.

My father had been dead a few years, but there was always that hope I'd have a wedding to dedicate to his memory. Maybe name a kid after him. But it was all gone, once again. She had been my last chance. They say women like older men, but it wasn't true in my experience.

The first week after her departure I lingered on the couch, watching my box set of *A Nightmare on Elm Street*, and writing some bad poetry. There wasn't a real plan yet, but the idea of placing just the right poetry stanza on her Facebook wall was a start.

> *You left me on sheets of white, my skin*
> *growing older with the leaves of Fall.*
> *I wait, next to a dying cigarette*
> *for you to turn our door knob, without knocking.*

No, that wasn't going to do it . . .

> *I wait for you, bottle in hand, like Bukowski without the*
> *talent, come hold my glass, to keep it steady.*

The weeks passed and my poetry became increasingly worse. I finally convinced myself to postpone the attempt, at least until finding a suitable poet to plagiarize. One has to be careful what he posts on the wall of Facebook.

I finally decided on a different approach to my problem, one that included my ex in no way whatsoever. I'd spend some quality time with the working girls, at least until I came up with something better. There was a void that needed to be filled, and anything resembling dating or begging was not appealing to me at the moment.

When the idea initially hit me last night, hiring Alisha had seemed like the way to go. She was just the right amount of sweet. I might even get my Bundy book back, if she hasn't sold it already. But now, I realize that would break one of the rules. Never hire the same girl more than once in a given month. It gives them the upper hand, and they tend to manipulate more cash from you during these encounters, due to familiarity. So Alisha was a no. The last thing I need right now is more games.

I decide to get things going, and call the agency that provided Alisha. The operator who always answers picks up. She sounds like she's in her forties, an edge to her voice, a voice that wasn't really friendly as much as it was matter of fact. I had decided to call her Cold Annie.

"Hello."

This would be oft-putting to a new caller, just the ominous *hello*, and not *this is such and such escorts, would you like a blonde?* There was no menu to choose from, just a suspicious female voice that was ready for an undercover cop attempting to arrange some company. During the last few calls I'd made a point to be polite and friendly to Cold Annie, even when I knew there wasn't going to be much sent my way.

"Yes, I would like some company tonight. Could you please tell me what girls are available?"

"Certainly. I must stress however, that this is a companion service only. What actually happens between the two of you is between two consenting adults."

"Of course."

"We have two girls tonight, Alisha and Josie. Alisha is Puerto Rican, Josie is Caucasian. You will have to contact them for more details after you choose."

Alisha was Puerto Rican?

"I'll go with Josie."

I feel like I should say something, to make sure Cold Annie knows I'm not racist. *I've been inside Alisha*, I could say, *and it was very, very nice.*

She rattles off the contact number before I can say anything, and promptly hangs up. I grab another beer from the fridge and down almost all of it before dialing the number.

The phone takes a moment to begin ringing and my bottle is half-empty by the time a soft voice comes on the line after a loud click.

"Hello?"

"Hi, is this Josie?"

"Why yes, it is. Hi, baby."

Her *hello* was significantly less sexual than the words that followed, her use of the word *baby* dripping with perversion. *Perversion* is the best word to combat a word like *loneliness*.

I ask her how she is, having fun saying her name, Josie. Josie, Josie, Josie. She puts a giggle behind everything she says to make sure she's got my business, which is unnecessary. Why else would I be calling her? Of course my intention is to give her my business.

She gives me her prices, never going into detail about what the money will actually get me. Typical phone etiquette for this kind of thing. I might be a cop, for all she knows. I finish my beer, laughing at the thought. I hope she didn't hear me gulping it down over the phone . . .

"So are you in a hotel, baby?"

No, I'm sitting on the couch in my living room, eyeing an oil painting my ex-girlfriend bought. One we had argued about in length when it came time to hang it. She had been very adamant about its placement, and the painting had hovered over the television ever since. It's one of those painting only a woman would pick out, an abstract thing, about motherhood in some way. That's how she interpreted it anyway. I only noticed it when the sun would bounce off the colors as I tried to watch television in the mornings.

216

"No, Josie, I'm sitting on a very expensive couch, in my home. Come join me on it."

We finish up our conversation with the less sexy details of where I'm located. I had lied about the couch of course, it was older than me, but Josie isn't getting paid to sit on her ass anyway. Unless that was my itch.

After I hang up, it dawns on me just how messy the place has become since the girlfriend left. Josie should be here in less than thirty and I'm getting a short twinge of self-consciousness, so the empty bottles and pizza boxes strewn across the carpet are quickly gathered up. My trash is full, so I take the bag downstairs and slip it into the neighbor's bin.

Soon enough there's a dainty knock on my door, and I meet Josie. My first thought is, *she's old*.

She's also pretty, a brunette built like most late forties brunettes who pretend they're still in their tweens: thin waist, random strands of hair dyed various colors (red in this case), and signs of cheap Botox. She also has a large purple bruise framing her left eye that looks like a bad mascara job, but isn't.

We exchange pleasantries, and then she invites herself in, proceeding to give herself a personal tour. She leans into each corner, taking the place in with her painted-up eyes. She even looks under the bed. Afterwards, she turns to me, not at all embarrassed.

"Sorry. I had to make sure you were alone."

I tell her I'm not into gangbangs and she gives a short laugh. Not so much an icebreaker as a statement of fact.

Josie sits on the bed to put her heels away. She's wearing a body-hugging dress with a flower pattern. I try not to stare at her swollen eye. She's also wearing pantyhose. Women *never* wear pantyhose anymore, at least in this part of the Midwest. It's a lost art, yet another reason to spend money this way.

She stretches her arms back, announcing her breast as she drops the raincoat. "So . . . what do you want to do?"

"You want to lay on the bed with me?"

"Okay. I need the money first, sweetie."

I count out two-hundred sixty, all twenties, and hold them out. She smiles, and takes the wad from my hand. Walking over to the nightstand where her purse sits, she bends over long enough for me to stare. Then she strips down to her lingerie, lace black.

We crawl into bed together, and she snuggles up next to me, just like *she* used to. Josie traces my neck muscles. "So what do you like?"

"We can just talk for a bit, if that's okay."

"Okay."

"This neighborhood—do you get a lot of calls?"

"Uh, a few. I've only been working for about three months. I quit for a while."

She lays her leg across me and I reach my hand out, to slide it under her hair. She winces for a split second. She catches me looking at her eye.

"I'm sorry, I should have said something. It," she says, pointing at her eye, "happened in a car accident. Does it bother you?"

I put on my sweet side and lean over to kiss the bruise. Prostitutes love tenderness. Unless they happen to be a Dom.

"You only paid for an hour, you know. Do you really want to spend it talking?"

She crawls on top of me after losing her remaining garments. She puts on a good act, and I start to think she's really into it. I lean into her as she slides down me and try to kiss her, but she pulls away.

"No kissing."

There's an awkward pause, then she notices the painting, giving it a look that's close to serious. Women must think about motherhood like men think about sex. I squeeze her hips to get her attention back where it belongs.

218

She speeds up. Her dark hair hides her face, leaving me a view of her lips, parted wide. The first time my girlfriend and I had sex, she hit me faster than this, and after she came, apologized. I'd asked her why. She never answered, so I had finished up and we never spoke about it again.

Sometime while thinking about *her*, Josie had started kissing me. I suppose she must've felt bad for pushing me away, but it doesn't matter now. I've lost it.

Josie rolls off after a few minutes of trying to fix me. We still have time left on the clock. To save face, I pull out my pre-prepared joint (Alisha had been kind enough to roll my entire bag for me) and offer it to her, which she says is sweet of me, of course.

"You seem really cool," she says. "Why don't you have a girlfriend?"

I don't feel much like talking after that. She gives me a number to call, one different from the agency. Her cell phone, she claims. Of course it's fake. I've been down that road before.

The next few hours go by faster with each drink, until the cooler is empty, and I'm alone with the television. It's a late night matinee, and stale Doritos from here on out.

Somewhere in this mess is a photo album, the only pictures of my mother squared away inside the glossy pages. Part of me wants to find it, and dig through it. Add her to the list of women I'm currently missing.

The front door opens suddenly and I fall off the couch, waiting to have my head smashed in by a blunt object. Could this finally be my pimp encounter? Does he bludgeon customers who can't keep it up? But nothing happens, so I sit up and face the intruder.

I really wish it was a pimp. But it's *her*.

She looks like she's been living out of her car. Hair tied back like a fast food worker, eyes wet and tired. She must've missed me.

"I'm sorry," she says, "I didn't mean to scare you—"

"No, it's okay . . ."

"I should've knocked."

"It's okay."

"How are you?"

I'm not prepared for this. My dignity gone, I slip back into my couch mold and look for my beer before realizing I don't have one. Instead of sitting, she just stands there, making me more self conscious.

"Why are you here?" It comes out sounding spiteful, and maybe it should. She left me, after all. It's always the hardest for the one who gets left behind. She needs to know I'm hurt.

She paces in her old tennis shoes, the tongues fat from soaking up dirty rainwater. Her pacing knocks loose little bits of dried mud that she kicks under the couch. Funny, since she used to throw such a fit when I didn't take my shoes off at the door.

"I wanted to talk to you. I've been calling you."

Her hair is the color of the room, a dismal tone. She folds her hands over her belly like she's a girl of six, patient as a Sunday dress. "Why haven't you answered your phone?"

"I broke it. It was an accident."

"I was worried."

Why is she putting on this caring act? She's left me alone for weeks, what's so different about today? She must be feeling guilty for dumping me for financial reasons. I look at her, keeping my face blank. There's a touch of impatience waiting behind her eyes.

"Look, I just thought we should talk about this. I know, okay?"

Know what? She waits for a response but I don't give her one.

"I know you cheated on me."

"What? I never—"

220

"I looked through your cell phone. When you went out for Chinese that weekend. I'm not stupid."

She must've seen the escort service number. The operator was female, and answered the phone, *a business phone*, with hello. She must've thought—

"I called the number, and *she* answered. The bitch was evasive, wouldn't tell me how she knew you. How long were you seeing her?"

Jesus. *I was cheating on her with Cold Annie?* Hardly. I had better taste than that. Besides, I had always been faithful, even when she didn't put out as much as she should have. I only used the escorts so I could forget. A man's memories are all tied to sex. Would she understand that?

"I wasn't seeing her. Or anyone. You've got things all mixed up."

She starts tearing up, her expression crunched with anger. There would be no reasoning. "I had thought . . . I actually wondered what it would be like to give you a child. And you were fucking around on me the whole time? I sat on this for weeks before leaving!"

I didn't do anything wrong, yet I can't look at her. Feeling guilt for something I didn't do.

Give me a child?

"It doesn't matter. I came by to tell you I'm leaving. For good. You fucked up, Jeffery."

She looks at me like I'm supposed to say something, apologize maybe. *For what?* I didn't do anything.

She turns away, and walks past the painting she loved, the one I sacrificed my own criteria of taste for, just to make her happy. I'd given her so much, and she's walking out like it's no problem. Why is it so easy for women to just dismiss a meaningful relationship?

"Don't you want the painting?" I ask.

She stops and looks at me, somehow looking more angry and hurt than before. "I bought that for us," she says. "No, I don't want it anymore."

She slams the door, causing empty beer cans to fall to the floor from various heights. I don't entertain the thought of going after her for one second. I'm not playing into that. *Just forget.*

I dig out my Grandmother's Bible, and flip to the book of *Daniel*, where I had stashed some money away for times like this. I button my jeans on properly and look for my coat. I need more beer. Maybe vodka this time.

"Hello."

The woman I'm not having an affair with, Cold Annie, answers the phone, and proceeds to tell me who's available. Do I feel like Korean, or Caucasian tonight? There's not many Koreans on the menu most of the time. But I don't feel like messing with the language barrier tonight. My hearing's not so good anymore, making foreign accents a real struggle. Cold Annie's most certainly going to think I'm racist after this one. *You just don't pass up Korean.*

An hour passes before the girl arrives, and she's surprisingly young.

The girl is wearing grey nylons, raised to the knee. A green dress with a side-split covers her lower half, a button-up blouse of grey silk covering her breasts. Her hair hangs loose, let down like it's the end of a long day, which it might be. I try not to think about that sort of thing when dealing with these women. I'm here to forget, not make new memories.

She waltzes into the apartment, and I watch as she inspects the place.

"You're not a cop, are you?"

I tell her no, and pull out my Alisha-rolled beauties. She walks across the carpet, betraying the supposed thickness of it as her heels create loud *thunks*. She stops at the painting that has become a magnet of sorts for female eyes. She tells me it's lovely, and I understand now, that I must burn it.

Mitchell Bess

Little Rock

The smell of sanitized filth still lingers
in my conscience, repressing the memory
of the surgeon's intended thievery
of my left testicle. *Did he say "left?"*
I tried to speak though the anesthesia
left me with just enough to grab her hand
as she was shaving my pubic hair.
I know she had sensed the exigency
as she sought the certainty in my chart.
I smile, remembering the erection
her small yet warm and strong hands had coaxed.
Arousal was something unexpected.
What a queer and simple man I must be.
I woke in another room with that smell.
They showed me how to change the bandages
as I found a new balance. Days at sea
will now be challenged as I resisted
the urge to keep from leaning to the left.
I lit a cigarette and wondered if
I would be offered medicinal pot
now that cancer had replaced a gonad
with a tumor. Sixteen-hundred hours and
I was shuffling to the door when she came
to my room and told me to look her up.
No. Little Rock was just too far to drive
for that.

LAURA DIMMIT

South on Interstate 55

For seven hours we sat in the sticky warmth
of the minivan—a blur of coloring pages and eating
the legs off of animal crackers doled out.
Only snatches of rumors handed down the center stripe—
two big-rigs, oil gushing onto the jumpsuits of the hazmat
workers, fire trucks screaming the wrong way down
the exit ramps. The tape of James Taylor's
Greatest Hits wore out completely, and all we were left
with was WGKX, *Today's Best Country*. We could
have gotten out, stretched our legs, but every minute
seemed like the last, how much longer could it take—
and now I barely sit through the end of a disappointing
movie or shopping lines at Christmas. Knowing how
patience falls away with age, I can't imagine that whole day
without wireless, the same three trees to count leaves on,
one billboard with thirty-two syllables, sixteen vowels,
the night sky of Memphis lit up on the horizon,
lamps filling in the dark windows one by one.

KERRY JAMES EVANS

The Patient Curse

> Night is the beginning and the end
> and in between the ends of distraction
> waits mute speculation, the patient curse
> that stones the eyes, or like the jaguar leaps
> for his own image in a jungle pool, his victim.
> —*Ode to the Confederate Dead*, Allen Tate

I. *The Jaguar*

It must have been the great sewing machine.
Tide well off by now, my grandfather
> would stand at attention, salute the morning.

The chickens in the coop would answer.

Springfield, Missouri: between me and the local blood bank,
the Confederate dead sealed behind an iron gate—
their tombstones unmarked, unworthy in death
> to be named among the living.

Beneath this clay, their blood taps the coffin's frame.

> My blood taps the coffin's frame.

My A-negative blood blazoned into the dog tags strung
> from my neck—

taped quiet to my chest, as if the clank of my dog tags
might disturb the living, the rows of timothy
     draped along the rows of tombstones.

I must claim this mind—

what my grandfather could not escape with his flat feet,
           his ego.

Not even my father.
    Driven by the stench of cotton fields burning.

My blood is the rope slung over the oak, the noose,
and who am I to live among the living,
when the dead walk the marrow of my bones?

They march in columns.
     They chant the old cadences.

I have followed my father to the river's mouth, witnessed the baptism.
I am the first son. I will fire the last shot.
       I am the gunpowder

and the blast, the bullet striking the coffin of my
grandfather
locked behind that iron gate. I am the echo to the grave—
the flooded grave afloat in a river of blood, and I am the river.

     I am the Confederate dead.

II. *Dead Hand*

They already told me what you are about to say
—thunder forms a melody—

your cigarette breath dropped to sand
like a soldier's wedding band.

A single mother for fear of prosthetics,
rotgut and night terrors, a dead hand

ripping wool blankets marked
with the capital letters: US from an open window.

The sun has a way of boring through fabric
regardless of where it is made.

You deny that a soldier can also be a good man,
but what do you know of sleep?

What can we know but cruel indifference?
I write poems for liars. You know who you are.

III. *Promotion to Serve as Guide-on Bearer for the Army National Guard's 110th Engineer Battalion, Company A*

And so it was, he had toothbrushed his toilets, his sinks.
He had avoided Iraq and Afghanistan,
though the upper-echelon of command
encouraged his father's aspirations
for a political career—

                    what a theatre might enable.

He passed on ironing uniforms,
resembled tinfoil rusted in rain,
traipsing through the armory's double doors
to stand at a bent position of attention.

Dubbed: *The leaning tower of pathetic* by his platoon sergeant.

It took a year of leaning for the higher-ups
of the 110th Engineer Battalion, Company A
to order a private meeting, break free

the guide-on

that saw action at Normandy, that fell to German gunfire
more than three dozen times, the blood
still stained on the embroidered castle

—top-right parapet.

They called him in to what seemed like a medieval
ceremony
known only to the dead:

a curtained room of cadence

and camouflage, men of rank—men he spoke to
only when spoken to.

They placed the stick in his hands.

They asked him to carry the dead beyond bone-filled pastures
—hold them as one and honor their blood.

IV. *Customs and Laws of War*

Terror is a sack over your head,
   and in the old way, bending

to your knees, steel rusting
   at your neck—and in this moment,

the moon, blood-orange
   and brimming, raises the ocean
      to high-tide. As any morning,
         you woke to your rifle,

prayed to your God;
   whether on a rug or a floor, dust
      carried light through a window.
         The sun's indifference to your life

has prepared you for this,
   the moon has allowed it.
      There is no remembering
         once you cross that river.

V. *Love Song*

How long do you think it took for the prostitute to get me off?
Like you have ever walked into a brothel, wife.
Like you would suck my dick.
A little late for credulities, don't you think?

This is the tone of a bad soldier.
A good soldier, like a good dog, knows obedience.
I was never a good soldier.
Like Hephaestus, iron fits best in my hands.
I am no Adonis.

It has been six years and our marriage stinks of slag.
We should take up the duct tape and marry ourselves to the bed.
You should give up the love song.
There is no other way to say it.
I had the dog put down.

VI. *Removing the Body*

Tanker rolled over; my father clutched
his door while four lanes of traffic
stood columned at a standstill
on the Capitol Beltway. Cars
backed down the on-ramp
despite blooded sirens—
my father's tumored kidney a jarred,
shrunken globe. After surgery,
we waited a hospital day, moseyed
the hall around the nurse's station,
where he counted tiles,
gripping the IV pole—
remembered penance for demerits
received in the Army's Officer Candidate school.
Called his sergeant *Dingo*.
                    D-I-N-G-O—Dingo was his . . .

Cadence for the anaesthetized,
morphine-induced Colonel
who, in eight months
will call me with asthma,
a foreclosure and a nonexistent
pension. His tractor, however, will pick
every rock from that gutted yard
of switch grass and weed,

plant Bermuda, and though the clay
seems redder now,
at forty-eight, he is young
enough to remember his father:
a green beret moonshiner
nicknamed Bruno,
who denies to this day
leaving my father on Bee Mountain,
where he counted each step
home, picking up rocks
from Hackelburg to Brilliant,
and, upon reaching home,
taking a drunken belt.

When the tanker collapsed
over the guardrail
and spilled jet fuel
onto the road below,
a cigarette led the march
of combustion.

Kidney: archaic nature or temperament.
A woman screams at smoke.
The love of men is the back of an eye socket.

Slit in the side, the kidney flared
—and to see the tumor
was to see the years.
I know too well the story
of cancer. What a man
can keep from his wife
and how it can eat
out the gut in middle age.
In old age. It is a repetition
of conscience and the glory

of a strong-armed man
kneeling before all.
Mercy has no name.
The willing forget the violence,
bow on the back porch to stares
—watch hummingbirds
beak sugar water from feeders
in a yard long burned
to the acidic decay of pine needles.

VII. *The Claiming*

The gray and gone drop turpentined coffee
into tin cans, suffer the worms
borne into their feet

after marching without boots or socks.

The same generals command the same troops.
Wilderness, Virginia: my brother
walks the fenceposts

with their rusted nails and decay.

He finds a bullet, and, at eight years old,
asks my father about the man
who fired his bullet.

In this way, a soldier is taught to claim life.

The claiming is the trench, the Mason Dixon Line,
the line after line of bullet-torn uniforms,
the boundary

between the living and the forgotten.

Daniel Iacob

Revolution of 1989

My parents never talked about
the revolution of 1989, to them
it never happened. It came and it went,
a distant storm that blew away
the old government and left a new
one in its place. Nothing more.

My uncle, though, would gloat
with excitement as I pestered
him with questions.
He was in the midst of the storm,
a revolutionary is what
he called himself.
He was one of the thousandths marching
towards the palace, yelling
"Down with Ceausescu!"
My eyes were wide open as he described
the gunshots, the insanity, the triumphant
cries when Ceausescu fled his palace
by means of a helicopter.
That same day the general of the army
shot himself, and the army shot
Ceausescu and his wife three days
later, on Christmas.
The revolutionaries disbursed like rats
into the city to wash their hands clean,

while the communist party
exchanged their uniforms for suits,
their guns for psychology.

The jobless remained jobless,
the homeless homeless.
The orphans
kept on sniffing paint.

Once in a while, when things were bad,
not that they were ever good,
they would rebroadcast Ceausescu's execution
on television, and I would watch
his solemn face as they led
him and his screaming wife to their death.
"They died like the dogs they were," my uncle
would proudly proclaim and I had the
revolutionaries to thank, although,
I never knew what I was thanking them for.

DANIEL IACOB

Killing

His face was the making of a painting
in which the artist got tired of the delicacies
of life and slashed onto his canvas the outline
of a face in three quick strokes. Instead of wrinkles
and sagging skin, he had jagged lines cut across
his cheeks like rivers flowing through a valley
and his skin was pulled back, making the overall
appearance of his face look like caked mud,
dried out by the anguish reflecting
from his eyes, buried deep below his forehead,
staring out like two hollow caves. He came
every few months to visit my grandfather
and they would sit in the parlor with the door
closed, talking of things I was told a boy
should not hear. Their meetings always reminded
me of a confessional and I knew
it had something to do with his left hand
missing below the wrist, by the way
he held his left arm inconspicuously behind
his back, out of sight.
Something about the missing left hand
explained the odd way he carried himself
as if he were trying to disappear,
or the way he looked at me made me
think that if you stare at yourself for too long
you are not yourself anymore but a ghost.
One day after he left, I asked my grandfather

what happened to his hand.
He told me that they fought together
in World War II and a year into battle
he took an ax and chopped his hand off.

I asked him if that made him a coward.

He said that there is nothing cowardly
about not wanting to kill
and wanting to live.
He told me that the first time Stefan
killed a person he lost something
far more important than a hand.
He said if you make through this life
without killing anyone,
consider yourself blessed.

MEREDITH S. W. LOWRY

Ena

Having to walk out my front door
with a migraine chipping away like ice,
I thought I had it bad.

Meeting my shrink's mother
with her Blockflöte and star of David,
the embarrassment of asking
if Yom Hashoah was a holiday,
filled me with pin-pricks
hot on my face when I stood
under an April moon
on her front stoop.
We both played alto flutes,
Vivaldi and Telemann,
made from pear wood
by a German craftsman.

Thinking I had it bad
in the concentration camp
my father ran, Ena Tarrasch
wrote *Farewell to Fear*
about the time she stood
the only Jew girl child
in front of her class, that matron
snatching her from family
like catching a fly
in the barrel of a gun,

listening to it buzz in her ear,
satisfying like the sharpening
of knives to a butcher.

We shared the fear of being chased,
running with our eyes
swiveling compass needles,
stumbling along tracks
in two worlds: her old trains
loaded with exhumed culture,
mine with its German heritage
newly built across Kansas,
alone with the clacking wail.
But she taught her son
the beauty of the cello
and he taught me
that the scars I bear,
the mental illness oozing
from my pours like eczema,
are something only good
to look back on as I put
the soothing music of my recorder
to the acrid memory of my lips.

HEATHER COOK

The Second Coming

I got my period at the age of twenty-two. It came in the night, stealthily, after a prolonged anorexia-induced absence. I'm not sure what caused its resurgence. My best guess is that some internal mechanism clicked, simply determined that six years was far too long for a woman to go without a regular menstrual cycle.

So I suppose a more accurate statement might be: I got my period *again* at the age of twenty-two. When I finally understood what was happening to my body, I sat on the edge of my bed and wept. "Please," I pleaded, addressing no one in particular, "just make this go away."

People who deny the perks of anorexia are liars. The non-necessity of grocery shopping and the lack of monthly bloodshed are both terribly convenient. Of course, the disorder has its drawbacks—most notably osteoporosis. At the age of twenty-one, I learned that my bones were fifty years older than the rest of me. By this point, my doctor had been touting the benefits of oral contraceptives for a good, long while. Our first conversation about the matter was a tad one-sided.

"Heather," he began, attempting to capture eye contact, "your body needs estrogen. Surely you understand that."

"Yes, but what would the estrogen *do* to me?" I squeaked, as if dared to ingest a vial of poison.

He knew to proceed with caution. "Well, women often find that they feel better. Sometimes there's weight gain. There's usually development of the breast tissue." When I scowled in disgust, he informed me that most women were pleased—no, elated—by the prospect of possessing an ampler bosom. He went on to recommend Seasonale, a form of birth control that (allegedly) puts the period on a three-month delay.

Initially, I met my doctor's advice with resistance. While the promise of four cycles per year didn't sound altogether unbearable, it couldn't beat my impressive track record of zero. Agreeing to take a calcium supplement, I opted to continue with my own tried-and-true method of period suppression: overexercise and calorie restriction.

After the night of the crimson flood, however, the Pill's appeal increased exponentially. Rather than add another hour to my extensive workout regimen and subtract another rice cake from my meager daily rations, I called my doctor to request the drug. It took me six months to fill the prescription. I wanted to see if my condition was some sort of grand fluke. Apparently it wasn't. Upon purchasing my sixth box of tampons, the diagnosis seemed official. I had Menstruation. Two days later, I choked down the first tiny, white tablet. My rationale was simple: four is less than twelve.

Fifty-two tiny tablets later—none yet pink—I still couldn't decide whether synthetic estrogen suited me. I was inclined to say it didn't. In a perpetual state of hunger and fatigue, I couldn't tell whether my ravenousness and exhaustion were hormone-related or merely symptomatic of my decade-long war on health. Either way, I found this estrogen business highly suspect. My breasts were sore, my body was seven pounds flabbier, and my brother kept asking why I seemed to hate life so much. His question was a fair one. Though I never pinpointed the exact source of my newfound cantankerousness, I think it might've had something to do with the occasional bouts of excruciating pain.

I woke in agony. The sensation in my lower abdomen was unsettlingly familiar—startling, gnawing, then wrenching.

Rolling onto my stomach, I huddled in a tight ball. Finding no relief, I sat up, drew my knees to my chest, and began rocking back and forth. Again, to no avail. As often happens when I stagger into an unpleasant situation, I engaged in bewildered conversation with myself.

"I know this feeling," I whispered.

"Don't be stupid," I replied.

"I'm telling you, this feels like—"

"Don't even say it. It can't be. Can it?"

"I wouldn't think so. I'm taking the white pills right now. The *white* ones, damn it." Unable to sleep, I thrashed away the covers and rose, at three in the morning, to get ready for my college classes.

Menstrual cramps and I have a long, sordid history. My freshman year in high school, I missed a grand total of twenty days, most of them spent curled on my bed in the fetal position, waiting for the triple dose of Extra Strength Tylenol to offer minimal but welcome respite. I always regarded these spastic fits as a design flaw, a bodily defect in need of personal mastery. Annoyed with my feminine weakness of will, I would sometimes punch myself in the uterus, tear out of bed, and fly into an angry rampage of housework. Such episodes usually ended badly, with me lying once again on my mattress, praying for infertility and whimpering like a pathetic fool. Eventually, I took matters into my own hands and conspired with my good friend Ana to murder Aunt Flo. We succeeded too. But six years later, the bitch was back, somehow resurrected from the grave.

By early afternoon, I was bleeding profusely. The increasing potency of the pangs rendered both sitting and reclining impossible. Though I had endured my classes by popping Advil every half hour and welting my wrist with a rubber band, these temporary fixes gradually lost their effectiveness. Clutching my gut, I paced the house. When, ache-weary and anguished, I could stand the torment no longer, I braced

242

my body against a wall and let out a guttural scream: "Life isn't worth this!" My brother found this declaration alarming. Upon returning home from work that evening, my mother treated me to an impromptu emergency room visit. When a man with a clipboard asked for a description of the pain, my response consisted of a single, gasped term: "Deep." After a forty-five minute stopover in the waiting room, I was escorted to my first pelvic examination.

I imagine the most unique thing about my initial pap smear was that it occurred only days before my twenty-third birthday. My stance on gynecological checkups prior to this incident had been an admittedly unhealthy one. No period, no sex, no need. Right? If the on-call doctor didn't believe my claim to virginity before squeezing in the speculum, he certainly did afterward. The contraption wouldn't open. As he and the nurse searched the facility for a device between sizes 'pediatric' and 'normal-person,' I busied myself with the clichéd practice of counting ceiling tiles. There were twenty-three, excluding half-tiles and the ones that served as fluorescent light fixtures.

I left the hospital that night with Vicodin in my system, a prescription for codeine in my pocket, and orders to continue taking the Pill. I also left with the reassuring knowledge that my cervix was immaculate. Seeing as how one can tell a lot about a woman by the cleanliness of her cervix, I was glad the doctor had found mine exceptionally tidy.

As I sat in the parking lot of the local twenty-four-hour pharmacy, waiting for my allowance of codeine, I replayed the doctor's verdict: "Right now, the Pill and your body are in conflict. Your body is saying, 'I need to menstruate,' and the Pill is saying, 'I won't let you.' In the end, the Pill will win. It just takes time."

I envisioned the Pill and my body locked in an epic battle. But which entity represented the forces of evil, and which one was fighting on my behalf? Though it was my body that had always been cast in the role of villain, it was the antagonistic Pill that now appeared to worsen my cramping. After all, weren't these new supercramps—sneakier, stronger, deadlier than ever before!—more severe than anything I had experienced at the age of fifteen? And where did my poor osteoporotic bones fit into the struggle? Perhaps they were a separate character, a victim in need of rescue. Maybe the Pill and my body were really in cahoots, working toward the same noble goal of restoring bone density. So did that make my fat-phobic brain the true enemy? Sinking into a lethargic haze, I became confused by the whole muddled analogy and realized that painkillers and twenty-one-hour spans of wakefulness probably weren't conducive to coherent thought.

"When are you going to take that thing off?" my mother prodded, nodding in the direction of my braceleted wrist. Three days after my emergency room excursion, I still hadn't cut off the laminated hospital tag. This seemed to disturb her, as did my eagerness to embrace the pain brought on by the warring factions within me. True, I trusted neither body nor Pill. But I knew that, in abandoning the contraceptive, the soothing, sweet siren song of comfortable emaciation could easily lull me back into a state of semi-starvation. The nine-year stint of anorexia had proven as much.

I suppose I was proud of the hospital bracelet. This manacle of femininity had evolved into a trophy, a tangible symbol of all I had gained, both figuratively and literally. In a rare demonstration of bodily acceptance, I wore the tag for a week, showcasing it on my arm as a wounded veteran might display a Purple Heart on his or her uniform. I brandished it freely, without shame, like a glorious badge of honor. I had earned it.

ANNA ROBB

Thump

The owl hit us parallel and in the upward motion
of an arc, rolled across the windshield and was gone.
We felt the double waste of it—the bird
and whatever small thing it held swallowed
back into the dark, and the car still hurtling forward
suddenly something we wanted nothing of.
It was too much. You turned toward home,
both of us blinking hard, startled, but more than that,
aware of the blood pounding through us like the echo
of that feathered thump, the night's quiet rebuke
pulsing with our breaths. Slower, slower still, but not gone.

ANNA ROBB

The Closest Thing

Maybe not heaven, but the closest sane thing,
this warm Sunday in November. Driving you home
I pass your street, just to sustain the moment—
the calm, the windshield warmed by the sun,
you and I aimless and happy, singing
out the open windows. We drive a circuit
through the town I've never left and to which you drifted,
somehow, to become as much my family as anyone.
I think of our friend, who worked up the courage
to write what she couldn't say, that there was no god
for her, and hadn't been for years. I think of her
sitting there every week, to let her children go on
believing. Her silence is its own prayer.
In the parking lot behind your building, the cabs
sit four abreast and idling, hanging on to the lull.
Too many guys on. One will go off clock before long,
or else loop downtown. But now they steal time,
and we do, too: companionable, finite, alive.

Isaiah Vianese

Hummingbird

When we were in love
and lived together
my days were full with him,

but things fell out—as they
too often do—and he moves
further and further away.

On a walk, I saw
a hummingbird drink
from lilies in the park

and watched for a long while.
I knew there was sweeping
to do, the sink to scrub,

but I watched the bird
move from flower to flower.
Perhaps my love will come back

or he will not.
I will live with that.
And the hummingbird—

his wings made him float
without a tether, without
a breath of wind.

ISAIAH VIANESE

I Do Not Remember Much About Our Trip to India

Mostly, I remember standing naked
in the hotel bathtub, water
up to my ankles, washing your clothes,
wringing them tight against my body.

Sometimes you helped. Sometimes
you completed other tasks: wrote in your journal,
ordered room service (tea and French fries),
found something to watch on TV.

I did not know that I was already losing you.
Maybe it was the heat. Maybe it was the songs
repeating on our iPods—two different creatures—
or that we did not make love enough.

Maybe homophobes there and elsewhere—
we can always blame them.
I remember missing you.
I do not remember what happened after that.

ISAIAH VIANESE

Winter Song

The neighbor's cherry tree
hangs low with snow.

While his father salts the step,
a young boy swings his shovel

up into the branches
to force the frozen weight free.

If Houseman were here,
he might wish this boy

many springs to admire
the tree in flower, many Easters

fragrant with blossoms,
but one should wish the boy winters

joyful as this, the lasting
kindness to love a tree,

even though it is gray with sleep.

KAY NIELL DUVAL

First Gifts

Asserting resurrection, you break forth
    through acid oak leaf
    and rock hard clay
squeeze through gravel
    root and stone
multiply like loaves and fishes
    in the shady places
      of my yard

Forgive me bulbs tubers
    rhizomes and corms
I have failed to keep the faith
I have not watered you
    in dry seasons
I have not covered you
    against the winter
    with layer on layer
      of rich warm
        mulch

Without reproach, you rise to bless me
    tender mercies
      from tender shoots
from earth's gracious table
    my daily portion
bread and wine
    generously served

In penitent shadow,
   I welcome your light
unaccountable beauty
   unnameable hues
jonquils and daffodils—narcissus all—
   crocus, snow iris
   muscari and scilla
   hyacinth, snowdrop
   and Lenten rose

Handmaidens of grace, apostles of hope
   you pardon my presumption
   you absolve my neglect
for another year you mark me paid
   no charge you say
      no charge

BURTON RAFFEL

Yet Another Poem

"Goddess," I asked, trying not to smile
too loud, "how many years have you and I
spent together? how many years rolled by?"

"Poet," she said, and though her lips stayed closed
she filled my ears with crystal laughter, "suppose
a number far too long, what have you lost,

"knowing I speak your name?" "O you I adore,
it ought to be enough that you are not bored,
you have not vanished, your doors have never been closed."

"Don't fret yourself, you all too human poet,
with fears like fame, while you have me, and know
nothing I hold in my hands can be lost." "I'm growing

"ashamed, as my time slowly lapses, and your eyes,
only your eyes have seen these hard-won lines,
your eyes alone, and all I hear is silence.

"Who in this world will call me poet?" "Your times
have no existence in mine. Whatever shines
for me will sooner or later be seen in their eyes."

DUSTIN MACORMIC

To the Woman in My Bed:
If You Want to Know the Truth

Early mornings, before your eyes
open and invite in the light,
the sun and window pane
conspire to illuminate all
the imperfections of your
body. I think about a favorite
book of mine that you left

on the porch to become turgid with
rain water—soaking through
the pages, smearing the now
illegible inscription. Which is,
in part, why I take issue with rain
when it taps on the window. And though
I can never recall the names of clouds,

I despise them, especially the heavy,
grey ones. Names can be difficult
to remember—for four eternal
seconds as I stand to draw
the curtains, making a case
for you against the unforgiving
light, I forget yours.

Maria Savvenas

How She Dances at Her Own Wedding

Her parents are from a part of Greece that keeps
the traditional dances intact. But as it is in America,
a prima-ballerina of a company in South Carolina
dances the men's dances
      like a man,
            in her own words.

In her own words, I remember her,
just before her wedding night, crouched down
on the bathroom floor of the reception hall
with her enormous skirt bunched up, her skinny, long arms
securing it staunchly white above her waist,
      saying
            I started my period.

In grand plie, as in the reception, yet no longer pivoting
in tsamiko dance like the male leader typically spins,
while the band, her father, and her brother
      celebrate
            the professional dancer

throwing money and singing to her,
as is a tradition in the bridal bedroom,
and what isn't normal to anyone else
except herself, for a minute or two,
is how she stands, serenaded and shameless,
      backstage
            naked at her own curtain.

Maria Savvenas

The Farmer

At first he talked about common
ancient coins he'd find on the farm,
but when he spoke about an Isis coin he found,
I was surprised to hear how much he knew
about the period when Greeks worshipped the Egyptian goddess.
Another day he spoke about a silver coin with gold
hidden inside, a rare coin Alexander the Great
gave to his sergeants. Like a song
within a song, the newspaper ran
a story that day about coins just like it,
a satellite image mapping where

on the island the coin could be found.
But the farmer already knew where it was.
We looked at the coin, and its official
photograph mapped out on the table
in front of us, next to
a sliced melon fanned out across the table
and a few joints gone up in smoke all afternoon.
Turned out he knew his history.

That evening we mimicked
the way the coin rested. I wasn't sure
who'd get to keep the coin
or how it ended up there.
Once I felt certain
he deserved to find a coin
ministries in Greece could take
a house for, I wished he'd keep it.

He'll Be Okay

Jonny woke up because his stepfather's Silverado had old shocks and couldn't take the gravel driveway. His head bounced hard on the back of the seat so he sat up and held himself real tight against the door. Mark stopped the truck when it reached the old converted farmhouse and he got out. Before Jonny had the chance to gather himself, Mark opened the door to the back seat of the cab.

"I got something to show you" Mark said. He waved his hand and started off to his workshop. Jonny sat with his hands in his pockets looking down.

"Just go, please." His mom said from the front seat. She undid her seat belt and turned her upper body in the seat. Her eyebrows were raised and she looked over her glasses. The freckles on her forehead fell into deep skin crevasses "Please." Jonny slid out of the truck and started after his stepfather. The grass was wet with dew and the air was cold but it was early enough in the evening that a person's skin could still remember how warm it had been earlier in the day. Crickets were singing. Crickets and stray dogs were the only sounds the country had to offer and Jonny hated that. His hands were buried deep in his jean pockets. All the sonic space could hide anything. Nothing could hide in the city. Every passing person or dog barking could be heard, and anything heard could be seen right out the window. But out here a something might make a noise a mile away and it would carry so far it could be anything by the time it was heard. The workshop was a wooden shed about thirty yards from the house and Jonny was taking a long time to walk it. He hadn't ever seen anything interesting come out of that workshop.

"Here it is." Jonny was just in earshot when Mark said this, but he didn't walk any faster. Mark stepped out into the doorway of the workshop. "Come on." He said. Jonny took his time. He would get to the doorway when he did. It was just fine with him.

Mark had a long cardboard box in his hand. When Jonny made it to the door Mark put his hand on Jonny's shoulder. "Come in, check this out." It felt like four in the afternoon inside the workshop and the room smelled like spray paint. There were scraps of plywood and piles of sawdust built up in the corner. Jonny had never been in the workshop before. Not to say he had never been invited, Mark had asked him if he wanted to help him varnish cabinets or build a slot car track and other silly, stupid stuff like that. Jonny always said no and stayed in the house with whatever book or movie he could find. He was surprised to see the walls were wood paneling; then again, he didn't know what else they might be made of. Leaning up against the back wall there was something big beneath a blue tarp. Only the wooden stand and four caster wheels were visable. Mark stood next to it smiling. Jonny gave it a good hard look, scanned it up and down trying to figure what it could be.

Mark handed the box to Jonny.

"You know what it is?" Jonny took the box and got to work tearing the tape and pulling cardboard tabs out of out of little slots. "It's a twenty-two. A Crickett." Jonny pulled the gun from the box and held the silver barrel at arms length. The black butt of the gun hovered above the concrete floor. Jonny put his hand beneath the stock and held it like a long black fish he was trying to sell.

"You ready?" Mark said. He pulled the tarp a couple of times. When it was on the floor a black jagged wolf shape, ten feet long, five feet high, stood against the wall of the workshop. Spray painted on the wolf, near the shoulder, was a big red heart. Jonny didn't say anything. He didn't know anything to say. He had been afraid of werewolves since the last time he visited his dad, two weeks ago. They stayed up late and watched "The Wolfman" with one of his father's pretty blonde film students. Even though he fell asleep with his head in the girl's lap only thirty minutes into the film, it was enough to get him good and scared. When he got back to the country he had bad dreams that drove him into his mother's bed. Mark had been giving him a hard time about not sleeping in his bed. He made jokes about Jonny driving a wedge between Mark and Jonny's mom. Jonny couldn't tell if this big wolf shape was a joke at his expense or not.

"Alright, You ready?" Mark said again. "Help me push this thing, will you." Jonny stared right at the spray painted heart. He hoped the plan wasn't to put this thing in his bedroom. "Come one, I'll steer. Let's get this outside." Jonny put down the gun and put his hands on the back of the wolf. It felt rough.

The two pushed the wolf out the workshop door and positioned it right against the outside wall. Mark trotted back inside after the gun and left Jonny in the dark with the wolf. It swayed, just a little, when the wind picked up. Jonny shivered at the same time. A light attached to the outside of the workshop turned on.

"Check it out." Mark said as he walked back outside. Only Jonny's eye's moved for the duration of the demonstration. He watched Mark tuck the gun under his arm as he pulled a small cardboard box from his shirt pocket. Mark held a bullet in front of his face so it caught the light.

"Better for shooting werewolves with, right?" He said. Mark pulled the bolt and loaded the gun. With butt of the gun rested against his shoulder, Mark aimed right at the red heart of the wolf. Jonny took a step back. After a deep breath, his stepdad shut one eye. Jonny had never seen him look this confidant. Usually Mark spoke slowly around him in a flaccid tone. He stuttered on occasion. Most of the time, he always tried to get on Jonny's level by taking a knee so he could look him in the eye, but had a hard time keeping his ballance. Mark was steady and his knees were straight and locked as he pulled the trigger. The wolf shook hard and a splinters from the center of the heart flew off into the workshop revealing a little spot of the brown wood. And the sound the thing made when it smacked against the wall, it shot right through Jonny. He stood straight up.

"That ought to help you sleep tonight." Mark said. He pulled the bolt and loaded it again. "Give it a try?" He held the gun out barrel first. Jonny took it. He held the butt of the gun against his shoulder the way he had seen Mark do. His arm stretched around the butt and because the gun was too long it caused a little pain in his shoulder. Jonny pointed the gun. He tried his best to steady his hand and squint one eye the way he had seen people in movies shoot guns. His eyes blinked open and shut as his finger squeezed the finger. There was a little kick back, not much, but his head still pounded at the sound.

"How's it feel?" Mark said. Jonny didn't say anything. He stood, squinting his eyes, staring at the wolf looking for the place his pellet hit "Give it another go." Mark handed Jonny a bullet. After Jonny took it, Mark put his thumbs under his braided belt. Jonny pulled the bolt and loaded the gun. He aimed at the wolf. He fired and pulled the bolt and reloaded and fired again.

Mark laughed a little bit. "Think you can take care of any werewolves that might come around tonight?" Mark held his flat palm out to his stepson, the bullets sat on top. "Here you go." Mark said. "I'll leave the target out so you can get more practice tomorrow." Jonny took the box of bullets and clutched them tight.

"Come on, let's go in." Mark said.

Jonny took the gun with him. He used it like a walking stick putting the butt on the ground every other step. It was a clear night.

Inside the house Jonny's mom told him to wash up and head to bed, so he started up the stairs clutching his gun and bullets.

"No." She said. "Leave the gun down here." Jonny stopped and held his gun to his chest.

"It'll be fine." Mark said. "He knows what to do with it." Mark turned to his wife. "We put the safety on. It'll be fine." Jonny's mom gave Mark a sharp, mean look and Jonny thought something was going to happen or someone was going to yell. But Mark just looked back and told her it would be fine. He lowered his eyes and said everything would be fine and she softened. She relaxed her eyebrows and let the corner's of her mouth level.

"Fine." She said. "But don't shoot it in the house. Jonny continued up the stairs. The gun was with him when he brushed his teeth and took it with him into his bedroom. He propped it up against the wall by the bed. He put the bullets on his bookshelf, which was full of little wooden cars and dinosaurs that Mark had made for him. The worst of them was a magic propeller. Mark tried to show him how to make it spin by rubbing a dowel on a ridged handle. Jonny never got the thing to work. He tried and tried but never once did the propeller spin in Jonny's hand. Jonny put his pajamas on and waited under the covers for his mom to come tuck him in. Mark came too. He leaned on the doorframe while Jonny's mom came in. She tucked the blankets under his body and kissed his head.

"I mean it." She said. "No shooting that thing in the house." Jonny told her okay and he wouldn't do it. Mark chuckled from the doorway. She the left the room and closed the door. Jonny wiggled the sheet out from under him.

260

The howl came around four in the morning. It was long and gritty. Jonny turned away from the window and closed his eyes. The howl came again, this time closer. Jonny got up. He paced back and forth from the far wall to his bedroom door thinking maybe he could wear himself out, make himself so tired he would just crawl back in bed and fall asleep. He heard the howl again so clenched his fists and fought his shaky nerves all the way across his bed to the window. He hoped not to see anything in all that country silence, and he wasn't sure he did. Wind pushed the tall grass in the field across the street. It all moved in the same except a little patch moving the opposite direction. Jonny stared at the anomalous patch of grass and he shivered. He sat back on the corner of his bed. Usually, this would be the point where he would run into his mother's bedroom and push his way between her and Mark. Jonny looked out the window. The ripple was still coming closer. Jonny rubbed his face. He slid off the bed and took steps for the door. He made it halfway across the room and stopped in front of the bookshelf. Jonny grabbed the bullets. Jonny got his gun. He crawled back across his bed and opened the window. Cold air pushed it's way around Jonny as he pulled the bolt and loaded the gun. He sat on his knees and tried to keep the gun steady on the windowsill. He kept his finger hovering above the trigger but he waited for something to push him. He heard that howl again. He swallowed and saw the red heart from the wooden target when he closed his eyes. He squeezed the trigger. There wasn't anything. Not anything but the sharp sound of bullet leaving the barrel. Jonny's posture sank. His body folded up and the gun fell back into the room. Jonny's eyes started to get wet. He pulled himself up to the window and looked out. Teasing him in the grass was the ripple. He pulled the bolt, loaded a bullet, wiped his eyes and set the gun back on the window. He fired again. Something yelped and the howling started again. He wiped moisture from his eyes so he could look for movement in the grass. The thing in the field was coming right towards the house. It yelped and howled some more. Jonny kept loading and firing the gun until the box was empty and his bed was full of shells.

"Jonny!" His mom was at his bedroom door. Mark was behind her. They both came in and looked out the window. They saw an old hound dog lying in the street. Mark left the room. Jonny's mom took the gun from her son and he let his body crumple into her body. He started crying, slowly at first with small tears, but they got bigger until small streams carved through his cheeks.

"Let's go to the kitchen." His mom said. She set the gun on the bed and hung her arm around her son. They left the room and walked down the stairs. He sat at the kitchen table and sniffed and wiped his cheeks with the sleeve of his pajamas.. His mom sat across from him and she didn't say a word. Her face was stern, but she didn't tighten her mouth or breathe heavy. Her foot didn't start tapping on the linoleum. Jonny was slumped in his chair. He straightened up when the front door slammed shut. Mark walked into the kitchen and went straight for the sink. He filled a glass with water.

"Is everything okay?" Jonny's mom asked.

He looked at the floor. "It would take a million in one shot to kill a dog with that gun." Yeah," Mark said. "that dog just got up and walked off. Mark sat down at the table. He had finished the water and spun the glass on its edge. "He'll have bit of a limp," Mark looked up right at Jonny. "but he'll be okay." Mark sat at the table.

"Why don't you go back to bed." Jonny's mom said.

Jonny ran his sleeve under his nose and got up from the table. He went to his room and shut the door. Before turning out the light he went to the bookshelf and grabbed the propeller and the dowel. He sat on the edge of the bad and rubbed the dowel up and down the ridges. The propeller only twitched. He tried moving it slower and faster, he he the thing differently with his hand closer to the ridges and farther away, he even tried pinching it between his thumb and index finger, but it only twitched. Jonny threw the toy at the base of his book shelf. It landed with a thunk. On the blue carpet the pale wood propeller looked pathetic. It looked like something that shouldn't have gotten the best of anybody and certainly didn't deserve to be thrown. Jonny slid off the bed and started to walk towards the toy that lay on the floor, but something out the window caught his eye. He saw Mark walking out of the field across the street with a shovel and even though it was the same cold night, he had sweat on his forehead. Jonny picked up the propeller and sat back on his bed. He started rubbing the dowel over the ridges again. He curled his knees to his chest and put his back against the wall and fell asleep with the dowel in his hand.

Laura Lee Washburn

Oceania: Images from Postcards I Forgot to Buy for Paul

1. The man, U.S. Marine, I'd guess
early morning, Maui airport,
sun coming up, the mountain
Pu'u Kukui, his wife,
her mother, his crutches,
one half of one of his legs
missing.

       2. Asian girl, maybe seven,
outside International Market, bowing
her violin, night, case open for coin.

3. The tan and slick hawker
rubbing salty exfoliant
across the sleepy tourist's forearm.

4. All-woman-(all-40s-or-50s, all-large,
all-aloha-dresses)-band on the street.

5. Monkey Puzzle trees faultless
as children's drawings of Christmas,
all stick, spike and triangle, easily
two houses high.

       6. 400 black swans
suddenly when the boat slows,
thoughts of Jarrell, their feathers
and waste murking water.

7. The mate yelling *look down*,
look down, and oh! when
we follow her advice.

8. The
woman swimming in wetsuit
and flippers, hands held
in perfect discipline behind her back.

9. New-fangled windmills, giant,
only a few white arms visible
over volcanic mountains.

10. Sheer drops straight down,
thin roads.

11. Men and women pedaling
uphill or bursting on crowded streets
and jetties down or over steps.

12. The taxi driver's massive
greenstone, papaya slices
ripe with 16 times the vitamins
of any given apple.

13-17. Barramundi,
Darling Harbour litter, the fur
seal scratching its neck, shuddering
decks between train cars,
Katherine Mansfield's childhood bed.

18. The American soprano dressed
as a soldier, no, you'd want her
in the red dress, Carmen's entrance,
solo, smashing out her cigarette.

III. Archival Treasures

JOHN DUVAL, TRANSLATOR

From *The Great Will* of 1461 by François Villon

(A meditation on the fragility of life, with illustrations drawn from ancient and contemporary times: Eloise and Abelard, Alcibiades (the handsome Athenian general whom Medieval writers mistook for a woman), Joan of Ark, Thaïs the prostitute, the serial black widow who murdered Buridan, kings, emperors, and popes. . . . —including a few stanzas in appropriately out-dated language—jd)

Paris dies. So does Helen.
Whoever dies dies in hurt,
his wind gone and his breath failing.
His liver crushes on his heart.
He sweats. God knows how he does sweat.
No one can make his trouble less.
No wife or children can he get
to pawn their body in his place.   320

Dying swells his neck and bends
his nose; he shakes and he turns pale;
his joints and nerves bulge and distend;
his flesh puffs and his veins pull.
Body of woman, so beautiful,
smooth and polished, dear and tender,
will you, too, come to this? You will,
or else straight up to God ascend.   328

Tell me where, in what country is
the lovely Roman Flora now?
Thaïs? and Alcibaides
her closest cousin? Where can be found
Echo, talking when a sound
sounds softly over pond and river,
her beauty beyond human bound?
And where are the snows that fell last winter?   336

Where's the scholar, Eloise,
whose love Pierre Abelardus won,
then lost his balls (such are Love's fees:
he's monked and shaved.) Likewise, ask on
for her who ordered Buridan
be bound up, gagged, bagged, and slithered
from an upstairs window into the Seine?
And where are the snows that fell last winter?   344

Where's the White Queen, white as lilies,
who with a siren's voice would sing?
Where's flat-foot Bertha, Beatrice, Alis,
Haremburgis, who governed Maine,
and our brave Joan, whom Englishmen
burned in Rouen at the town center—
Where are they, Mary, holy Queen?
And where are the snows that fell last winter?   352

Prince, don't even ask for them,
not this week, not this year either.
You'll only get the refrain again:
Where are the snows that fell last winter?

Who else? Where is the third Calixte,
last of that name upon the long
pope list, who reigned four years? Where is

Alphonse the King of Aragon?   360
Or the gracious duke, Duke of Bourbon?
Or Arthur, duke of Breton men?
Or Charles the Seventh? Where's he gone?
Might as well ask for Charlemagne.

Likewise, the Scottish king, where is
he now, his half face all aflush,
purple as an amethyst
from his chin to his eyebrows?   368
And the known monarch of Cyprus?
And where, alas! is the King of Spain,
whose name I don't recall what was?
Might as well ask for Charlemagne.

I'll just quit asking. Why persist?
The world is nothing but illusion.
Death keeps coming. None resists.
None gets a stay of execution.   376
Well, one more question, in conclusion:
where's Ladislaw, king of Bohagne?
And where's his grandpa? Ask that question,
might as well ask for Charlemagne.

Where is the Dauphin of Auvergne?
And the brave Breton du Guesclin?
And the good old Duke of Alençon?
Might as well ask for Charlemagne   384

Lo! be he the Apostolic Pope
y-clad in surplice, who doth tie
his waist with nought but a stole, to rope
the foul fiend with and choke the lies
from out his mouth, e'en he doth die
dead as his lowliest sacristan,

buffeted roughly out of life,
swept away by the wind and gone.   392

Be he the lord of Constantinople,
Emperor with fist of gold,
or he of France, that King most noble
above all monarchs most extolled,
he who in praise of God hath built
churches and convents, who hath won
reputation in this world:
swept away by the wind and gone.   400

Or be he yet the wise, whilom
Prince of Vienna and Grenoble
or he of Dijon, Salins, or Dole
or his eldest son, or, for example,
mark ye any of his people,
trumpeters, heralds, or hangers on,
however comfortable at table:
swept away by the wind and gone.   408

Princes are destined unto death
and others living, everyone.
It mattereth nought if they be loath,
swept away by the wind and gone.

Since popes and kings, kings' sons and sons
conceived in queens' wombs—all Their Graces
lie cold and dead and under stones
while others take their royal places,   416
me, a poor pedlar of sweet phrases,
will I die, too? Yes, sir, but let
me sell my wares and take some wages
first, and then, come honest death!

Below is the original French from the most famous of these lines, usually known as the "Ballade of the Ladies of Times Past," ll. 329–356, edited from the 1489 Printed Edition.

Dittes moy ou ne en quel pays
Est Flora la belle Rommaine
Archipiada ne Thays
Qui fut sa cousine germaine
Echo parlant quant bruit on maine
Dessus riviere ou sus estang
Qui beaulté eust trop plus que humaine
Mais ou sont les neges d'entan   336

Ou est la tressage Heloys
Pour qui fut chastré et puis moyne
Pierre Esbaillart a Saint Denis
Pour son amour eust ceste essoine.
Semblablement ou est la royne
Qui commanda que Buridan
Feust getté en ung sac en Saine
Mais ou sont les neges d'entan   344

La royne blanche comme ung lys
Qui chantoit a voix de seraine
Berte au grant pié.Bietris/Allys
Harembouges qui tint le Maine,
Et Jehanne la bonne Lorraine
Que Anglois brullerent a Rouen
Ou sont ilz vierge souveraine
Mais ou sont les neges d'entan   352

Prince n'enqueres de sepmaine
Ou ilz sont ne de cest an
Qu'a ce refrain ne vous remaine
Mais ou sont les neges d'entan

272

RICHARD TURNER

Henigan Introduction

First head of English and Speech at "Normal School #4," Virginia Craig retired in 1952, ultimately giving her name to Craig Hall which housed the English Department beginning in the late 1960's. There Dr. Robert Henigan advised and taught students, studied and wrote from his office on the third floor east, and himself retired in 1989. Truly a Renaissance man, he taught Shakespeare, Milton, and T. S. Eliot. When he retired, it was said the department had to hire three teachers to replace him. Irish, Henigan loved Yeats and Heaney; from Nebraska, he offered a seminar on Willa Cather.

His poem "Acquainted with Craig Hall" is closely modeled on Frost's "Acquainted with the Night," even keeping to the terza rima form. Some of the surprising details (janitor, bell, the shut mouth, clocks) seem dictated by Frost's images. But Frost's theme of one defiant, telling time by the moon alters in Henigan's classroom setting. Henigan's tone seems saddened, his theme frustration. The crux occurs in the penultimate stanza: students, unable to grasp the heights of poetry, unable to believe in the mystery, can only watch the temporal clock and hope for their grades ("Absolutes in which the world rejoices"). The scholar-teacher's high goals suffer defeat. Bob Henigan returned from World War II with a Bronze Star and malaria. He set high standards for himself as well as his students. He was dedicated, and often melancholy.

273

ROBERT HENIGAN

Acquainted with Craig Hall

I am one acquainted with Craig Hall.
I have walked up the stairs—and down the stairs.
I live here winter, spring, and fall.

I have gazed at rows of plastic chairs.
I have passed the janitor at night
And hung my head, embarrassed at his stares.

I'm asked to make distinctions, wrong or right,
Absolutes in which the world rejoices.
But we must walk together toward the light.

I have shut my mouth and stopped the sound of voices,
Waiting for the bell that never rings,
While students quietly review their choices.

They do not choose to see Pegasus's wings,
Nor to believe in beings mystical.
How can they care what song a poet sings

Where clocks can't tell them any time at all?
I am one acquainted with Craig Hall.

JAMES S. BAUMLIN

Introducing Robert Wallace (1932–1999): Poet, Editor, Teacher, Springfieldian

Dear Bob,
It was great to hear from you, and at such length. You are still the smoothest typer ever to come out of Springfield. I like the look of the *Deciduous Review* and would be happy to be a judge for the Spring issue. I think it's a wonderful thing you're doing, giving that kiss of print to these young writers.

Written in 1978, the above letter came from no less a luminary than John Updike, Wallace's undergraduate housemate at Harvard, with whom he kept a lifelong correspondence. Updike mentions the *Deciduous Review*, a literary magazine that Wallace published at Case Western Reserve, where he had taught for years. As editor of Bits Press, Wallace published some of the best known poets of his times: Richard Armour, David Daiches, Stephen Dunn, X. J. Kennedy, Ted Kooser, Mary Oliver, Linda Pastan, Howard Nemerov, Laurence Perrine, Richard Wilbur, and Miller Williams— not to mention his friend Updike, for whom he published several now highly-collectible chapbooks. (The living writers that Wallace lists in the lecture following were virtually all personal friends and correspondents; together, they formed a literary coterie, to which Wallace himself belonged.)

Though he left the Ozarks to study and teach elsewhere, Wallace remembered Springfield as "a small-town sort of city with lots of trees, pleasant even in the Depression." In "Melinda Lou," a poem from *Girlfriends and Wives* (1984), He writes nostalgically of his home and his first childhood sweetheart:

Six, in ringlet curls,
on Normal Street. . . .

275

> You biked, played hide-
> and-seek and kick-the-can,
> played guns, played nurse
> with me and Homer Ice, . . .
> and moved to Kansas.

"The houses are still there / on Normal Street," the poet continues, "smaller by forty years, / and shabbier." "And you," he ends, "are, once a decade, / when I look, small, sweet, / and golden in the locket of my heart, / dead, or in Kansas." In 1998, Wallace wrote to SMSU archivist, Jenni Boone:

> I did grow up on Normal. Lived at 456 (two doors west of Kimbrough) from 1ˢᵗ grade till 1946 . . . . It seemed quite normal to live on a street called Normal, which of course in those days I didn't connect at all to the "Normal" school that was then STC (& is now SMSU).

(And is now Missouri State.) Like the following lecture and everything else quoted in this present introduction, Wallace's letter to Boone is housed in Special Collections and Archives at Missouri State University: after a life of literary wandering, at least his literary remains have come home.

For Wallace, writing, editing, and teaching poetry were equal passions, interconnected. A generation of American poets learned its craft from his textbook, *Writing Poems* (1982), now in its eighth edition. The piece following, "On Not Teaching Poetry," is an undated, unpublished lecture. Making reference to his *Poems on Poetry* (1965), it is likely a work of the late 60s or 1970s. There is an "anti-establishment" strain running through his writings at this time, as one might expect from a vocal opponent of the "war in Indochina." Expressing the spirit of Susan Sontag's *Against Interpretation* (1966), Wallace's lecture serves as a reminder to today's teachers and students: freedom and pleasure remain at the center of aesthetic experience, which poetry gives in abundance. "The job," thus, as Wallace's lecture declares, "is to get poetry out of the schools and back under the bedsheet."

276

ROBERT WALLACE

On Not Teaching Poetry

The problems—like the pleasures—of teaching poetry are obvious to anyone who has tried it in the classroom. Yawns from the back row, the chilly indifference from bright students who see in physics or political science the golden landscapes of the future, and—possibly most disheartening—the bumbling and myopic eagerness of the loyal few, who find symbols where there are none, who hurl jargon ahead of them like bridges, who blindly argue for the magic of l's and s's and r's that sound like running water or tiger growls, who can freely associate and see anything but the poem on the page. These last are most embarrassing, for they give us back our nonsense with a vengeance: to whom we have perhaps done the greatest disservice, since they are willing to believe us. But, I suspect, we know that we have failed them all. And, I suspect further, we know that we have somehow managed to fail ourselves.

Something seems to be wrong. Wrong despite our elaborate system of literary training—despite the courses and theories in teachers' colleges, despite the carefully contrived syllabi and textbooks (complete with meticulous questions and study hints and even, sometimes, diagrams that should set an engineering student's fears at rest). And wrong despite lectures like this one, symposia at meetings of English teachers, articles in *The English Journal* and *College English* on "'The City in the Sea': A Re-Examination" or "The 'Death Wish' in 'Stopping by Woods.'" Wrong despite Project English and the efforts of the Advanced Placement program. I do not intend to belittle these efforts, many of which are valuable and necessary; but, despite them and although the new criticism and the art of analysis have become inescapable in our schools and in that great leveler, Freshman English, and although English departments in the colleges are thronged with majors, something is fundamentally awry. Every year we send out thousands upon thousands of products of the system . . . *and they don't read poetry*. They have lost, or perhaps never acquired, the habit, the joyful skill of reading poetry. Like ourselves, they queue up for the latest movie, buy tickets months in advance for the newest play, rush out to buy the most recent novel for a perfect evening at home. But they are apt not even to know about new books of poems, much less look forward eagerly to them. A new book of poems, in a nation of nearly 200 million, is lucky to sell 200 copies. Few libraries trouble with them. A runaway best-seller may go to 10,000 copies—once or twice a decade—although the texts we require students to buy sell into the hundreds of thousands of copies each year. And I suspect the sales of Chaucer or Spenser or Donne or Pope or Wordsworth are negligible from year to year. *Is it unfair to suggest that the result is strangely disproportionate to the effort?*

And our "younger" poets turn out to be in their forties or fifties before we hear of them. I imagine that more literate Americans know the names (if not the poems!) of Yevgeny Yevtushenko and Andrei Voznesensky than of *our* thirty-year-old American poets. Wendell Berry, Larry Rubin, Donald Finkel, Sylvia Plath (now dead), Robert Sward, Frederick Seidel, David Slavitt, Tim Reynolds, Lewis Turco, Robert Bagg, Robert Mezey. The names of those nearer to forty may be more familiar: Allen Ginsberg, Theodore Holmes, Paris Leary, Kenneth Pitchford, Peter Davison, Frank O'Hara, Carolyn Kizer, George Garrett, Robert Bly, John Hollander, W. S. Merwin, James Merrill, John Ashberry, Gregory Corso, Robert Creeley, Henri Coulette,

Philip Levine, Donald Peterson, James Wright, Anne Sexton, Robert Watson, David Wagoner, Philip Legler, May Swenson, X. J. Kennedy, Donald Hall, Galway Kinnell, A. R. Ammons, David Ray, Robert Pack, Maxine Kumin, Charles Gullans, George Starbuck, Adrienne Rich. Here are some in their forties—a few will begin to stand out: Edward Field, Davie Ferry, Edgar Bowers, Daniel Hoffman, Alan Dugan, Denise Levertov, Jon Swan, Jane Cooper, Philip Booth, Donald Justice, Joseph Langland, James Dickey, Arnold Kenseth, Vassar Miller, Alan Ansen, W. D. Snodgrass, Samuel French Morse, Kenneth Koch, William Jay Smith, Barbara Howes, Anthony Hecht, William Meredith, Howard Nemerov, Reed Whittemore, Robert Lowell, Robert Huff, Howard Moss, Richard Wilbur, Edwin Honig, Louis Simpson (the Pulitzer Prize last year), Jack Gilbert, John Logan, Gene Baro. And just to test you, a few in their fifties: Elizabeth Bishop, Robert Fitzgerald, Charles Olson, E. L. May, Richmond Lattimore, John Berryman, Jean Garrigue, Delmore Schwartz, Winfield Townley Scott, and Theodore Roethke and Randall Jarrell if they had lived. Stanley Kunitz and Robert Francis are in their sixties, as John Holmes would be had he lived. Our students and graduates know the names of few of these, and I doubt whether the teachers of poetry in our schools and colleges would do much better. I suspect that the reading of poetry for pleasure is pretty much a dead art, even among those who profess it. And I submit that 50¢ a line—seven dollars for a sonnet that may last as long as English does—is pretty poor pay, but represents the value our society places on poetry. I'll pass on without trying to assess the responsibility for our culture, a matter I'm probably not competent to discuss, and without trying to deal with the blame which poets certainly share, which is a bitter topic for a different audience.

This failure of the teaching of poetry is stranger still since children—the raw material fed into our machine—*do* trust literature, poetry, and enjoy it gaily and unsuspiciously.

They are our primitives, delight in the magic of language, and even use poetry for solving the practical problems of their world: "Eeny meeny miny mo" or "One potato, two potato, three potato, four." And they employ it as name magic to protect themselves, without realizing what they are doing and without knowing that they are dealing in tetrameters or assonance: "Pudden-tane; ask me again and I'll tell you the same"; or to hurl insults: "Nancy pancy." We may well wonder what has happened to this natural impulse to use and enjoy language poetically by the time they have become the dour, resisting students we often see in Freshman English classes . . . and never see again.

The problems are complex and difficult, and easy blame like easy solutions will miss the mark. Generalizations are hard, since what is or should be done at any given level will in part be determined by what has been done before or what is to be done next. Always we must begin where the students are, and take them as far as we can.

When the subject, "Teaching Poetry," was suggested to me, I thought I would talk about some of the luck I've had with poems in the classroom and why I thought it happened. But as a poet, I kept bringing the Greek horse of poetry into the Trojan walls of criticism. The concomitant of teaching poetry is *studying* it, and the very word sends a chill through me. A poem is not to *study*, answer questions about, take examinations on, but to *read* or *hear* for pleasure. The experience of poetry—of any literary work—should be *joy*. The first essential in any art is *delight*. Horace said that poetry should "teach and delight," not that it should "be taught." The *poem* will do the teaching, if any is to be done, just as it will do the delighting if it is left to its own powers and if we do not claim more for it than it does for itself. The first necessity is to read, that is, enjoy, relish, follow, lose one's self and self-consciousness in the pleasure of the poem. Only then may one ask questions, or be asked questions, without danger. If this joy is sufficient, it will support—indeed, will stimulate—any amount of learning and study. Judgment, criticism, may come after we like the work of art. But the joy must come first. Knowing that Old Whiskers is going to ask some sharp questions in class in the morning and that there will be a two-hour examination at the end of term, alas, can set up a deadly environment for understanding poems. I remember the profound relief of a girl to whom I'd been trying to teach prosody—when I accidentally said that I don't *analyze* every poem I read. Her eyes lit up to know that she hadn't been wrong about what to do with a poem. You don't ask questions of it *unless you want to*. Any work of art requires what I shall call *the necessary ignorance*—which is a little more than "willing suspension of disbelief," but not much more. We must submit ourselves to the poem or painting, ignorant as barbarians, willing to go the way it takes us, unable to go any other way; prepared to feel first and, if necessary, to think later. C.S. Lewis (in *An Experiment in Criticism*, pp.7–8) has imagined a family in which the confusions of literary activity are plain:

> As there are, or were, families and circles in which it was almost a social necessity to display an interest in hunting, or county cricket, or the Army List, so there are others where it requires great independence not to talk about, and therefore occasionally to read, the approved literature, especially the new and astonishing works, and those which have been banned or have become in some other way subjects of controversy. Readers of this sort, this "small vulgar," act in one respect exactly like those of the "great vulgar." They are entirely dominated by fashion. They drop the Georgians and begin to admire Mr. Eliot, acknowledge the "dislodgement" of Milton, and discover Hopkins, at exactly the right moment . . . Yet, while this goes on downstairs, the only real literary experience in such a family may be occurring in a back bedroom where a small boy is

reading *Treasure Island* under the bed-clothes by the light of an electric torch.

Beginning with the necessary ignorance will probably lead on to more sophisticated levels of reading and thinking about what we read. If we have encountered something we like, we will want to talk about it—whether at a cocktail party or in a classroom—and to listen to the best talk about it we can find; we call that criticism. But these "higher" levels of activity cannot truly exist without the foundation of ignorant joy, carelessness about why we are made to feel strange or special by a poem as long as we do—or, to change the metaphor slightly, without the intimate and unforced reading in the *cellar* of ourselves, when we are alone with the book.

I read all these signs as a *failure of joy* and, in some measure I suspect, we all are ill from it. Its clearest evidence is the sort of cultural fright which makes us *suffer* through poems or concerts or trips through a museum because we think we *should* like these things, because it is expected of us. Of all the boredoms, cultural boredom may be the worst, because it teaches us at rock bottom to feel—we would never dare say or perhaps even think it—that the classics are bores. Once burned, forever shy. I think that poems can compete with baseball and girls *on their own terms*, for there is enough of life to allow for what Cotton Mather called "a little recreation of poetry," if we can contrive not to convince our pupils—and ourselves—that poems are miserable duties. Good reading is a series of self-discoveries; we must learn to keep our hands off until they happen, if they do. We shall not be worse off if they don't happen of themselves, for we could never have forced them. We may invite, but we cannot bully.

As a poet, I sometimes feel that the job is to get poetry out of the schools and back under the bedsheet. Our students who read Donne or Pope or Frost because we make them— and so often read them badly and convince themselves they're missing nothing—in fact read Ginsberg or Ferlinghetti or Kahlil Gibran under the bedsheets after the lights are out. Or Ayn Rand. Perhaps if we forbade them to read Donne and Spenser (as being too sexy) and tried to argue that "Trees" is a finer poem than "On His Blindness," if we *taught* Call-him Gibberish and turned up our noses at Wallace Stevens, we might find we had won our battle. Cultural rebelliousness is a fact of youth; and we might get it on our side. This of course is a pipe-dream. But the contamination of literary joy in the classroom seems to me to be the principal fact we have to deal with. These young people discovered Salinger's *The Catcher in the Rye* and nearly wore it out under the bedsheets *until it got into the schools*. When I first started teaching nine years ago, it brought a light into every eye. Several casebooks later, two weeks ago, talking with a class about what they'd like to read, they shrugged it off as blandly as they did *The Return of the Native*. *Catcher* seems to be joining *Lord Jim* and *A Passage to India* in that literary limbo we are responsible for. I think *Catcher* is a very good book, though a very different one from what our students once upon a time thought they were reading. But no matter of that: they *were reading* it and probably would have discovered somewhere along the line what its real virtues are. Now they are beginning not to read it at all.

Well, what are some of the things we—the shoe pinches me with the worst—what are some of the things we are doing to poetry in the classroom that we shouldn't be doing?

The first thing seems to me to be *hurrying* the student along too fast. I see two kinds of dangerous hurry. One simply is expecting—wanting!—students to read at a level of sophistication they aren't ready for. We push our preferences backwards into the schools. What we teach in Freshman English this year will be taught in Advanced Placement courses in the schools next year and in regular courses in the year after. In one school I visited, "Sir Gawain and the

Green Knight" was read I the eighth grade, and a full-scale, ten-week, all guns blazing study of Yeats was going on in the eleventh grade. This begins to leave nothing to teach in college, producing bored "we-have-been-there-before" attitudes which make any learning nearly impossible. This is part of the objection to reading snippets of things in school courses—Books I and II of *Paradise Lost*, only Lilliput from *Gulliver's Travels*—which entitle students to feel, and say, that they've *done* these things and are waiting for some still greater miracles of college. Every college English teacher looks for and can tell sad tales about those dangerous students who have already "done" it. (But of course they have never read Walter Scott or Anthony Trollope or Robert Herrick, nor enough of Dickens, and they will be surprised that anyone can take Campion or Ben Jonson seriously.) And in many cases, we know, they haven't really made much sense of *Moby-Dick* or Kafka—have in fact been burned by over-exposure to Yeats and "Heart of Darkness" or "The Secret Sharer" and the critical magnifying glasses we like to use. We are all tempted to teach as we have learned, to import into a schoolroom or undergraduate classroom methods and levels of discussion we have encountered in our own classes in college or in graduate school.

Over the years I have come to think that the greatest virtue of my school education—aside from the endlessly poetic hours I was required to sit in the hall facing a clock— was that I was under-exposed to the best or even good poetry. I recall being ecstatic in the fourth grade over a piece called "Somebody's Mother," and my favorite poets for years were Robert W. Service (the only poems owned in our household), James Whitcomb Riley (a 39¢ copy of which a strange lady bought me when I was staring, penniless and obviously yearning, at a department store book counter), Eugene Field, Ogden Nash, and Richard Armour, in about that order. We read "Evangeline" in the eighth grade, but I

284

don't think I thought of it as poetry. Thanks to the glorious ineptness of Miss May Berry in the tenth and eleventh grades—I suspect she liked poetry, but couldn't bring herself to try to persuade the sarcastic football players on the back row to sample anything loftier than *The Reader's Digest*—and to a dreadful advising system which let me skip the senior lit course, I managed to reach college with a marvelous and teachable ignorance. I was ready for whatever was served up. I remember being surprised, in English I at Harvard as a freshman, that my classmates already seemed to know who Chaucer was. My achieved ignorance was even more of a triumph, as I had been writing poems of my own since the fourth grade—when "My Pup and Me" was printed in the city newspaper.

A second, more dangerous kind of hurry is that automatically produced by deadlines, for quizzes or papers, or even by our expectations for class discussion. A genuine response to any poem requires a certain leisure, and, as you know, will develop naturally only through many readings over a long period of time. More perhaps depends on where *we* are in our reading skill and pleasure than on the poem. I suppose it is possible to like a poem and read it for years without ever making very much of it—"The Waste Land" might be a good case in point—enjoying its sound or the color of its imagery, without saying or having to say what it means. This is why poets and novelists so often seem to turn aside questions about what they meant or whether they meant this or that. It is perhaps more important for the reader to find out *for himself* than for him to be told. T.S. Eliot remarked:

> I know that some of the poetry to which I am most devoted is poetry which I did not understand at first reading; some is poetry which I am not sure I understand yet: for instance, Shakespeare's.

And yet we create an artificial reading situation in the schools, demand of students a full, analytical account of a poem they have read once, maybe twice, the night before. Nothing is easier than to set up a kind of critical shooting gallery in the classroom and knock over, rather miraculously, on by one, rabbits the students have never seen. And by so doing, intimidate them as readers forever. It is no wonder they deliver to us so much nonsense, fail to see the poem for its symbols or techniques. It is no wonder they rush to the library or some criticism, for they know that only in that way can they find whatever it is that will satisfy us when we turn on them from the desk. In truth, perhaps we should admit, many of them never *read* the poems at all. It is not enough that we know we are not demanding more of a response than an intelligent first reading, because, whatever we say, we act in class and grade papers and exams as if we expected the impossible. And, sweet innocents, they try to give us what they think we want.

This leads me to the second main thing we shouldn't be doing, or at least doing as we do. The use of criticism as a teaching activity is fraught with dangers. We demand analysis at a high level without being sure that the joy requires it or even makes it possible. Students lose sight of the poems, are afraid to react themselves, lope off unhappily to introductions and books of criticism because of the kind and level of response we expect. We scare them to death. And they end up seeing books through other books . . . which isn't seeing them at all. Criticism, what ought to be forgotten, is too often what is remembered. There is a vast gulf between clearing away difficulties and adding them.

We are all victims of the over-powering criticism of our time. I sometimes wonder whether we haven't come to believe that books, poems, are less something to *read* than something to *say something about*. That is the clear implication of our class discussions, papers, exams. I know our students believe it. That is why over-reading is their besetting sin. That is why we are buried in our own jargon about myth and form and symbols and structure. That is why they tell us meaninglessly that a poem is in iambic tetrameter or that there is an anapest in line three. That is why they say l's—nonsensically—mean something. That is why, without ever seeing the poem itself, they retail a lot of guff about Existentialism, Jungian psychology, phallic symbols, or good and evil in *Alice in Wonderland*. They don't do all this because they enjoy it; they do it because they think we expect it. Our danger isn't in bringing up readers who can't tell a hawk from a handsaw, but readers who can't tell either one from a symbol. The net effect of all the criticism in which we are immersed and in which, willy-nilly, we immerse our students, is to destroy the very *life* of the literature we value.

Let me put my point in a simple statement of C.S. Lewis's, which will be true till the end of time. "*It is always better to read Chaucer again that to read the critics.*" I submit that will be true no matter how many times one goes through *The Canterbury Tales*. It is always better to read Chaucer again than to read the critics. If that leaves us spluttering "But" and "Still" and "On the other hand," so much the better. We need a little gravel in our craw. It is always better to read Chaucer again than to read the critics.

There are two additional dangers in criticism in our teaching. One is what I might call the *judgment fallacy*, the belief, which criticism inculcates, that we must make judgments about and among works of art. We may want to do this, but we don't have to. Perhaps we should do it as little as we can. Milton is not a better poet than Herrick because his subject is bigger or more important. You see this judgment fallacy at its worst when our reviewers condemn John Updike or Richard Wilbur for not being Dostoyevsky or Rimbaud. The cultural, philosophical, or political importance of a work of art is the *last* thing that matters, never the first. In one of the quality reviews this fall, Robert Frost is niggled at because he lacked what the critic calls a "tragic howl." By such standards, I can't imagine how Shakespeare could ever have managed "hey nony nony" . . . nor where we would be without it.

The other critical danger is that we are led to teach *difficult* poems because there is more to talk about, more to unravel and explain. It is a deal easier to make a class go on for an hour with "The Canonization" than with "Drink to me only with thine eyes." At least without falling into nonsense. And when students begin to see that difficulty is an important criterion for what we consider good poetry, I don't blame them if they vanish forever into James Bond and *The Reader's Digest* and never come back. The appropriate response to a poem is silence, not talk. We must somehow learn to teach by being *quiet* enough.

The worst villains are texts with questions and apparatus and study hints, which blight the pleasure by implying that poems are things to ask questions about, to *study*, not to enjoy, which set out to satisfy interests the student didn't know he had (and probably *didn't* have). Publishers, who know what things sell, are concerned more about the prose than about the poems it is meant to buoy up. When Mr. Taaffe and I were hunting a publisher for our anthology, *Poems on Poetry*— an effort, by the way, to let poetry teach itself—one publisher didn't even want to see a list of the poems, but was eager to have the prose he assumed must pad the book, ten or fifteen thousand words at least. In the end we weren't able to avoid having some little introductions, if we were to get the book published at all—which I recommend you ignore if you read it.

One generalization: Critical activity is illegitimate whenever it is answering questions the reader hasn't yet asked.

The third thing we shouldn't be dong in *enforcing taste*, which is an extension of the critical function and the judgment fallacy. To tell the student that what he likes is a bad poem may be awakening, but I suspect that more often it kills off his liking for anything. He becomes afraid to like anything, or hides it, for fear of being berated. Those analytical texts are again the worst offenders with their invidious comparisons and outright assaults. Brooks and Warren's murderous attack on "Trees" no doubt finishes off the poem, and it may also finish off the student. I have gone into class armed with their deadly—deadening?—logic and found myself in the end facing increasingly stubborn in beleaguered partisans of "Trees," "The Little Toy Soldier," and no doubt that favorite of my own once-upon-a-time, "Somebody's Mother." It is a combat I doubt if we can win. I doubt if we should try. Bullying isn't discovery. In fact, I'm not so sure anymore that "Trees" and "The Little Toy Soldier" are bad poems. We may have outgrown them, and we may hope that our students will. But if they do not, or cannot, it would be grossest folly on our part to abuse and possibly ruin for them what they are capable of reading and liking. I don't mean that we shouldn't have preferences or make them known. The best defense against bad poems is the introduction of good poems; and I believe that in due time, however long and wasteful it may seem to us, Marvell and Yeats and even Milton will replace Kilmer and Ogden Nash and James Whitcomb Riley. But we must be willing to wait. The folly is in expecting all readers to be like ourselves in the end. Literature is not a kingdom, however wise may be the philosopher we would choose as king, but a delightful anarchy in which only fools pretend to be kings. We should be glad that this is so. It would be humorless to insist that no one can be truly a meaningful and cultured human being without a taste for Dryden. And it may be equally humorless to insist that no pupil can have our blessing unless he has abjured "The Little Toy Soldier" and proved he relishes John Donne. The classics in a sense judge us, not us them. I do not like Shelley and am no doubt the worse for it. But it will hardly do to force the issue. Any honest response is better than a very elaborate, even correct, but dishonest one. C.S. Lewis makes this point (in *The World's Last Night*, pp. 38–39):

Suppose you had spent an evening among very young and very transparent snobs who were feigning a discriminating enjoyment of a great port, though anyone who knew could see very well that, if they had ever drunk port in their lives before, it came from a grocer's. And then suppose that on your journey home you went into a grubby little tea-shop and there heard an old body in a feather boa say to another old body, with a smack of her lips, "That was a nice cup o' tea, dearie, that was. Did me good." Would you not, at that moment, feel that this was like fresh mountain air? For here, at last, would be something real. Here would be a mind really concerned about that in which it expressed concern. Here would be pleasure, here would be undebauched experience, spontaneous and compulsive, from the fountain-head. A live dog is better than a dead lion. In the same way, after a certain sherry party, where there have been cataracts of *culture* but never one word or one glance that suggested a real enjoyment of any art, any person, or any natural object, my heart warms to the schoolboy on the bus who is reading *Fantasy and Science Fiction*, rapt and oblivious of all the world beside. For here also I should feel that I had met something real and live and unfabricated; genuine literary experience, spontaneous and compulsive, disinterested. I should have hopes of that boy. Those who have greatly cared for any book whatever may possibly come to care, some day, for good books. The organs of appreciation exist in them. They are not impotent. And even if this particular boy is never going to like anything severer than science-fiction, even so,

The child whose love is here, at least doth reap
One precious gain, that he forgets himself.

290

I should still prefer the live dog to the dead lion; perhaps, even, the wild dog to the over-tame poodle or Peke.

And while I am quoting, let me call in Mr. Eliot again:

I do not know whether little girls have a different taste in poetry from little boys, but the responses of the latter I believe to be fairly uniform. *Horatius at the Bridge, The Burial of Sir John Moore, Bannockburn,* Tennyson's *Revenge,* some of the border ballads: a liking for martial and sanguinary poetry is no more to be discouraged than engagements with lead soldiers and pea-shooters. The only pleasure that I got from Shakespeare was the pleasure of being commended for reading him; had I been a child of more independent mind I should have refused to read him at all. Recognizing the frequent deceptions of memory, I seem to remember that my early liking for the sort of verse that small boys do like vanished at about the age of twelve, leaving me for a couple of years with no sort of interest in poetry at all. I can recall clearly enough the moment when, at the age of fourteen or so, I happened to pick up a copy of Fitzgerald's *Omar* which was lying about, and the almost overwhelming introduction to a new world of feeling which this poem was the occasion of giving me. It was like a sudden conversion; the world appeared anew, painted with bright, delicious and painful colours. Thereupon I took the usual adolescent course with Byron, Shelley, Keats, Rossetti, Swinburne.

Eliot goes on to describe a third phase of his reading, which he dates from his twenty-second year, in which what I have called the necessary ignorance, a deliberate ignorance, can exist side by side with a critical awareness. This is very sophisticated activity, no doubt, and some readers may never reach it at all; most of us will be blocked off, as I am from Shelley, from ever achieving the necessary ignorance with

291

certain authors or books. (This leads to a consideration of how we read at the highest level—not of real readings but of creating a kind of "ideal" reading which no actual experience can ever more than approximate—which is beyond the scope of this too short hour.)

These problems will look very different at different levels in the educational process. I suspect, for instance that the college's expectation of a serious *interest* in its students is legitimate; the university isn't the place to evangelize for poetry—it may be way too late—although we'd be witless if we didn't take the world as we find it. We must, of course, all of us, keep separate in our minds reading (the exaltation which we value) and studying (the perception of the reading experience itself), for the main pedagogical problem seems to me to be delight. In general, let me suggest some positive ways of *not* teaching poetry.

1. I suggest a return to, or at least a major shift in emphasis toward, the *factual* in examinations and papers. Spot passages to be identified, words or phrases to be glossed, plots to be summarized, paraphrases. Research—factual, biographical—instead of critical papers. Our students are drowning in a morass of interpretive and critical activity for which they are not, and perhaps can never be, prepared. It is fair at the various levels to require them to read certain works, and to ask them to prove it, but it is neither just nor tactful to demand that they deliver us a certain kind of response, that—God help us—they prove that they *like* it. What goes on between the student and Donne or Dryden is a private matter. I suspect that we shall find that more does on than we might believe, and certainly more than goes on when we force the student to work up a response which, most of the time, will not be his nor even genuine. And the jungle of gobbledygook in their writing will vanish over-night and the

critical creepers that entangle the poems will shrink up and disappear, leaving the poems healthily and fully in the center.

2. I suggest that, instead of further educational prose, we invite real live poets into the schools, and I am thinking more even of the high schools and grades than of the colleges, where already a valid tradition is beginning to persist. There are plenty of poets around, and they would be glad to come and would cost very little. Most of them can read and talk about poetry, their own or just poems they like, with an authority and pleasure that will be infectious. A number of our best poets have even written books of poems for children. Some have already made their way into the schools—John Ciardi and William Jay Smith, whose forays into the grades are well-known. I wager no third-grader, or tenth-grader, in a school Mr. Ciardi has visited will ever think poetry is sissy stuff. If a school system—or the Foundations—would put up the cash to have poets visit around in the schools for half days now and again, I suspect a lot of the problems of teaching poetry would turn out to have been solved.

3. I suggest that we all might do more in reading poetry aloud, ourselves, or having the students read to each other, since poetry is essentially an oral art. The noise a poem makes can be exciting and may be the easiest way into it. If we cannot have the poets themselves visiting the schools or teaching in them, we can have good collections of records of poets reading and use them frequently. I'm thinking of grade schools as well as high schools and colleges. We very much need a series of recordings of contemporary poets designed for use in the grades, and maybe some films.

4. I suggest not only that we resist texts with teaching aids—in which poems are harnessed into dragging sledges of numbered prose—but that we need more and better

anthologies of *contemporary* poems, which publishers resist because of copyright fees. It is cheaper to use "Ozymandias" again than to get Wallace Stevens or E.E. Cummings or Richard Wilbur. It seems clear to me that we ought to begin in grade school with *contemporary* poems, since they are likely to be a lot easier to understand than poems still posturing in the manners of earlier centuries. Even grade school libraries should be flush with as many recent and uncondescending collections as can be found or milked from publishers. (An excellent anthology of sports poems, *Sprints and Distances*, just out, should be put in reach of as many hands as possible.) These books will be coming along in the next decade, and it will be up to the teachers in the grades and in the high schools to be looking for them and to insist that the money be found for them when they show up. (I proposed to one publisher a paper anthology of really up-to-date poems for use in the schools, and was told there would be no market for it. Our publisher of *Poems on Poetry* doubts that many of the schools—for which it seems to be perfect—will be adventurous enough to pick it up for senior lit courses and advanced placement sections. They think teachers prefer the fat, old-fashioned walruses of textbooks with the endlessly reprinted "Ozymandias," but I don't believe that. If the teacher is bored, it is certain that the pupils will be. And, wherever the money or the will can be found, in schools or colleges, poetry rooms like the Woodberry Room in Lamont Library at Harvard should be set up—with books, records, comfortable chairs, smoking privileges, jack-record-players.

5. I suggest we can do more to let students *choose* the poems or poets they want to read. The burden of proof will thus be partly on them. If good enough texts are used and if libraries are vigorously up-to-date, it should be easy enough for them to come enthusiastically back to the classroom with something they *want* to talk about. And since talking

about poems may be a dangerous activity, even we in colleges might think more of requiring students to memorize poems they like. It may strike us—and them—as old-fashioned and mechanical, but it may be better than a lot of things I know we are doing. Like the factual exam, it might take the pressure off in just the right places.

6. Finally, I suggest that we experiment more than we have with teaching poetry-*reading* by teaching poetry-*writing*. Students, especially in the grades, are full of artistic impulses we might take advantage of. We should find ways of encouraging and directing a playfulness with words. Writing is one way of getting technical questions asked, and getting the student to ask the questions is the art of teaching in a nutshell. Several years ago I taught a television workshop in writing verse for school children in Philadelphia, including some fifth graders. I am convinced that grade-schoolers can learn the rudiments of prosody and technical alternatives—which they will need if their efforts are not to peter out into the mere repetitions of expressionism, the dullness of which they will see soon enough. A well turned couplet, they will find, is more fun to have written than a scraggly bit of free verse. And a quatrain more fun yet. We might even expect a revival of limericks! I am not promising any miracles, but I think students can be led on just as they now are in art or music in the schools. What surprises me in fact is that when we think of teaching art or music in the schools we think of the students as *doing*, but that when we think of teaching poetry we think of them only as consumers. All this will take a lot of skill and tact on the part of teachers, and I can see the difficulties becoming more and more formidable as one goes on toward and into a high school curriculum. It may be necessary for the teachers to write poems themselves before it can be made to work. Courses in writing and in teaching

writing may be wanted in our teacher training, and poets may be needed in summer institutes for English teachers.

None of this is meant as a map of where we are going, but it is at least one poet's tour folder. It is enough if I can suggest some possible directions . . . and that we may find, one morning, that our ways of teaching poetry—or *not* teaching it, as I would have it—changed quite as much as the new arithmetic is altering the educational landscape.

Regulations for Irvington Hall

I. HOURS.

1. Meals. All students must report for meals promptly at the hour set. In case they are prevented by some activity of the school or for some other reason which is acceptable to the matron, they may report after the meal hour, providing they serve themselves and wash their own dishes.

2. The hour from 6:30 to 7:30 shall be set aside each school day as the recreation hour. It is expected that students shall participate in some kind of wholesome recreation at this time. This regulation is made in the interest of health and school work. After 7:30 study conditions must prevail throughout both halls. A violation of this regulation shall be considered as a gross indifference to the wishes of ambitious, earnest students, and therefore shall be treated as a most serious offence. This regulation admits of the following exceptions:

(a) During the summer term the study hours begin at 8 o'clock.

(b) When students have out of town guests they shall be accorded special privileges, which are merited by their general conduct and the individual case. The matron is to be the judge in determining these exceptions.

(c) Guests who are residing in the city are expected to observe the dormitory regulations when at the dormitory, and should be so advised by their friends.

(d) Saturday evening of each week may be set aside as social evening. At this time the young men of the school may be invited to the dormitory. On this evening the recreation hour may continue until 10:30 o'clock. The too frequent requests for exceptions to regulations on the part of any individual student shall be considered as sufficient evidence to merit a special investigation of the general standing of the student in the college.

3. The light will be flashed at 10:30 o'clock and turned out at 11 o'clock for 30 minutes, at which time they will be turned on again. The study hour extends from 7:30 o'clock to 11 o'clock. Students who are unable to prepare their lessons in this time should so report to the president of the school.

4. On Friday and Saturday nights all students will be expected to be in their rooms by 11 o'clock. Any violation of this regulation will be reported by the matron to the women's welfare committee of the college, except in case of a party who have an approved chaperon. In this event the responsibility shall be placed entirely with the chaperon.

5. It is expected that proper reverence be shown for the Sabbath day. A spirit of quiet should prevail during the day, both in and about the dormitories. It is not expected that students will practice upon the piano or other musical instruments or play inappropriate selections which may not only disturb the residents of the dormitory, but may prove quite offensive to the neighborhood. The hours from 2 o'clock to 4 o'clock Sunday afternoon will be known as "quiet hours." At this time absolute quiet must prevail throughout both buildings. All students are expected to be in their rooms by 10:30 o'clock Sunday evening. It is expected that all the girls of the college be regular in church attendance.

6. On one evening in the week the swimming pool at the Y. W. C. A. is available for the college girls. Any girl in the dormitory will be permitted to go to the swimming pool under the following conditions:

(a) She must return by 9:30 o'clock.

(b) She must present to the matron a signed request from the physical director.

II. CHAPERONS.

It is expected that the girls living in the dormitory observe the same regulations concerning chaperonage that would be observed in their own homes. A group of the older girls in the dormitory who are approved by the matron and the women's welfare committee may serve in the capacity of chaperons. It is expected that the young women of the dormitory will not partake of meals in public restaurants as the guests of young men, without a chaperon, except in the case of relatives and then the kinship should be closer than that of a cousin. Under no conditions will a resident of the dormitory be permitted to go to the station unless she is accompanied by someone who is approved by the matron. It is understood that no resident of the dormitory will go automobile riding after night with young men, under any conditions whatsoever.

III. REGISTER.

In order that the whereabouts of the dormitory girls may be known at any time, both for their convenience and protection, girls who go out during the evening hours are expected to register proper information, including the hour of departure and return.

IV. BATHROOMS.

It is expected that each girl will leave the bathroom in a clean and tidy condition after use. It is further expected that the rights of the other girls shall be observed by each individual in the matter of use of the bathrooms.

V. LUNCHES.

It is strictly forbidden to serve lunches in the rooms, with the exception of fruit. This regulation is made to prevent mice, roaches and other rodents from invading the rooms, as well as in the interest of the health of the students. The college will undertake to provide for the girls suitable provisions for light lunches.

VI. IRONS.

The college will provide at least four electric irons and ironing boards, to be at the disposal of the girls. Each girl will be expected to pay an incidental fee each term of $1.00 to cover the expenses incurred in connection with the use of the iron, sewing machine, laundry equipment, etc. The girls are cautioned to always disconnect the iron after use, in order that there may be no danger from fire.

VII. PICTURES.

Pictures may be put on the walls of the rooms, providing sharp, short thumb-tacks are used. The girls are expected to take the same care of the walls and furniture of their rooms as they would in their own homes.

VIII. TELEPHONE.

The telephone may be used by the girls at any time, providing their social conversations are limited to four minutes. One of the residents of the halls will be designated by the matron to answer phone calls during the meal hours, but in no case shall girls be called to the telephone during meal hours except in emergencies. The one answering the telephone will record on a slate attached to the wall near the phone, the name of the girl called and the numbers which are calling. Telephone calls of a private nature may be made from the matron's room, with her permission.

IX. HOT WATER.

Hot water will be provided after 3 o'clock each day in the week in sufficient quantities for all students, provided it is not wasted. It is expected that students observe ordinary precautions here as elsewhere.

X. COMPLAINTS.

A dormitory committee composed of a member to be elected from each floor will be organized for the purpose of developing a complete understanding between the residents of the dormitory and the management. If any of the girls living in the dormitory desire to complain about the quantity, quality or variety of food served there, or other types of service afforded by the dormitory, it is expected that they will make such complaint to the committee-woman of their floor, or the matron. It will be considered very bad form to complain of the food or services unless the complaint is registered with those who can modify conditions.

"Regulations for Irvington Hall." 1911. Poster. *In 1911, women attending Fourth District Normal School in Springfield, Missouri, lived in Irvington House, the girls' dormitory. The poster above survives, giving "house rules." My, how times have changed.*

Notes on Contributors

C. D. ALBIN received the Master of Arts in English from Southwest Missouri State University on July 25th, 1984, and now teaches English at Missouri State University-West Plains. His poems, stories, and reviews have appeared in a number of publications, including *Arkansas Review, Cape Rock, Flint Hills Review, Georgia Review, Harvard Review*, and *Natural Bridge*.

JESSIE ALEXANDER-EAST is an alumna of the Missouri State University Creative Writing Program. She is currently the youth services coordinator of the Mid-Continent Regional Library system in Kansas City.

WALTER BARGEN has published thirteen books of poetry and two chapbooks of poetry. His most recent books are *The Feast, Remedies for Vertigo, West of West*, and *Theban Traffic*. His poems have recently appeared in the *Beloit Poetry Journal, Poetry East, River Styx, Seattle Review*, and *New Letters*. He was the winner of the Chester H. Jones Foundation prize in 1997, a National Endowment for the Arts Fellowship in 1991, and the William Rockhill Nelson Award in 2005. In 2008, he was appointed to be the first poet laureate of Missouri.

JAMES S. BAUMLIN is Professor of English at Missouri State University and is an editor for Moon City Press.

TITA FRENCH BAUMLIN is Professor of English at Missouri State University. A PhD in Shakespeare, Early Modern drama, and Rhetorical Theory, she was Editor of the scholarly journal *Explorations in Renaissance Culture* 1994–2006, co-author of *The Instructors' Manual for the HarperCollins World Reader* (HarperCollins, 1994), and co-editor of *Perpetual Adolescence: Jungian Analyses of American Media, Literature, and Popular Culture* (SUNY P, 2009; with Sally Porterfield and Keith Polette), *Post-Jungian Criticism: Theory and Praxis* (SUNY P, 2004; with James S. Baumlin and George H. Jensen), and *Ethos: New Essays in Rhetorical and Critical Theory* (SMU P, 1994; with James S. Baumlin). Her essays on *Venus and Adonis* and *The Taming of the Shrew* were judged "best of" published Shakespearean criticism in the later half of the 20th century and reprinted in collections of *Shakespearean Criticism* (Gale P, 2006 and 2000), and articles on Shakespeare and related subjects have been published in such journals as *College English, Studies in English Literature, Papers on Language and Literature, CEA Critic, Rhetoric Review, Renascence*, and most recently in the *Continuum Handbook for Renaissance Literature* (London: Continuum, 2010; ed. Susan Bruce and Rebecca Steinberger). Her new interests are in fiction and creative nonfiction; she edited *Yankee Doric: America Before the Civil War, A Novel*, by Burton Raffel (Moon City P, 2010), and her own works-in-progress include a novel and several short stories.

MITCHELL BESS is from Cape Girardeau, Missouri. He graduated at forty-six with his BS in Professional Writing with a minor in Creative Writing from Missouri State University in December, 2010.

BEN BOGART is a graduate of Missouri State University, having earned a Bachelor's and two Master's degrees. His work has appeared in *Elder Mountain* and *Moon City Review*. Ben currently lives in Kentucky with his wife, Gina, where he is a PhD student at the University of Louisville.

ANTHONY BRADLEY is a student of Creative Writing at Missouri State University. He has previously been published in *Red Ink Journal*.

LIZ BREAZEALE is a junior at Missouri State University, majoring in Creative Writing. This is her first published work, the winner of the *Moon City Review* Short Story Competition.

KEVIN BROCKMEIER graduated from (Southwest) Missouri State University in 1995 before receiving his MFA at the Iowa Writers Workshop. He is the author of two collections of short stories and three novels, including 2011's *The Illumination*. He has received three O. Henry Awards, the PEN USA Award, a Guggenheim Fellowship, and an NEA Grant.

SARA BURGE received her MFA in poetry from Southern Illinois University Carbondale and currently teaches at Missouri State University. Her first book was published by C & R Press in fall of 2010, and her work has appeared in *The Virginia Quarterly Review, River Styx, Cimarron Review, Court Green, MARGIE, Juked,* and elsewhere.

MICHAEL BURNS taught and ran the Creative Writing program at Missouri State University for over twenty-five years. He is the author of several collections of poetry, and has had his poems published in many journals and anthologies. He now lives in Kentucky.

LEE BUSBY is currently a graduate student at Vermont College of Fine Arts. He graduated with a Master's in English from Missouri State University in 2008. He has previously published poems in *Poet's Ink Review, Red Ink Journal,* and *Sunken Lines,* and won the Best Poem award in *Moon*

City Review in October 2008. His chapbook, *Wild Strawberries*, has been accepted for publication by Finishing Line Press.

LANETTE CADLE is an associate professor of English at Missouri State University. Her poetry has previously appeared in *Moon City Review*, and has also appeared in *Connecticut Review, Crab Orchard Review,* and *Arkansas Review*.

MARCUS CAFAGÑA is author of two books, *The Broken World*, selected for The National Poetry Series, and *Roman Fever*. He has published poems in numerous journals and anthologies, and served as co-editor of *Moon City Review* 2010. He coordinates the creative writing program at Missouri State University

JOEL CHASTON is a distinguished professor of English at Missouri State University. He received his doctorate at the University of Utah in 1988, and taught at Brigham Young University and Western Michigan University before joining the faculty at Missouri State in 1989. Among his publications are numerous scholarly articles and four books in the field of children's literature, including *Bridges for the Young: The Fiction of Katherine Paterson*, and *"Number the Stars" by Lois Lowry: A Literature Guide*. At Missouri State University, he has received awards including the University Award for Excellence in Teaching and the University Award for Excellence in Research, and holds professional memberships in the Assembly on Literature for Young Adults and the Children's Literature Association.

BILLY CLEM completed the MA in English at (Southwest) Missouri State University-Springfield in 1998. He teaches writing, Multicultural Literatures, and Women's Studies at Waubonsee Community College, outside Chicago. His work has appeared in *Lodestar Quarterly, Moon City Review*, and *Elder Mountain*.

CLARK CLOSSER, emeritus professor of English, retired in 2010 after thirty-two years of teaching at Missouri State University. He designed and occasionally taught English 205, Creative Writing: Nonfiction. "The Summer I Carried a Gun" is an essay from his autobiography in progress, *Death on Valentine Street*.

HEATHER COOK earned a bachelor's degree in Creative Writing from Missouri State University, where she is currently pursuing an MA in English. She lives in Springfield—alone, but with her sense of irony.

KRISTEN CYPRET is a reader for *Moon City Review*. She is an English major with an emphasis in Creative Writing at Missouri State

University. Her work has appeared in *Brilliance* through The American Library of Poetry.

LAURA DIMMIT is currently a senior Creative Writing major at Missouri State University.

SUSAN DUNN graduated from Missouri State University with a Master's in English in 2001 after working on her undergraduate degree at the same institution for over 18 years. She now teaches English at Anoka Ramsey Community College in Minnesota. Her poems have been published in journals such as *Willow Springs*, *The Chiron Review*, and *Mississippi Crow*.

JOHN DUVAL has received two translation awards from the Academy of American Poets, a National Endowment for the Arts grant, and a grant from the Washington, D. C., Council of the Arts for Banishèd Productions to stage readings from his *From Adam to Adam: Seven Old French Plays*. Most recently, Kathleen DuVal and he published the anthology, *Voices of a Continent: A Colonial America Reader*. He met his wife, Kay, in 1965, when they were both teaching at Missouri State University. Last spring he came back to teach a workshop in literary translation for Missouri State language students. This year he is a Visiting Fellow at Wolfson College, Cambridge University, completing a translation of *The Song of Roland* for Hackett Publishers.

KAY NIELL DUVAL completed her PhD in English Literature and taught at Darton College in Georgia and the University of Arkansas after teaching at Missouri State University from 1965–68. She has spent the academic year 2010–11 at Wolfson College, Cambridge, UK, researching and writing her book about the Brontë sisters' religion and their art.

ANDY EATON was born in 1981 in San Diego. He earned a BA in English at Missouri State University and an MLitt in Creative Writing from the University of St. Andrews in Scotland. He divides his time between Northern Ireland and the Ozarks, where he teaches English.

JEN MURVIN EDWARDS was a top 25 finalist in the Glimmer Train Press July 2010 Very Short Fiction contest. She has been previously published in *The MacGuffin* and has work forthcoming in *Palooka* in Spring 2011. Her graphic fiction has appeared in McGraw-Hill's (Jamestown Education) *World History Ink* series and the *Chickasaw Adventures* educational comics series (Layne Morgan Media). She currently teaches creative writing at Missouri State University in Springfield, Missouri.

KERRY JAMES EVANS is currently a PhD student in creative writing at Florida State University. His poems appear or are forthcoming in *Agni, Beloit Poetry Journal, New England Review, New Letters, North American Review* and elsewhere. His first book is entitled *Bangalore* and is due from Copper Canyon Press in 2013.

BRANDON FUNK was raised in Ozark County in southern Missouri and attended Missouri State University from 1995 to 2004, completing his BA in English in 2001 and MA in English in 2004. He has lived in the Twin Cities region in Minnesota since 2005 and has taught English at a regional community college for much of that time. His interests outside of academic life include cooking, reading naturalist literature, and any outdoor activities—from fishing to birding to making good coffee from northern lake water.

SHERI GABBERT is an undergraduate student at Missouri State University with majors in creative writing and philosophy. Her work has also appeared in *417* Magazine.

ANA GARCÍA BERGUA was born in Mexico City in 1960. She is the author of the novels *El umbral* (1993), *Púrpura* (1999), *Rosas negras* (2004), and *Isla de bobos* (2007), as well as the short story collections *El imaginador* (1996), *La confianza en los extraños* (2002), *Otra oportunidad para el señor Balmand* (2004), and *Edificio* (2009).

D. GILSON is a graduate of the MA in English program at Missouri State University. Currently he is an MFA candidate in poetry and nonfiction at Chatham University, where he is also a supplemental writing instructor. His work, which focuses on outsider status in the Ozarks, has appeared or is forthcoming in *Elder Mountain, The New York Quarterly, elimae,* and *Plain Spoke.*

JESSICA GLOVER graduated from Missouri State University in 2009 with a MA in English. Currently, she is a PhD candidate in the English department at Oklahoma State University.

JULIE HENIGAN holds a PhD in English and Irish Studies from the University of Notre Dame, but grew up in Springfield, a member of the (Southwest) Missouri State University English department family. She has worked as a teacher, musician, oral historian, archivist, and folklorist, and is currently teaching as adjunct faculty at the Ava campus of Drury University.

Her poems have appeared in *Ozark Review, Orbis, Outposts, Manhattan Poetry Review, Dal gCais*, and *Moon City Review*.

ROBERT HENIGAN taught English at (Southwest) Missouri State University from 1961 until his retirement in 1989, specializing in several areas, notably modern poetry. In 1965, at the request of then department head George Gleason, he founded a modest campus literary magazine which he dubbed *Type*—the forerunner of the current *Moon City Review*. Dr. Henigan published poems in *Quoin, The Ozark Review, Jumping Pond, A Different Drummer, The Springfield News-Leader*, and in *Original Essays on the Poetry of Anne Sexton*, ed. Frances Bixler. He also left behind a legacy of students who love literature.

DANIEL IACOB was born in 1988 in Suceava, Romania, just before the 1989 collapse of the communist regime. Since coming to the United States in 1997, he has lived in New York, Seattle, and Springfield, Missouri.

TOSHIYA KAMEI's translations include Liliana Blum's *Curse of Eve and Other Stories* (2008), Naoko Awa's *Fox's Window and Other Stories* (2010), and Espido Freire's *Irlanda* (forthcoming). His other translations have appeared in *The Global Game* (2008), *Sudden Fiction Latino* (2010), and *My Mother She Killed Me, My Father He Ate Me* (2010).

LORA KNIGHT is a Creative Writing graduate student at Missouri State University. Her work has appeared in *Cave Region Review*.

TED KOOSER served two terms as U.S. Poet Laureate, and during his second term won the Pulitzer Prize for poetry.

MEREDITH S. W. LOWRY earned her BS from Michigan State University in 1978 in Clothing & Textiles, with a focus on weaving. She moved to Missouri in 1981 and attended (Southwest) Missouri State University for two years, filling the necessary requirements to attend nursing school. After working as a Special Procedures Nurse for nine years and as Nursing Supervisor for a home health agency for two years, she returned SMSU to study Creative Writing from 1999–2001. She has since become a Universalist Minister and spends free time writing, weaving, making jewelry, and sewing.

DUSTIN MACORMIC is a graduate teaching assistant at Missouri State University. His work has also appeared in *Mid Rivers Review*.

MILLER MANTOOTH writes on a typewriter while wearing his finest beard. He received an MA in English from Missouri State University in 2009, but he did so under a slightly different name. He is currently in the MFA Writing program at Vermont College of Fine Arts, where he is also not known as Miller Mantooth. He loves his grandmother dearly, though, and Mantooth is her maiden name, so he chooses to honor her in this small way.

TRAVIS MOSSOTTI's poetry has appeared or is forthcoming in the *Antioch Review, Cincinnati Review, Hunger Mountain, New York Quarterly, Poetry Ireland Review, Subtropics,* and many other journals. In 2009 he won the James Hearst Poetry Prize and an Academy of American Poets Prize. His first book *About the Dead* has been a finalist for the National Poetry Series, The Journal Award in Poetry, the Tampa Review Prize for Poetry, and the Brittingham and Pollak Poetry Prizes. His poem "Decampment" (appearing in the winter 2010 issue of *Southern Humanities Review*) has recently been adapted to screen as an animated short film (www.decampment.com).

ANDY MYERS is a Creative Writing student at Missouri State University where he has studied fiction with Richard Neumann, W. D. Blackmon, and Brian Shawver. In the Fall of 2009 he was asked to read at the Moon City Student Invitational reading.

ALLYS PAGE is an undergraduate in the English Department at Missouri State University.

BENJAMIN PFEIFFER is an alumnus of the Missouri State English Department. In addition to his writing he has worked as an editor, most recently as Managing Editor for the Kansas University MFA graduate student literary journal.

BURTON RAFFEL writes, "Translation is an art, but a secondary one. Though his publishing record does not show it, Burton Raffel has always focused most intently on his poetry and fiction." As an editor and translator, he has published more than one hundred books.

ANNA ROBB teaches and studies creative writing at Missouri State University, where she earned her Master's in English in May 2011.

MARIA SAVVENAS is a graduate teaching assistant at Missouri State University. She is working towards a Master's of English in literature.

JENNER SHAFFER earned his BA in Creative Writing from Missouri State University in 1997, and served with distinction as a diesel mechanic with the 101st Airborne Division in the U.S. Army from 1997–2000. Since earning an MA in Writing in 2004, he has taught English at the collegiate and secondary levels, and served as a Teacher Consultant for the Ozarks Writing Project, a chapter of the National Writing Project. He lives and works near the Lake of the Ozarks, Missouri.

BRIAN SHAWVER taught in the English Department at Missouri State University from 2005 to 2010. He is the author of the novels *Aftermath* and *The Cuban Prospect*, and he currently teaches at Park University in Kansas City.

ROLAND SODOWSKY grew up on a small ranch in western Oklahoma. He has three degrees from Oklahoma State University and studied Old High German as a Fulbright Scholar in Germany. He has taught linguistics, literature, and creative writing at OSU, the University of Calabar in Nigeria, the University of Texas, Sul Ross State University, and Missouri State University where he is a Professor Emeritus. He has published poetry, short stories, or novellas in *Atlantic Monthly, American Literary Review, Glimmer Train, Midwest Quarterly*, and many other literary magazines. His collection of short stories, *Things We Lose* (U. Missouri P), won the Associated Writing Programs' Award for Short Fiction. He received the National Cowboy Hall of Fame Short Fiction Award for *Interim in the Desert* (TCU P), the Coordinating Council of Literary Magazines-General Electric Award for fiction, and has been a recipient of a National Endowment for the Arts award. Now retired from Missouri State, he and his wife, the poet Laura Lee Washburn, live in Pittsburg, Kansas, where he, his brother, and his son are engaged in a continuing battle with the mesquites and cedars on their family homestead.

ALEXANDRA TEAGUE's first book, *Mortal Geography*, was published this spring, and her work has also appeared in *Best American Poets 2009, The Missouri Review, New England Review, The Iowa Review*, and elsewhere. She has just finished a semester as a Visiting Professor of Poetry at University of Arkansas in Fayetteville, and is very happy to be spending this Spring writing poetry, thanks to an NEA grant.

RICHARD TURNER is an emeritus professor of English at Missouri State University.

JENN VELSACO-CAFAGÑA is a 1994 graduate of Missouri State University and currently works as a children's librarian for the Springfield-Greene County Library District. Her poems have appeared in *Between the Leaves: A Gathering of Writings by Booksellers* and *Type*. She lives in Springfield, with her husband and son.

ISAIAH VIANESE graduated with his MA in English from Missouri State University in May 2010. His chapbook, *Stopping on the Old Highway* (recycled karma press) was published in 2009, and his poems have appeared or are forthcoming in the *Blue Collar Review, The Fourth River*, and *The Other Herald*. He lives in New York.

FRANÇOIS VILLON was an innovative and influential French poet during the fifteenth century. Villon's poetry reflected his tumultuous life; he spent much of his thirty years in exile and imprisonment. His works include the *Testaments* and the *Ballade dse Pendus* and have been revisited by artists such as Dante Gabriel Rossetti, Ezra Pound and Galway Kinnell.

ROBERT WALLACE was born in Springfield, Missouri, graduated from Harvard University in 1953 and later received a Fulbright Scholarship to St. Catharine's College at Cambridge. Wallace served in the army for two years and afterward published his first book of poetry, *This Various World and Other Poems*. Wallace began his teaching career in 1957 at Bryn Mawr College and taught at Sweet Briar College, Vassar, and Case Western Reserve University. Wallace published six books of poetry and the textbook *Writing Poems*.

SARAH WANGLER's poems have appeared most recently in *Best New Poets 2010, Superstition Review*, and *Cardinal Sins*. She is a Michigan native and an MFA candidate at Oklahoma State University in Stillwater, Oklahoma. She also holds an MA in English from Northern Michigan University in Marquette, Michigan.

ERICA WARREN acquired her MA in English at Missouri State University and is a lifetime resident of the Springfield area.

LAURA LEE WASHBURN is the Director of Creative Writing at Pittsburg State University in Kansas, an editorial board member of the Woodley Memorial Press, and the author of *This Good Warm Place: 10th Anniversary Expanded Edition* (March Street) and *Watching the Contortionists* (Palanquin Chapbook Prize). Her poetry has appeared in such journals as *Carolina Quarterly, Quarterly West, The Sun, The Journal*, and *Clackamas Review*. Born in Virginia Beach, Virginia, she has also lived and worked in Arizona and in Missouri where she was an Instructor at Missouri State University from 1992 through 1997. She is married to the writer Roland Sodowsky.

BRUCE WEST is a professor of photography at Missouri State University. He exhibits his photographs widely throughout the United States and Europe. His photographs are included in major public and corporate collections such as the Library of Congress, the Victoria and Albert Museum, and the Houston Museum of Fine Arts.

SATARAH WHEELER is a writer from Southwest Missouri. She received her Bachelor's in Creative Writing from Missouri State University in December of 2009

SHANNON WOODEN is both alumna and faculty member of Missouri State University, teaching British literature, critical theory, and creative writing. She has published on literary representations of science and literature, gender studies, popular culture, and contemporary fiction. This is her first published short story.

CHAD WOODY works and lives in Springfield, Missouri, with his wife Heather. Current projects include *Junk Apocrypha*, a book of selected woodcuts, engravings, and etchings, and an illustrated children's collection entitled *Uncle Knuckle's Preposterous Narrations*.

MEG WORDEN lives, writes in Portland, Oregon, with her husband and son, and her tiny dog. Meg has been published in *Ascent* and has written columns for the *Lovely County Citizen* in Eureka Springs, Arkansas. She is currently a regular contributor on www.thenervousbreakdown.com and www.fictionaut.com.

Moon City Press is a joint venture of the Missouri State University
Departments of English and Art and Design.
With series lists in "Arts and Letters" and
"Ozarks History and Culture,"
Moon City Press
features collaborations
between students and faculty
over the various aspects of publication:
research, writing, editing, layout and design.

CPSIA information can be obtained at www.ICGtesting.com
Printed in the USA
LVOW062257090113

315090LV00002B/7/P